Mercenaries in the
Classical World

Mercenaries in the Classical World

To the death of Alexander

Dr. Stephen English

Pen & Sword
MILITARY

First published in Great Britain in 2012 by
PEN & SWORD MILITARY
An imprint of
Pen & Sword Books Ltd
47 Church Street
Barnsley
South Yorkshire
S70 2AS

ISBN 978-1-84884-330-1

A CIP catalogue record for this book is
available from the British Library.

Typeset by Concept, Huddersfield, West Yorkshire.

Printed and bound in England by
CPI Group (UK) Ltd, Croydon, CRO 4YY.

Pen & Sword Books Ltd incorporates the imprints of Pen & Sword Aviation, Pen & Sword Family History, Pen & Sword Maritime, Pen & Sword Military, Pen & Sword Discovery, Wharncliffe Local History, Wharncliffe True Crime, Wharncliffe Transport, Pen & Sword Select, Pen & Sword Military Classics, Leo Cooper, The Praetorian Press, Remember When, Seaforth Publishing and Frontline Publishing.

For a complete list of Pen & Sword titles please contact
PEN & SWORD BOOKS LIMITED
47 Church Street, Barnsley, South Yorkshire, S70 2AS, England
E-mail: enquiries@pen-and-sword.co.uk
Website: www.pen-and-sword.co.uk

Contents

Preface

I first had the idea for writing this book several years ago whilst I was writing my book on the army of Alexander the Great. It struck me at that time that perhaps the best general works on mercenaries were those of Parke and Griffith published in 1933 and 1935 respectively. A great deal of scholarship on various aspects of mercenary service has appeared since that time, but a re-examination was somewhat overdue.

The subject is of interest to me, and I hope others, because it is intimately linked with the development of warfare throughout the ancient world; the gradual and sometimes painful move from armies consisting of largely untrained citizen hoplites to the highly trained and effective field army of Alexander.

As a final note of introduction, I should say what this book is intended to be and what it is not. It is not an exhaustive academic examination of every reference to mercenary soldiers in the surviving sources; that would be an enormous undertaking. This work is intended to be an accessible narrative of mercenaries and their activities from the Archaic period in Greece to the death of Alexander the Great.

By way of acknowledgements, there are a number of people who helped in various ways with the writing and production of this book. I would like to thank Elizabeth for her never-wavering love and support, and for her unending patience; Phil Sidnell and the team at Pen & Sword for making this book, and my earlier three, possible; David Stanford, my copy editor, for his tireless and outstanding work, going above and beyond what I could ever have expected; and my family for their continuing encouragement and support. Finally, I would like to thank Peter Rhodes for reading an earlier rough draft of this work and for the many helpful comments he made; it is undoubtedly a better work for his insightful input.

Finally, I would say that this work owes a great debt to the many scholars who have come before me, and to the body of work that they have produced.

I hope that in some small way I can add to that work. Despite the various people who have seen, read and helped with the production of this book, any remaining errors are entirely my own.

Any dates within this work are BC unless otherwise indicated.

Introduction

What is a mercenary? It would seem prudent (and indeed, an obvious place to start this investigation) to attempt to answer that question. We cannot, after all, chart the rise of the mercenary soldier to a position of great prominence in the military affairs of the ancient world without understanding who and what they were.

One of the earliest modern authorities on Greek mercenaries, Griffith, stated that 'the professional soldiers of the ancient world were mercenaries.'[1] This view seems to be an attempt to develop that held by the other great early scholar of the Greek mercenary soldier, Parke, whose view was that the history of the mercenary was the history of the development of the soldier from amateur to professional.[2] As we will see, mercenary service did indeed lead to an increase in professionalism throughout the period of the ancient world, but the view of Griffith does not do justice to the complexity of the situation.

Professional soldiers (and defining that term is not necessarily easy) certainly existed in the ancient world, and they would generally not have considered themselves as mercenaries. The Spartans, for example, were either professional or very close to it, but they certainly were not mercenaries; nor were the Theban Sacred Band or the *pezhetairoi* of Alexander the Great. We can easily conclude that professionalism does not automatically confer the status of 'mercenary'.

Another oft-used aspect of military service, that some have taken to be a defining feature of mercenary service, is that of payment.[3] Mercenaries were certainly paid; that was (and remains) the *raison d'etre* for the individual soldier. As with the status of professionalism, however, the mere fact of payment did not automatically make a soldier a mercenary. For example, perhaps from as early as the Persian Wars, rowers in the Athenian navy were paid for their service.[4] The Macedonian soldiers in the armies of Philip and Alexander were also paid, but again, neither the Athenians nor the Macedonians in these examples would have been considered (or called) mercenaries in the ancient world.

Therefore, in order to get to the heart of what a mercenary was in the ancient world, I think we must look at a modern parallel. Modern warfare changed markedly from the end of the Second World War to the modern period. The Geneva Convention, which was written in 1949, shortly after the end of the Second World War, did not really address the issue of mercenary service, as it had not been a feature of that great conflict. The Geneva Protocol, in 1977, however, rectified that omission because of the increasing prevalence of the mercenary soldier on the modern battlefields of the world.[5]

Article 47 of the Geneva Protocol defines a mercenary as someone who:[6]

- is specially recruited locally or abroad in order to fight in an armed conflict;
- does in fact take a direct part in the hostilities;
- is motivated to take part in the hostilities by the desire for private gain and, in fact, is promised, by or on behalf of a party to the conflict, material compensation substantially in excess of that promised or paid to combatants of similar ranks and functions in the armed forces of that party;
- is neither a national of a party to the conflict nor a resident of territory controlled by a party to the conflict;
- is not a member of the armed forces of a party to the conflict;
- has not been sent by a state which is not a party to the conflict on official duty as a member of its armed forces.

Not all of the elements of the definition of the Geneva Protocol are relevant to the study of the ancient world, but it is an excellent starting point. From this, we can say that the key point is that mercenaries were paid, but to remember as well that the reverse does not hold. Therefore, we need to say that not all soldiers who were paid were mercenaries, but all mercenaries were paid. In which case, mercenaries fought without a political imperative. Soldiers in a national army will fight for many reasons, but they will often centre around concepts of duty, loyalty and patriotism, besides those of career and personal advancement. Mercenaries would have felt no such compunction (although we will return to this point shortly); they fought because they were being paid to do so.

This does not mean, however, that they would simply fight for the highest bidder; once they took service in an army they tended to remain loyal for the length of their service with that employer, rather than tout their services from general to general, as we may otherwise expect.

The major feature of the Geneva Protocol definition of a mercenary that does not apply to the ancient world is the concept of active service in a conflict. Many mercenaries did, of course, see active service, but there are several examples of cases in which they did not, and yet the troops involved were certainly mercenaries, those on garrison duty being the prime example. We will see during our discussion of the reign of Alexander the Great that his mercenaries were largely employed in two ways: as part of a reserve heavy infantry line in the set-piece battles (where they frequently did very little of the actual fighting unless the Persians were to break through) or as garrison troops in the major cities of the ever expanding empire.

Mercenaries in the ancient world were typically foreigners. They were frequently, although not exclusively, Greeks, fighting in whatever conflict was active at the time, and for whomever could afford to pay them. Persia and Egypt were often ready employers of professional mercenaries, as were Carthage and Syracuse.

The concept of political imperative is a very interesting one in the ancient world, particularly in relation to the status of being a foreigner. The resident aliens in Athens (metics) were undoubtedly foreigners, and were paid for their service to the state. Metics who fought for the state did so after volunteering, which would seem to place them outside of the realms of the mercenary.

Considering the evidence, I think we can come to a basic definition of mercenaries in the ancient world:

- They were paid.
- They fought without a political imperative.
- They were typically foreigners and usually had no personal interest in the conflict.

The major drawback with the definition is the third point; there were examples where soldiers whom we would likely call mercenaries took up arms against an individual or a state, but not directly *for* their home state. Consider, for example, the Greek mercenaries fighting in Persian service against Philip and particularly Alexander. Many of them had a significant political and personal desire to see the Macedonians defeated, and to see Greece free once more. Thousands of them fought, as foreigners for pay, against the Macedonians. They may well have held significant political views but they were not compelled to fight for Persia; they chose to do so, and I think that is the key issue in considering the status of those men.

The Greeks did attempt to stop Greeks fighting for Persia, or anyone else, but with little evident success. The League of Corinth, established by Philip and continued by Alexander, issued a decree essentially outlawing a Greek from taking up arms against another Greek. This was a direct attempt to stop Greek mercenary infantry fighting for Persia. Philip knew that those troops would be his biggest obstacle in any future invasion of Persia, and he was attempting to legislate to remove the problem. We will see the numbers of Greeks in Persian service declining throughout the period of Alexander's conquests, but I will argue this had very little to do with the decree, and was simply because Darius was not an attractive paymaster once Alexander began the conquest of Persia. Darius' access to the sources of Greek mercenaries was also limited shortly after the invasion of 334, and on top of this Alexander hired mercenaries in huge numbers.

The definition above leads us to the very interesting question of when does mercenary service end? In other words, when does a mercenary stop being a mercenary? The major time when this would occur was when they were no longer employed by a paymaster. Perhaps the most famous example of this is the march of the 10,000. Once Cyrus was killed, they no longer had any hope of being paid and their status as mercenaries should therefore have changed. What we call them at that point does not seem overly important, perhaps unemployed mercenaries or bandits; either way they were then simply a very large band of soldiers in a foreign land trying to get home (and seeking a new paymaster, of course).[7] Their actions would tend to label them as bandits as they lived off the land and pillaged what they needed to survive, through necessity. Though plundering would not have been new to them, nor to most mercenaries, plunder, or its promise, was often a significant part of the incentive package for mercenaries. In fact, on many occasions in the ancient world, mercenaries derived their salary entirely from plunder rather than through a regular wage, as we would understand it today.[8] The distinction, therefore, between piracy and plunder on the one hand, and mercenary service on the other, is not one that can be kept completely clear.

In some ways, the ancient Greeks seemed a little uncomfortable with the concept of mercenary service, and as a result they never coined or used a single overarching word equivalent to our 'mercenary'; they, in fact, created several words to describe mercenary service. The most commonly used Greek word at the start of the Classical period was *epikouros*, meaning something like 'helper'. This was in the sense of a soldier who was fighting with (perhaps alongside) other soldiers, the soldiers of the city-state.

The multivalent Greek word *xenos* (for a foreigner) was also sometimes employed of mercenaries; its use began during the fifth century but certainly went beyond that. It was a word, however, that was also used to describe very many other types of individual, too. This is the term that Xenophon exclusively uses to describe the Greek mercenaries in the service of Cyrus the Younger in 401.

During the later fifth and into the fourth century, the term *misthophoros*, from *misthos* (wage) and *phoros* (bearer or carrier), becomes common, indicating one of the essential elements of mercenary service as discussed, although it did not exclusively refer to mercenary service. This was the most common term used by Greek historians writing during the Roman period to describe Greek mercenaries.[9]

There were occasionally derivatives of these, too; the Thracian mercenaries employed to help defeat a Spartan invasion at Lechaeum in 390 were called *xenikon* (foreign corps).[10] Whichever term we choose to use, there does seem to have been a development from the Archaic period through to the fourth century; from *epikouros* to *misthophoros*.[11] One other term that is used occasionally is *stratiôtai*, although this is more typically the base word for 'soldier' but has been variously translated as mercenary or professional soldier; either way, there is certainly a juxtaposition with the citizen soldier.

A Note on Sources

As historians we must be fully aware of the sources for the material we discuss, and indeed of their limitations. This section is not intended to be a comprehensive examination of those sources, but more of a brief overview to present the reader with a sense of where our information comes from. More information will be presented throughout the course of this work that will support and build upon what is said here in this introduction.

Mercenaries were not an invention of the fifth century; they are almost as old as warfare itself, although it is true to say that large-scale source evidence only starts to appear for the period of the fifth century and later. Having said this, we are not lacking entirely in earlier evidence. Diodorus and Herodotus both tell us of Greek mercenaries in the service of the Egyptian Pharaoh Psammetichus; Herodotus describing them in rather derogatory terms, whilst Diodorus is more neutral. Diodorus also makes a single reference to mercenaries in the service of Corinth in the seventh century.[12] We also know of mercenaries in the service of the Athenian tyrant Pisistratus and his sons in the late sixth century. The tradition in regard to Pisistratus' use of mercenaries, and indeed their use by other autocrats and tyrants, is not a positive one. For example, Herodotus and Aristotle present a picture of armed mercenaries juxtaposed against an unarmed and disenfranchised populace.[13] Herodotus makes frequent references to the tyrannical use of mercenaries, whilst Diodorus notes that this was not a phenomenon exclusive to Athens, but notes other autocrats who also employed mercenaries as a bodyguard, and thus as a basis of maintaining power.[14]

The fall of the Pisistratid tyranny in Athens saw a change in attitudes towards mercenaries. Prior to this they had been employed as the tyrants' bodyguard and therefore had a prominent role in the tyranny. This being said, they were therefore heavily linked to that tyranny in the popular consciousness; mercenaries were the tools of the tyrant. This appears to have also been true beyond the boundaries of the Athenian polis.

In the early fourth century, we have information from a number of sources. In his *Life of Agesilaus*, Plutarch tells us of the shame felt by Spartans at their defeat to a body of mercenary peltasts led by Iphicrates. Plutarch notes:[15]

> Whilst Agesilaus was in the Corinthian territories, having just taken the Heraeum, he was looking on while his soldiers were carrying away the prisoners and the plunder, when ambassadors from Thebes came to him to treat of peace. Having a great aversion for that city, and thinking it then advantageous to his affairs publicly to slight them, he took the opportunity, and would not seem either to see them or hear them speak. But as if on purpose to punish him in his pride, before they parted from him, messengers came with news of the complete slaughter of one of the Spartan divisions by Iphicrates, a greater disaster than had befallen them for many years, and that the more grievous because it was a choice regiment of full-armed Lacedaemonians overthrown by a parcel of mere mercenary targeteers.

In this passage, Plutarch is either stating that citizen soldiers were of far greater worth than mere mercenaries, or at the very least that that was the contemporary perception (although the Spartans would have felt their citizens more worthy than any other, in any case); this is another view that seems prevalent throughout the Greek world. Many of Plutarch's biographies are a valuable source, but especially for supporting material for more historically biased writers. Always bear in mind, however, that writers like Plutarch (first century AD) and Diodorus (first century BC) were not contemporary with the events they describe. Other historians like Thucydides and Xenophon were contemporary, a fact that may colour your views as regards their reliability, as a contemporary is more likely to be able to garner first-hand information from participants in any given event.

Diodorus is also an important source for the employment of mercenaries in the fifth century, before the period covered by Thucydides. The latter historian produced one of the great works on ancient warfare, and it is surprising that he places very little importance on the significance or relevance of mercenaries throughout that war, and although he does make a relatively large number of references to them, most are only passing mentions.[16] For Thucydides, mercenaries were a peripheral issue in the Peloponnesian War (the war fought primarily between Athens and Sparta between 431 and 404).

Athenian political speeches are a further rich source of information, particularly those that survive from the fourth century. Isocrates wrote pamphlets and Demosthenes made speeches in which they expressed deep concerns about the growing use of, and reliance upon, mercenary soldiers. Demosthenes was concerned about the potential for mercenaries upsetting the natural order of the city-state, as they were not inherently loyal (only when monies were regularly paid), whilst Isocrates was heavily critical of the Phocians' employment of mercenaries during the Sacred War.

Two of the titans of Greek philosophy, Plato and Aristotle, were not silent on the subject of mercenary service either. Interestingly, Plato was critical of the individuals themselves, rather than of mercenary service *per se*:[17]

> Cyrnus, find a man you can trust in deadly feuding: he is worth his weight in gold and silver. Such a man, in our view, who fights in a tough war, is far superior to the others – to just about the same degree as the combination of justice, self-control and good judgement, reinforced by courage, is superior to courage alone. In civil war a man will never prove sound and loyal unless he has every virtue; but in the war Tyrtaeus mentions there are hordes of mercenaries who are ready to dig their heels in and die fighting, most of whom, apart from a small minority, are reckless and insolent rogues, and just about the most witless people you could find.

To compare, Aristotle believed that citizen hoplites were inherently braver because they had more to lose in battle; they were fighting to defend their homes and therefore felt death preferable to flight and safety, unlike the mercenary:[18]

> *Stratiôtai* turn cowards, however, when the danger puts too great a strain on them, and they are inferior in numbers and equipment; for they are the first to fly, while citizen-forces die at their posts, as in fact happened at the temple of Hermes. For to the latter flight is disgraceful and death is preferable to safety on those terms; while the former from the very beginning faced the danger on the assumption that they were stronger, and when they know the facts they fly, fearing death more than disgrace; but the brave man is not that sort of person.

The fourth-century writer, Aeneas Tacticus, also gives us some very interesting snippets of material from the many historical illustrations he gives in his under-read work *How to Survive under Siege*. He, like many of the other sources we have mentioned, is critical of the practice of a besieged city employing mercenaries. He was concerned that their loyalties would be to themselves first and foremost, rather than to the city, as would be the case with citizen soldiers, much the same argument that was employed by Plato and Aristotle. His concern was that there was always the possibility of betrayal because of bribery or some other act of self-preservation, although there are in reality few examples of mercenaries swapping sides at a crucial moment of a battle or siege. Perhaps the most famous example is the defection of the mercenaries commanded by Eumenes at Gabiene in 316.[19] This was probably rare because of the impact it had on the reputation of the mercenary soldier; if this occurred too frequently then the employment opportunities for all mercenaries as a group would decline because of a lack of trust on the part of prospective employers. Knowledge of this fact may well have made an individual mercenary, keeping an eye on his long-term employment, wary of defection unless circumstances were dire.

The Eumenes incident is also an indication of the importance of Diodorus as a source because of the vast time period he covered, down to the later Roman Republican period. His ability as a historian is often criticized, as is the quality and reliability of the material he left behind, but there appears to be a slowly increasing appreciation that he can add a great deal to our knowledge of this subject, and of history more broadly. Whilst he does not always present a negative picture of mercenaries, he does link them with tyrants; a standard criticism that perhaps means little, given the influences that Roman thought would have had on him (and indeed other writers of the Roman period).

Diodorus preserves a wealth of evidence, particularly of the fourth century, which saw a very significant increase in the use of mercenary forces. Diodorus makes only two references to mercenaries in his pre-fifth-century material, but from the fifth century they are quite common in his history, indeed they are mentioned in every book, from book 11 onwards, with the high point when his narrative enters the fourth century. He also pays great attention to the career of Cyrus the Younger and of Dionysius I of Syracuse, both of whom were great employers of mercenaries.[20]

The mention of Cyrus the Younger brings us to Xenophon and his great works on mercenary service. His work detailing the march of the 10,000 to Cunaxa, their defeat (despite being the superior troops) and their return to Greece, with all of the privations and deprivations that brought, is invaluable. The picture Xenophon paints of mercenary service is largely positive; but we must always remember that he was employed as a mercenary himself and was present during the march of the 10,000, and is therefore likely to have had a rather coloured view of their activities.

Regarding the sources, it is interesting that many present a relatively negative picture of mercenaries and of mercenary service, certainly when compared with citizen soldiers. The views of these aristocratic authors were not necessarily in tune with the views of the individual Greek citizens. Whilst the historians were generally suspicious of mercenaries and of mercenary service, individual Greeks do not seem to have had the same issues, given the numbers that regularly volunteered for service both inside Greece and beyond.

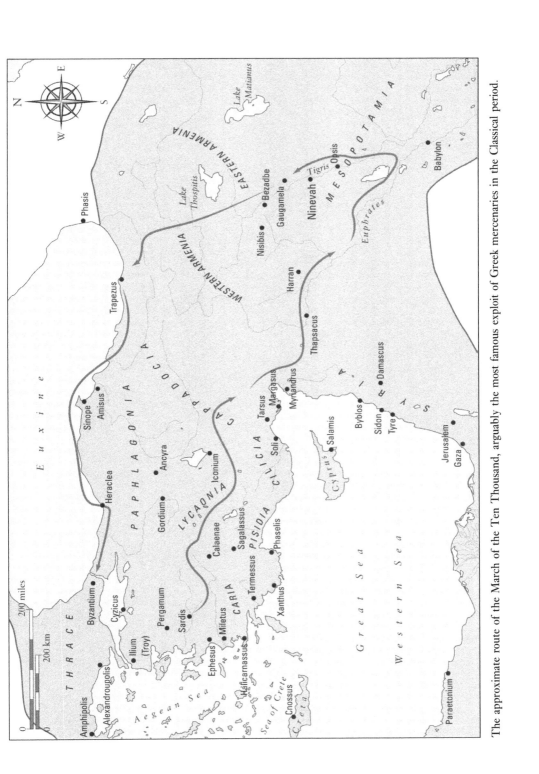

The approximate route of the March of the Ten Thousand, arguably the most famous exploit of Greek mercenaries in the Classical period.

Chapter 1

Payment and Remuneration

The most fundamental aspect of mercenary service, as we have already noted, was that of the provision of service in return for some form of payment or remuneration. In this chapter we will explore the payment systems and methods that existed.[1]

Employing mercenaries was not a decision that was taken lightly, because of the costs involved. Outside the Persian Empire, no employer could easily afford an open-ended agreement on terms of service, and thus most mercenaries were employed for a specific campaign, after which they would need to seek other opportunities. Therefore, it was often not in the financial interests of the mercenaries for wars to end quickly, or for one side to be comprehensively defeated, as their future employment opportunities would be limited as a consequence.

Although the employment of mercenaries was an expensive way of waging war, their professionalism led to their increasing usage throughout the Classical period and into the Hellenistic period. The cost, therefore, became a necessary burden of the state, and a means had to be found to bear that greater expense during times of war. States and individual commanders came up with a number of mechanisms to provide their mercenaries with the payment they required, and we will begin this chapter by examining some of those methods.

Methods of Payment

Direct payment in the form of coinage is the most obvious method of payment that we might imagine today, especially considering our modern market economies. Ancient societies, however, did not have the same relationship with money that we do in the modern world; the ancient economy was not as heavily monetarized as is ours. Even citizens in the richest of ancient societies, the Persian Empire, often conducted their business in the form of trade and barter, rather than direct purchase. It it also probably true to say that the Persian Empire did not make much use of coinage except for the payment of mercenaries.

This being said, however, payment in coin was often made, especially after the Athenian Empire had spread coinage over a wide area and made its use more common than it had been before the fifth century.[2] At the end of that century the Peloponnesian War continued the increasing trend towards payment in coin, and by the end of that war it was relatively commonplace for mercenaries to receive at least some of their remuneration in the form of hard currency. In the mid-fourth century, Diodorus tells us of an incident during the Third Sacred War (356–346, of which we will hear more later) where coins were struck specifically in order to pay mercenaries for their service:[3]

> After the death of Onomarchus his brother, Phayllus succeeded to the command of the Phocians. In an attempt to retrieve the disaster, he began to gather a multitude of mercenaries, offering double the customary pay, and summoned help from his allies. He got ready also a large supply of arms and coined gold and silver money.

He goes on to tell us more of the same incident:

> ... Phayllus, the brother of Onomarchus, when he became general, struck into coin a large number of dedications in order to pay the mercenaries.

Some of these coins manufactured from melted-down dedications survive, carrying the names of the Phocian generals Phayllus and Onomarchus, demonstrating that this minting did occur and suggesting that the payment in hard currency was not unusual by this time.

Therefore, the spread of coinage as a means of exchange and the spread of mercenary service appear to be linked. The spread of coinage did facilitate the hiring of large mercenary armies, which changed the nature of Greek warfare. It has even been argued that the minting of coinage and the subsequent payment of mercenaries in coin was detrimental to Greek society as a whole and was in itself a significant cause of the downfall of the polis system.[4]

Although coinage is the most obvious form of direct payment, and for many mercenaries this would have been the most important and desirable form of pay, it was by no means the only mechanism that was at the disposal of the paymasters. In order to understand the next form of payment fully, we need to understand something of the motivation for mercenary service. Some mercenaries were undoubtedly motivated by the prospect of a reasonable steady wage, and for these men service away from the front line would have been considered a choice assignment. Consider, for example, the mercenaries employed by Philip II of Macedon. He stationed mercenaries throughout Greece at strategically important locations, a policy adopted and greatly expanded upon by his son, Alexander the Great.[5] These men would have received a regular wage (not just in coin, as we shall see) and were in very little danger as long as there was no rebellion. For some, these postings would have been highly sought after, less so for others.

Many were motivated by mercenary service because they had no other way to make a living; there was no welfare state after all. Individuals needed to be able to feed themselves, and in many cases their families, and therein lies the second mechanism that commanders had at their disposal; some of the payment received by mercenaries was in the form of food and drink. Mercenaries, like everyone else, needed to eat more than they needed hard currency, and employers found a number of ways to make this happen. Some employers would pay the food bills for their mercenaries (a payment called *sitêresion* or *sitarchia*) or provide them with enough coinage to pay those bills themselves. This payment would have been separate from their wage, which sometimes fluctuated depending on employer, but this *sitêresion* payment appears to have been more stable.

Some employers paid something akin to travelling expenses (*ephodia*). Employers could also make payments in kind and simply provide food and sustenance for the mercenaries (*trophê* or *sitos*). For many commanders, this latter option would have been the simplest, and perhaps the cheapest solution, as they would be feeding their regular army anyway; a few more mouths would make little difference, and it would save potentially a significant amount of money, especially as the numbers of mercenaries employed increased. *Misthos* was also paid to mercenaries, and hence the common fourth-century name for a mercenary soldier *misthophoroi*. *Misthos* was akin to a regular wage or salary. This terminology developed as the employment of mercenaries developed and as terminology was required; because of this the terminology did not really evolve until it was needed in the mid-fourth century, along with the rise of the mercenary army.[6]

The extent to which these terms are specific or synonymous and inter-changeable can be (and has been) debated, but the important thing to note here is that the provision of food, or a payment specifically for the purpose of purchasing provisions, was an important pay structure at the disposal of a mercenary commander.

Mercenaries could also be paid a form of bonus for either length of service, or for particularly distinguished service, although this was relatively rare. The Syracusans gave Dion's mercenaries a bonus payment of 100 minae for success against Dionysius in 357, and we also know that Cyrus offered his mercenary army five minae each once victory had been assured. Xenophon tells us:[7]

> So the generals called an assembly and made this announcement; and the soldiers were angry with the generals, and said that they had known about this for a long time, but had been keeping it from the troops; furthermore, they refused to go on unless they were given money, as were the men who made the journey with Cyrus before, when he went to visit his father; they had received the donation, even though they marched, not to battle, but merely because Cyrus' father summoned him. All these things the generals reported back to Cyrus, and he promised that he would give every man five minas in silver when they reached Babylon and their pay in full until he brought the Greeks back to Ionia again. By these promises the greater part of the Greek army was persuaded.

As we can see, this was not an act of largess on the part of Cyrus but the promise of a bonus payment in order to keep the mercenary army intact after a period where their pay was evidently in arrears.

Alexander the Great also gave a bonus equivalent to two months' pay to his mercenaries (and everyone else in the army) after the Battle of Gaugamela in 331. This would not have acted as a motivation in the same way the Cyrus incident did before Cunaxa, because this was unexpected and was a bonus for services already rendered. Diodorus tells us of these bonus payments:[8]

> From the money which was captured he distributed to each of the cavalrymen six minas, to each of the allied cavalrymen five, and to the Macedonians of the phalanx two, and he gave to all the mercenaries two months' pay.

It is difficult to appreciate at first glance how generous these bonus payments were, but to put these figures in a context, in terms of ancient currency:

100 drachma = 1 mina
1 talent = 60 minae

We do not know with absolute certainty how much a cavalryman in Alexander's army would have earned as a daily rate (or what that payment consisted of), but around two drachmae a day is a typical estimate. Therefore, six minae, or 600 drachma, as a bonus payment (300 days' pay) seems a significant amount. The bonus paid to mercenaries, two months' pay, thus seems considerably less generous by comparison to that paid to the regular divisions of the army, but with Alexander this was to be expected. He was a significant employer of mercenaries, as we shall see later, but they were never the main component of his army, always being on the periphery.

The least frequently used and therefore probably the least important method of payment of mercenaries was in the form of land. The practice of allotting land for military service became commonplace in the Roman Empire, for both legionaries and auxiliaries, but it was rather less common in Greece, and certainly as a method of payment for mercenaries. One of the very few incidents of this form of payment was by Dionysius in 396. Diodorus again:[9]

> Dionysius ... offered the mercenaries, who numbered about ten thousand, in lieu of their pay the city and territory of the Leontines. To this they gladly agreed because the territory was good land, and after portioning it out in allotments, they made their home in Leontini.

The rarity of this form of payment is indicated by the circumstances of this incident. It was evidently a lack of funds that forced Dionysius to create this novel method. It is further interesting to note that once the mercenaries had accepted their allotment of land they seemingly settled down and no longer pursued the life of the mercenary, making this form of payment undesirable if the tyrant wished to maintain his mercenary army. Mercenary settlers were often not popular amongst the natives either, of course.

The final element of remuneration for mercenaries is one of the most important for the majority: booty. For many mercenaries, and indeed a great number of regular troops, booty was a major source of funds and a significant motivational factor in taking up mercenary service in the first place.[10]

The desire to enjoy the spoils of war is as old as Greek warfare itself; it is a central theme of the Homeric epics, where there is no clear dividing line between plunder and legitimate trading activities.[11] The traditional view amongst Greeks was that the conquered peoples and their possessions passed to the conquerors: to the victors belong the spoils. The desire for the acquisition of wealth as a motivating factor in warfare, both for the state and for individuals, cannot be denied. In terms of states, the distribution of plunder was even included as a clause in some treaties.[12]

Booty could come in a number of forms. It could be actual items of intrinsic value that could easily be carried away by the victor; this was probably a major source of this type of income for mercenaries. One such 'item' was the captured enemy; individuals captured in warfare automatically became slaves and were often sold after the battle to provide a major source of income for the state, some of which was likely to be distributed amongst the army. We see, for example, Alexander selling 30,000 Thebans into slavery after his Sack of Thebes in 335. The sale brought much needed revenue into the Macedonian treasury, some 440 talents, each Theban being worth on average eighty-eight drachmae.[13] The state could also sell any captured livestock and especially land; the scope for income from warfare was vast, if successful, of course.

Violence and plundering after a battle or siege reached something of a peak in the Greek world in the fourth century, with a number of cities being sacked and pillaged, although the Hellenistic period was arguably worse. It is entirely possible that this trend is linked to the increasing use of mercenaries, who saw plunder as a major source of income, a form of bonus payment for successful service. It is also likely linked to the generally parlous state of the finances of some of the major protagonists in the fourth century.

Individual rank-and-file mercenaries could become wealthy as a result of plunder, but how many actually did is an interesting question. The choicest artefacts would likely have been taken by regular state troops, with the mercenaries picking over whatever was left. Commanders would also have their choice of items before the lower ranks, and therefore, there may not always have been a great deal left worth stealing.

Some mercenaries undoubtedly did very well out of plunder, particularly the commanders. Xenophon, for example, made enough money from the expedition to Persia to enable him to make a dedication to Apollo at Delphi, and also to buy a plot of land in the Peloponnese, upon which he built a temple and an alter to Artemis:[14]

> Here Xenophon built an altar and a temple with the sacred money, and from that time forth he would every year take the tithe of the products of the land in their season and offer sacrifice to the goddess, all the citizens and the men and women of the neighbourhood taking part in the festival. And the goddess would provide for the banqueters barley meal and loaves of bread, wine and sweetmeats, and a portion of the sacrificial victims from the sacred herd as well as of the victims taken in the chase.

To perform such acts it would have taken a great deal of plunder, but as a commander and aristocrat, Xenophon was in prime position to receive more than his fair share.

We do also have some circumstantial evidence of the amount of plunder a rank-and-file mercenary could achieve.[15] Nicostratus, an Athenian who saw mercenary service overseas and died in the 370s, left two talents of property at his death. This estate was contested in court, and we have the speech of Isaeus demonstrating some of the detail of the case.[16] It seems impossible that this money could have come from a wage alone, or even with a bonus payment included. Some of this figure must have come from plunder, which he invested in property in Athens.

In terms of the collection of booty, Aeneas Tacticus presents us with a vivid and interesting picture from the perspective of a commander under siege:[17]

> After your defensive force has been concentrated in a specific place and the enemy are dispersed in search of plunder, now is the time to attack them, to cut off their routes of retreat with cavalry and to form ambushes composed of select troops.

The implication being that almost as soon as the siege had begun there would be raiding parties out looking for plunder and pillage. It is certainly true that foraging parties would constantly accompany an army looking for food and water, and it is not difficult to see plundering taking place alongside this. Whether these parties were large enough to reduce the size of the attacking force sufficiently to make a sortie viable is highly debatable, and I think unlikely, unless the attacking force was desperately short of supplies.

Aeneas Tacticus goes on to tell us:

> Attack the enemy where you are not unwilling to give battle and in doing so you will suffer no disadvantage. From my previous discussion you can see that it is advantageous to allow the enemy to plunder as much of your territory as possible, so that plundering and burdened with booty, he will be readily open to your vengeance and all that has been taken can be recovered and those who have committed aggression will receive just what they deserve.

I doubt that local landowners would support this policy, and there seems little evidence that it was ever actually adopted.

The fact of the victorious army owning the property, and indeed the person of the conquered, was never questioned; exactly who amongst the conquering army owned which part of the booty was, however, a major source of difficulty after a battle. We see this as a central theme in Homer in the dispute between Agamemnon and Achilles over Briseis.

The distribution of booty amongst the victors seems to have been a highly controlled affair. In theory, the commander of the victorious force took possession of all of the captured goods, including people and livestock. Much of the 'living' booty would then be sold; what was not would be distributed and then (likely) sold.

In general, it was the responsibility of the commanding general to organize the distribution and sale of the booty, and it tended to be distributed according to a series of unwritten rules. These rules would generally govern how much senior commanders, junior commanders and the rank and file would receive from the total.[18] Whatever remained would temporarily remain in the possession of the general until the army returned home. At that point, the remaining spoils would become the property of the state, no doubt after a certain amount had been squirreled away by the general for his own purposes. In terms of mercenary generals, there was no home state as such, so they could become rich beyond the dreams of their subordinates from the spoils of war.

The major city-states like Athens and Sparta had officials whose responsibility it was to assist a commander with the sale and distribution of booty, and likely to ensure the state received its fair share. Merchants and slave traders would be part of the baggage train of an army and would provide an immediate market for captured goods. The immediate market was, however, limited, and a sizeable amount of booty could cause a saturation of the market, with supply seriously outstripping demand, and the inevitable drop in price that this situation always brings. This occurred, for example, in Sicily after the failure of the Athenian expedition in 413.[19]

Some plunder could, however, be acquired outside of the strict control of the general and of state officials. We see from Xenophon again that towards the end of the *Anabasis* he organized a raid, with his closest friends, on a local wealthy estate, with the sole intention of gathering plunder. Xenophon presents this raid as a way of gathering plunder for himself and of helping out his closest friends. Whatever was collected on such raids was kept by those involved, although probably distributed along similar lines as those applied to the army as a whole, i.e. the commander receiving the lion's share and then progressively less gooing to those lower down the food chain. Mercenary armies were, therefore, remarkably dangerous to the civilians in areas where they passed. Xenophon tells us:[20]

> Xenophon set out and took with him, with the idea of doing them a good turn, the captains who had been his particular friends and faithful to him through everything. About 600 others too came up to him, trying to force their services upon him, but the captains turned them away, so as not to have to give them a share of the booty, which they regarded as being already theirs.

This is an interesting illustration of the views of the mercenaries at the end of the *Anabasis*, and likely illustrative of mercenaries and others more generally. Plunder was a way of life for such people, and as Xenophon says, they considered the property to be 'already theirs'.

Now that we have established the methods and mechanisms by which mercenaries were paid, we should turn our attention to the amount of pay and its regularity. In terms of the regularity of payment, the theory and practice of payment appear to differ significantly. It is not greatly surprising that sometimes mercenaries, and even the regular troops, were not paid at regular intervals. There are several reasons for this, but by far the most important would have been a lack of funds, which was a major cause of the increase in plunder during campaigns into the fourth century and beyond. Mercenaries would nominally have been paid on a monthly basis, as suggested by Xenophon in an address to his gathered mercenaries:[21]

> Now I promise, in case you set sail from here, to provide you with pay from the first of the month at the rate of a Cyzicene per month to each man; and I will take you to Troas, the place from which I am an exile, and my city will be at your service; for they will receive me willingly.

The above quotation from Xenophon illustrates the regularity of pay for the 10,000, but it is rare to have such information; for the most part, whenever rates of pay are cited they are always presented as a daily rate. In terms of administration on the march, monthly remuneration was no doubt easier to calculate and distribute.[22] Different forms of payment would be distributed at different times of the month, of course. Financial payments that were specifically intended for the purchase of food would likely be paid in advance, i.e. at the start of a month. No sensible commander would allow his troops to go hungry for the sake of keeping coin in his treasury for a few more days, to say nothing of the indiscipline that this would inevitably lead to.

There is some surviving evidence that expenses incurred by a mercenary whilst travelling to meet up at a muster point with his new commander would be met by the individual, and that part of his wage, the *ephodia*, would only be paid upon his arrival. We see this from both Callicratidas and Xenophon.[23] Xenophon gives us a very vivid picture of the different types of people who signed up to be part of Cyrus' mercenary army, and suggests that some would have funded themselves in terms of travelling expenses:

> For most of the soldiers had sailed away from Greece to undertake this service for pay, not because their means were scanty, but because they knew by report of the noble character of Cyrus; some brought other men with them, some had even spent money of their own on the enterprise, while still another class had abandoned fathers and mothers, or had left children behind with the idea of getting money to bring back to them, all because they heard that the other people who served with Cyrus enjoyed abundant good fortune. Being men of this sort, therefore, they longed to return in safety to Greece.

Some men were motivated to take up mercenary service by the fact that they were unable to make a living in any other way. Indeed, this trend would have gathered in pace through into the Hellenistic period, where it became a way of life. It was something of a vicious circle, with more opportunities leading more people to become dependent on that way of life. However, the fact that travelling expenses would likely have come out of the pocket of the mercenary himself would have ensured that those in absolute penury could not become mercenaries, at least not at any great distance from home.

It seems likely, however, that mercenaries did receive some form of up-front payments, likely for food at the very least. Diodorus presents us with a number of passages in which an employer would send a representative with large sums of money in order to hire new mercenaries. We see Alexander the Great doing this, for example, by sending recruiters back to Greece on more than one occasion. Diodorus also supports this view by his reference to a commander gathering funds *before* embarking upon a programme of recruiting a body of mercenaries. He tells us of the recruitment policy of Dionysus in 383, for example:[24]

> Now that Dionysius was well supplied with money, he hired a multitude of soldiers from every land, and after bringing together a very considerable army, was obviously preparing for a war against the Carthaginians.

And of the Carthaginian response:[25]

> Now the Carthaginians formed an alliance with the Italian Greeks and together with them went to war against the tyrant; and since they wisely recognised in advance that it would be a great war, they enrolled as soldiers the capable youth from their own citizens, and then, raising a great sum of money, hired large forces of mercenary troops.

These passages tell us that some form of advance payment was made to the mercenaries being hired, although perhaps not a great deal, as we also see in the other cited passages that some needed to pay their own travelling money. The same passages also tell us that mercenary armies were not cheap, and that the finances needed to be planned and in place up front.

How much mercenaries were paid is a rather more complex question to address. There are a number of reasons for this. It is partly a simple lack of surviving source material that makes reference to their remuneration, and partly for the reasons discussed above, that there were a great many ways a mercenary could be paid, not all of them easily measurable. It is also worth noting that what we have in the surviving literature is largely the theory of what mercenaries, or indeed regular troops, would have been paid. The reality may have been very different.[26] It is certain that there were periods where mercenaries would not have received any remuneration, perhaps because of a lack of funds on the part of the employer. In those instances the mercenaries could either desert in search of a more reliable paymaster, or stick with what they knew in the hope that the situation would improve. If the mercenary chose the latter course we would be unlikely to hear of this from the surviving source material and will assume a regular salary was paid.

It seems to be generally accepted that the wages paid to mercenaries fell from the fifth to the fourth centuries. It has been noted that by the fourth century the wage was little above a subsistence level, and that the cost of living had risen significantly during and after Alexander's conquest of Asia, making mercenary service very unattractive.[27] The more recent trend is to downplay the wage deflation argument in favour of saying that the wages may have fallen in the fourth century, but not by a great deal.[28] The reality of the situation is probably somewhere in between. It does seem that the wages for mercenary service did decline in the fourth century, but that mercenaries appear to have had a little more of a free rein in terms of the collection of plunder, which could have more than made up for the drop in base salary.

As noted earlier, however, the collection of plunder was not guaranteed, but there was an undoubted rise in violence in the fourth century and into the Hellenistic period. There were a number of factors for this, but mercenary activity was certainly one of them. There were notable exceptions in the fourth century, of course, in terms of the size of mercenary remuneration. Cyrus, Jason of Pherae, the Phocian generals and probably Alexander the Great were all generous paymasters, and we must therefore draw a distinction between those wealthy employers and the mercenaries who were employed to fight in a less lucrative war. However, as with modern salaries, there does appear to have been something of a significant gap between those at the bottom and those further up the pay scale: there was not one standard rate. Whatever the rate, there does not seem to have been a shortage of willing applicants when mercenaries were required.[29]

It has long been supposed, and it does seem logical (although there is no actual direct evidence to support this), that mercenary pay would have been linked in some way to the wages of regular troops in service overseas.[30] Of course, the word 'linked' is critical here; it is not the same as saying that pay would have been the same; it further seems logical that mercenary pay may have been a little lower. We will examine this in more detail later when we examine the situation in the Macedonian army.[31]

In terms of monetary value, Thucydides gives us a number of examples of the size of *misthos* payments (regular wages) made during the Peloponnesian War to both soldiers and sailors.[32]

Thucydides tells us:

> At this time when their ships were at sea the Athenians had the largest
> number of ships on active service and in fine condition, though there
> were similar or even greater numbers at the beginning of the war ... the
> total number of ships in service in the course of one summer was two
> hundred and fifty. This and Potidaea were particular drains on their
> finances. The men on duty at Potidaea were two-drachmae hoplites
> (receiving one drachma a day for themselves and one for their servant)
> ... All the ships were paid at the same rate.

The payment of one drachma a day does appear to have been the standard
rate for infantry and sailors during the fifth century.[33] Aristophanes
mentions this figure in the *Acharnians* in 425, whilst in 424 in the *Wasps* he
suggested that three and two obols a day were a standard wage.[34] The two
obols a day suggested by Aristophanes could well be a confusion with the
two obols of *sitêresion* (ration money) mentioned by Demosthenes and noted
earlier.[35] Plutarch also tells us that Alcibiades paid the sailors in his fleet
three obols a day (half a drachma):[36]

> Lysander, who had been sent out as admiral by the Lacedaemonians,
> paid his sailors four obols a day instead of three, out of the moneys he
> received from Cyrus; while Alcibiades, already hard put to it to pay even
> his three obols, was forced to sail for Caria to levy money.

Xenophon expands upon this story by noting Lysander's attempt to
persuade Cyrus to pay one drachma a day (six obols); the attempt ended in
failure, however.[37] This incident rather suggests that four obols a day was
above the regular *misthos* payment for the fifth century, for sailors at least.[38]

One of the first large-scale mercenary employers was Dionysius I, tyrant
of Syracuse (405–367). Unfortunately, we have no surviving evidence of
exactly what he paid his mercenaries or his regular troops. Diodorus does
tell us that he was generous, however, particularly when he needed to be:[39]

> From the Syracusans he enrolled those who were fit for military service
> in companies and from the cities subject to him he summoned their
> able men. He also gathered mercenaries from Greece, and especially
> from the Lacedaemonians, for they, in order to aid him in building up
> his power, gave him permission to enlist as many mercenaries from
> them as he might wish. And, speaking generally, since he made a point
> of gathering his mercenary force from many nations and promised high
> pay, he found men who were responsive.

Although we do not know with any certainty, as noted above, we can reasonably assume that 'high pay', as Diodorus puts it, was perhaps around the one drachma a day that Cyrus was paying his mercenaries.

The Army of Cyrus is the first large-scale mercenary army for which we have details regarding pay. During the early stages of the march, they were receiving one daric a month, around five obols a day. Once the true dangers of the campaign became known, and to maintain the army in the field, this was raised to around one and a half darics a month, about seven and a half obols a day; a phenomenal sum, based upon the other evidence we have seen so far.[40] Even if pay was declining generally in the fourth century, there were some high points in terms of salary expectations for mercenary service. If, however, this daric or daric and a half per month represented not only *misthos* but also *sitêresion*, then the picture would appear rather less generous. If the soldiers were expected to pay for their own food and equipment from their salary then perhaps the pay of Cyrus was not what it would first appear to be.

To an extent, they had the option of plunder, but this was limited during the outward journey at least.[41] When they were heading home it would have been a far more regular occurrence, and we have already seen that Xenophon himself was not immune to its lure. We do know that Xenophon never mentions free *sitos* (food) being issued to the mercenary army, and nor does he mention *sitêresion* at any point being paid on top of the one daric a month. In reality, we do not know exactly what is included in the daric payment, but it does seem likely that the troops were expected to purchase their own supplies from markets as and when they were available.

We have noted the general belief that the pay of mercenaries declined in the fourth century, although I think the reality is that pay probably did not decline markedly from that of the fifth century. We have very little surviving source material down to the death of Alexander (323) regarding mercenary pay. There are, in fact, only two pieces of surviving text that give us any real clue as to the figure.[42] The first of these two pieces of evidence is from Xenophon and is in connection with the decision of Sparta to allow members of the Peloponnesian League to contribute money, rather than troops, to the league.[43] As with the Delian League/Athenian Empire, this was something that strengthened the Spartan position as head of that league The League, or probably Sparta in actuality, agreed a figure that each participating state would pay in lieu of sending citizen soldiers to fight; the rate being three Aeginetan obols a day, equivalent to four and a half Attic obols (the standard currency we have been using in this discussion so far).

It seems logical to assume that the Spartans would set the payment at a level that was not below the level they would need to pay a mercenary to take the place of the citizen soldier from the League. If they had set the level lower, then either Sparta would have needed to make up the difference or she would have been able to hire fewer mercenaries than they would have had citizen soldiers from the member states. This latter course may not have been an issue for Sparta (or anyone else for that matter), as professional soldiers would likely have been of a higher quality than their citizen counterparts. A rate of four and a half Attic obols a day is probably a reasonable guess as to the base line *misthos* payment for mercenaries during at least the early part of the fourth century. If so, then it does represent a significant fall from the one drachma a day (six obols), which is the likely figure for the fifth century.[44] We must remember a point already made, of course, that the rate varied significantly between pay masters, and that there was not a single standard rate.

The second piece of textual evidence for the rate of pay of mercenaries in the fourth century is from Demosthenes' *First Philippic*, produced sometime around 351.[45] This is a piece of evidence noted earlier and is the outline of a plan put forward by Demosthenes that would allow the Athenians to put a mercenary army into the field in Thrace at a considerably lower cost than normal. Demosthenes proposed that the mercenaries be paid a *sitêresion* payment (ration pay) of two obols a day with no *misthos* payment at all. The mercenaries would be allowed virtually free rein to plunder Thrace and Macedonia as they saw fit in order to both further Athenian interests and to provide themselves with plunder. It is unknown if the commander would keep a measure of the plunder and return it to Athens, as was the normal practice with citizen armies, or if all of the plunder was to be theirs.

The financial element of Demosthenes' proposal was:

> You think perhaps that this is a sound proposal, but you are chiefly anxious to hear what the cost will be and how it will be raised. I now proceed to deal with that point. As to the cost then: the maintenance, the bare rationing of this force, comes to rather more than ninety talents; for the ten fast galleys forty talents, or twenty minae a ship every month; for two thousand men the same amount, that each may receive ten drachmas a month ration-money; for the two hundred cavalry twelve talents, if each is to receive thirty drachmas a month.

In the plan, both infantry and sailors would receive two obols a day, and a cavalryman one drachma (six obols).

The worth of this passage has been questioned most severely, given that it was a proposal of Demosthenes and it was never enacted.[46] Despite criticisms from scholars, I believe this passage of Demosthenes does have some value. We must assume first of all that Demosthenes was putting this forward as a serious policy proposition; I think we have no reason to assume anything else. Accepting this, if the figure of two obols a day, which Demosthenes clearly states is for *sitêresion* only, were unrealistic (either high or low) then its chances of becoming policy would be reduced. It seems reasonable to assume that this figure is very close to (if not actually) the figure mercenaries would expect to receive for the *sitêresion* element of their wage. This evidence only gets us so far, of course, because the proposal by its very nature does not give us any indication of the *misthos* element of a mercenary's pay.

There is one further inference that we may be able to make from this passage, however. Demosthenes was clearly attempting to raise and support a mercenary army at the lowest possible cost. The fact that he included a *sitêresion* payment at all implies that mercenaries would have demanded this (or some other form of up front payment) as a minimum and would not have been content to work entirely for the prospect of plunder.

At the same time as Demosthenes was making his proposal to the Athenians, the Third Sacred War was raging in central Greece. This war was one of the largest employers of mercenaries that the Greek world had seen; unfortunately, however, our main source for the war, Diodorus, gives us no specific figures as to how much those mercenaries were being paid. What he does tell us, however, is that the *misthos* payment made by the Phocians to their mercenaries was raised significantly on more than one occasion.

In three separate passages Diodorus gives us some very interesting information:[47]

> While these things were going on, [The Boeotians dispatching troops] Philomelus threw a wall around the shrine [Delphi] and began to assemble a large number of mercenaries by raising the pay to half as much again, and selecting the bravest of the Phocians he enrolled them and quickly had a considerable army.
>
> When it was clear that the Boeotians would take the field with a large army against the Phocians, Philomelus decided to gather a great number of mercenaries. Since the war required ampler funds, he was compelled to lay his hands on the sacred dedications and to plunder the oracle. By setting the base pay for the mercenaries at half as much again as was usual, he quickly assembled a large number of mercenaries, since many answered the summons to the campaign on account of the size of the pay.
>
> After the death of Onomarchus, his brother Phayllus succeeded to the command of the Phocians. In an attempt to retrieve the disaster, he began to gather a multitude of mercenaries, offering double the customary pay.

These three passages give us some very interesting general information regarding the actions of the Phocian generals. On two occasions, first in 355/4 and again in 354/3, they offered *misthos* payments that were fifty per cent above the standard level, and as the war went badly in 353/2 they offered double the base level. Despite the progress of the war, they evidently did not have any difficulty recruiting at these levels. If we were right to assume that the four and a half obols a day demanded by Sparta was equivalent to the early fourth-century *misthos* payment, and that the rate declined through the fourth century, as seems to be generally accepted, then a fifty per cent increase would likely reach a level of one drachma a day, or a rate equivalent to the fifth-century standard. The double rate would therefore have been around one and a half drachma a day, a generous sum indeed. We must remember, of course, that we have been discussing the *misthos* payment only, and it seems likely that a *sitêresion* payment of around two obols (if we accept the Demosthenes figure) a day would have been paid on top of that, which would give the total state requirement. A high wage would not have precluded the mercenaries also being able to plunder when the opportunities presented themselves.

The evidence for the later fourth century regarding mercenary pay is remarkably sparse; especially considering this is a period for which we have so much surviving material. We do know that Alexander's elite heavy infantry, the hypaspists, were paid forty drachma a month and that Alexander paid his allied troops one drachma a day.[48] The figure of one drachma a day applies to the allied infantry in the army, Odrysians, Triballians, etc., but not to the Thessalian cavalry. We have no evidence at all as to their rates of pay, except for the obvious statement that cavalry were paid more than infantry.

It has rightly been pointed out that we have no reason to believe, from the surviving material, that Alexander's mercenaries were paid either more or less than the allied troops.[49] It is perhaps worth noting that he used both in very similar ways; that is to say, as a reserve formation in the set-piece battles.[50] Having said this, however, there is no reason to assume that because different categories of troops were employed in a similar way they would have received the same pay and conditions.

In all of the surviving sources that deal with the remarkable career of Alexander, there is perhaps only a single clue as to the wages paid to the very many mercenaries he employed. In 331, whilst at Ecbatana, Alexander took a major military decision to undertake a significant reorganization of the army. This is not the correct place to analyse the changes that occurred; suffice to say that the previously indispensible Thessalian cavalry were disbanded.[51] They were not immediately sent home, however, but were offered the opportunity to sign up once again, but as mercenaries rather than allied troops. Most of the Thessalians did exactly this, although they were again disbanded as mercenaries not long afterwards, and they never again had the prominence in the army that they had during the initial stages of the war of conquest up to the Battle of Gaugamela in 331. This piece of evidence is very limited, but the numbers who signed up as mercenaries (i.e. almost all of them) implies that the mercenary cavalry were paid at least the same amount as the allied cavalry, although we do not know what that figure is exactly. If the mercenaries were paid substantially less, then signing up as mercenaries would have seemed a far less attractive proposition, and we would assume greater numbers would have chosen simply to return home with the great wealth that they had already amassed during the campaign in Asia.

Despite any attempts to demonstrate the contrary, however, the reality is that we simply do not know how much Alexander (or anyone else towards the end of the fourth century) paid his mercenaries. All we can do is speculate as to the level and suggest that it was fairly high, partly because of the supposition surrounding the Thessalian cavalry, and partly because shortly after the war of conquest began, Alexander was not short of funds and would have been able to be generous if it was required or desired.

Chapter 2

The Archaic Period

Warfare has been a constant throughout history, and throughout the history of warfare there were likely to have been mercenaries. The first positive evidence we have for the employment of Greek mercenaries, however, comes from the period towards the end of the great migration of peoples into the Greek world.

At the end of the Bronze Age, central Greece was torn apart by successive waves of invasion, or migration, by Dorians from Illyria.[1] The levels of violence that attended these movements of peoples are much debated and hence they are called either invasions or migrations. Either way, the Greek world was to change permanently. The new arrivals were Greek speaking, and as a result were accepted in some areas and lived peacefully alongside the native populations. In other areas, the native Greeks were forced to move in a generally southern direction into the Peloponnese. Many of these settled in the rough and mountainous terrain of the Arcadia region, a region that was to become a byword for mercenary recruitment in the Classical period.

Over the succeeding centuries a measure of cultural homogeneity developed, but there were enough differences to ensure that warfare between competing city-states was an ever-present threat. Long before the rise to prominence of the great city-states, however, there was a great deal of economic hardship in some parts of the newly settled Greek world. Arable land in Greece is generally quite fertile, but the problem is that there is very little of it, and it is particularly scarce in areas like Arcadia.[2] The hunger and economic hardships that this brought resulted in significant numbers of largely men who sought a living overseas. Sometimes, this meant working as mercenaries, but perhaps just as often as skilled tradesmen, such as the stone masons that worked at Persepolis.

It is in the light of these social difficulties in Greece that we see the first evidence of Greek mercenary activity, and it was not in Greece. It would appear that Greeks abroad during this period almost exclusively sought service in one region: Egypt.

Egypt

In Egypt, we see a period of around 150 years of almost unbroken mercenary service, beginning with the Pharaoh Psammetichus (664–610), and only coming to an end (albeit a temporary one) with the Persian conquest of Egypt by Cambyses. The beginnings of the history of Greek mercenary service in Egypt are a rebellion against an oppressive overlord and are related by Herodotus. Psammetichus, the Egyptian Pharaoh, was in revolt against the Assyrian domination of Egypt. In order to determine his course of action, he consulted the best-known oracle in Egypt at the time, that resident at the town of Buto. Herodotus tells us the tale:[3]

> He sent to inquire in the town of Buto, where the most infallible oracle in Egypt is; the oracle answered that he would have vengeance when he saw men of bronze coming from the sea.

Psammetichus apparently did not believe the oracle, but Herodotus continues:[4]

> Psammetichus did not in the least believe that men of bronze would come to aid him. But after a short time, Ionians and Carians, voyaging for plunder, were forced to put in on the coast of Egypt, where they disembarked in their armour of bronze; and an Egyptian came into the marsh country and brought news to Psammetichus (for he had never before seen armoured men) that men of bronze had come from the sea and were foraging in the plain.

This passage is interesting not only because it tells us a great deal about the development of Egyptian military equipment, and indeed that of Assyria, given that they were ruling Egypt, but also that voyages of plunder were not unknown. It would be incorrect to call these Greeks 'mercenaries' at this point; clearly, pirates would be more accurate.

With the arrival of the Greeks, Psammetichus saw the fulfilment of the oracle and immediately set about befriending these strange visitors. He apparently offered to take them into his service, employing them as mercenaries, and with their assistance won the freedom of Egypt.

Herodotus presents a picture of the Greeks arriving by chance, an accident of wind and tides, but Diodorus gives an entirely different picture of the Greeks being summoned by Psammetichus himself; if the latter version is to be believed then their arrival was not fortuitous but part of a planned uprising.[5] The details of the expulsion of the Assyrians and the victory of

Psammetichus are unknown, but we do know that after victory had been assured the mercenaries were offered the opportunity to settle in Egypt, at Daphnae on an eastern tributary of the Nile in the Delta. Herodotus again tells us:[6]

> To the Ionians and Carians who had helped him, Psammetichus gave places to live in called The Camps, opposite each other on either side of the Nile; and besides this, he paid them all that he had promised.

This was, of course, a strategically sensitive area, given that it controlled (in part at least) access to Egypt via the Arabian Peninsula. The route along the coast was the obvious way in which an invading army would move into Egyptian territory. The very fact of them settling in that location indicates the level of trust he built up very quickly with these men; a level of trust that, until recently, had not really existed.

Using these mercenaries as settlers was a very clever ploy by Psammetichus. He could not possibly afford to pay them, even during times of peace, so another method needed to be found to keep them close in case of further difficulty, either from without or within.

He could not allow large numbers of mercenaries to wander freely around Egypt; the damage they could cause (in terms of plunder) was immense. Neither could he casually dismiss them and send them back to Greece. These men were mercenaries, if not at the start (when they were basically pirates) then certainly later; they needed employment and they could very easily seek employment from the Assyrians or any number of other potential or real threats to Egypt. Given the lack of good quality Egyptian infantry (a situation that never really improved), Psammetichus would have likely felt that settling these men was a no-lose situation. If there was a further invasion or uprising then these men could be brought out of retirement to conduct a final campaign. He also likely hoped that they would help to train the young people in the towns where they were stationed, generally improving the ability of the citizen soldiers. Perhaps the mercenaries did this to an extent; and it is very interesting that they do not appear to have resisted the decision. Psammetichus appears to have ultimately been proved right, as:[7]

> A mixed race of professional soldiers grew up whom the Pharaohs employed on their campaigns against Syria and Ethiopia.

Having significant numbers of Greeks, be they mercenaries or not, was not uniformly considered positive by the native Egyptian population. As the influx of Greeks continued (because this was the only regular area of recruitment in the Archaic period for Greek mercenaries), the native Egyptians became restless. During the reign of Apries, for example, there were perhaps 30,000 Greek mercenaries in Egypt; Herodotus tells us:[8]

> Learning of this, too, Apries armed his guard and marched against the Egyptians; he had a bodyguard of Carians and Ionians, thirty thousand of them, and his royal palace was in the city of Saïs, a great and marvellous palace.

Despite their numbers, however, there was something of a popular nationalist uprising, during which Apries, who was seen as the person responsible for this massive influx of foreign troops, was overthrown and replaced by Amasis. The new ruler was well aware of the importance and potential usefulness of having a well-trained, equipped and loyal army of 30,000 Greeks at his disposal. After his victory, he did not dismiss the Greeks, but did seek to remove them a little from the popular consciousness. He acted to physically relocate them from the strategically important delta region (with its large numbers of native Egyptians) to Memphis, where they were employed as his bodyguards. Again, Herodotus notes:[9]

> The Ionians and Carians lived for a long time in these places, which are near the sea, on the arm of the Nile called the Pelusian, a little way below the town of Bubastis. Long afterwards, king Amasis removed them and settled them at Memphis to be his guard against the Egyptians.

The expression 'guard against the Egyptians' is particularly interesting here, and implies a link between mercenaries and tyrants that we will explore in more detail later.

Greek mercenaries were also to play a key role in the end of Egyptian independence when the country fell to Cambyses of Persia in 525. During that struggle, Greek mercenaries fought on both sides, but it was a single individual who did more than any other to bring defeat to Egypt. Herodotus attributes the success of Cambyses' attack on Egypt largely to Phanes of Halicarnassus. Phanes was evidently a high-ranking Greek mercenary in the military hierarchy of the Egyptian Pharaoh, Psammetichus III, but had ultimately become disgruntled with the conditions of his service in Egypt. Herodotus tells us that much, but fails to give any detail on exactly what Phanes' complaint was, telling us only that:[10]

> One of the Greek mercenaries of Amasis, a Hallicarnassian called Phanes, a brave and intelligent soldier, being dissatisfied for some reason or other with Amasis, escaped from Egypt by sea, with the object of getting an interview with Cambyses.

Whatever Phanes' reasons for dissatisfaction, we can only assume that they must have been very serious, given his actions. We have already noted that defection was neither a common nor a desirable trait amongst mercenaries, as it led to an unwanted reputation, and ultimately would affect the employment prospects of all. We must remember too that Phanes left his sons behind in Egypt, as well making them an inevitable target of the regime after his desertion became known.

The potential implications of such a high-ranking defection were not lost on Amasis, and he immediately attempted to track down the fleeing Greek. Phanes was ultimately tracked down and captured in Lydia, before he reached Cambyses, but he effected his escape by inducing his captors to become blind drunk, then slipped away into the night. Shortly afterwards, he reached the court of Cambyses and gained an audience with the Great King. Phanes formulated a plan as to how Cambyses could get a substantial army across the Arabian Desert and enter Egypt almost undetected, and before Psammetichus could react to stop him. Cambyses was perhaps lucky, in that, shortly prior to this, Amasis had died and his son, Psammetichus III, succeeded to the throne of Egypt. The transition between the two rulers would inevitably have led to a degree of stasis, and unfortunately for Egypt it was at exactly the wrong time.

The plan proposed by Phanes was to seek the assistance of, and ultimately befriend, the Bedouins of that region. Cambyses was, in Herodotus' words, 'anxious to launch his attack on Egypt', and was evidently persuaded of the potential of Phanes' plan.[11] It appears to have taken very little time for Cambyses to organize an invasion force, and we can assume that his troops were in a state of near-readiness, as the invasion was contemplated before the arrival of Phanes. Cambyses quickly launched the attack by marching towards the Arabian Peninsula, where he did indeed receive the assistance of the Bedouins, described in detail by Herodotus, although we do not know what he gave in return for their assistance.[12]

When Cambyses had successfully crossed the Arabian Peninsula, the two armies came face to face and made preparations for battle at Pelusium. Herodotus tells us:[13]

> Before the battle the Greek and Carian mercenaries who were serving with the Egyptians contrived the following against Phanes in their anger at his bringing a foreign army against Egypt: they seized his sons, whom he had left behind, and brought them to the camp, where they made sure their father could see them; then, placing a bowl in the open ground between the two armies, they led the body up to it one by one, and cut their throats over it. Not one was spared, and when the last was dead,

they poured wine and water onto the blood in the bowl, and every man in the mercenary force drank.

Once this hideous crime had been perpetrated by the Greek mercenaries in Egyptian service, battle was joined. The battle was hard fought and brutal – unsurprising, given its prologue. The Rhodians and Ionians on the side of the Egyptians were evenly matched by the Ionian and Aeolian Greeks employed by Cambyses and the Persians. Herodotus tells us nothing that would allow us an attempt at a reconstruction of the battle, save that the Greeks fighting for Psammetichus were slaughtered by their counterparts in Persian service. Whether or not Phanes survived the battle is not recorded.[14]

We have mentioned the figure of 30,000 Greek hoplites in Egyptian service at this time, and, given their quality and the general lack of quality of Persian heavy infantry, it seems a likely guess that the Persians would have fielded similar numbers of Greek mercenary hoplites too, but we have no positive evidence for this supposition. The victory was decisive for Persia; Egypt was under Persian control until c.404.

During each of the three main periods of Egyptian rebellion against Persian rule – first against Darius I, then Xerxes and finally Artaxerxes – Greek mercenaries fought on both sides. They were soldiers and showed no national or pan-Hellenic sentiment at all. On each occasion the fighting was vicious and no quarter was asked or given. Greek mercenaries cared little who their enemies were; they were professionals, after all.

At the end of the Persian occupation, when Alexander 'liberated' Egypt, Greek mercenaries were still to play a significant role in the life of the country. From the very first piratical raids that resulted in mercenary service, Greeks have a history spanning many hundreds of years of continuous mercenary service, with many and various paymasters in Egypt.

Greece

Aristotle is as responsible as anyone for creating the image that tyrants relied heavily upon mercenaries to prop up their regimes. Unfortunately for the tyrants, there is actually a great deal of truth in his assertion:[15]

> It is also in the interests of a tyrant to make his subjects poor, so that he may be able to afford the cost of his bodyguard, while the people are so occupied with their daily tasks that they have no time for plotting.

The bodyguard that Aristotle notes were the mercenaries, apparently employed by raising taxation on the ordinary folk of a city-state. The tyrant's priority was, therefore, maintaining his power through the employment of a bodyguard of professional mercenaries.

Aristotle does draw the distinction between tyrants at different periods in history. Those of the fourth century, and indeed those in Sicily, were undoubtedly military demagogues, whereas their earlier counterparts were men who generally came to pre-eminence in their cities because of civil or economic strife within their respective cities, and they, generally speaking, had a positive impact upon their respective states, even if some did maintain small mercenary bodyguards.[16]

The early tyrants, those of the seventh and sixth centuries, did not employ armies of mercenaries. They sometimes employed a bodyguard, as noted above, but even that was not a general rule. These mercenaries were few in number and were never asked to participate in territorial expansion in the same way as those in Sicily or in fifth-century and (to a greater extent) fourth-century Greece.

In order to judge the picture with regards to mercenaries propping up the rule of tyrants, we should examine some specific examples. Timagenes of Megara, Cýpselus of Corinth, Pisistratus of Athens and Dionysius the Elder of Syracuse all came to power, according to Aristotle, by acting as populist politicians and taking action against the wealthy in their respective city-states.[17] The result being that they were popular rulers and had a bodyguard voted to them. Whether or not they were mercenaries does not survive, but is often assumed.

Cypselus of Corinth and his son Periander in the seventh and sixth centuries were the first two tyrants of Corinth, and their rules demonstrate a significant development in terms of style, in many ways a forerunner of what we see from Pisistratus in the later sixth century in Athens. Cypselus was one of those seventh-century tyrants who rose to prominence, and remained so because of his popularity with the populace. We are also explicitly told that he did not keep a bodyguard. Periander, on the other hand, changed the character of the Corinthian tyranny somewhat, and he was aided in this by the maintenance of a mercenary bodyguard of some 300 strong. This force was entirely directed towards maintaining his powerbase; it was not large enough to be used for territorial expansion.[18]

The early tyranny in Sicyon is another example of one in which mercenaries were not hired as a bodyguard to support the regime. Aristotle describes the government thus:[19]

For the longest-lived was the tyranny at Sicyon, that of the sons of Orthagoras and of Orthagoras himself, and this lasted a hundred years. The cause of this was that they treated their subjects moderately and in many matters were subservient to the laws, and Cleisthenes because he was a warlike man was not easily despised, and in most things they kept the lead of the people by looking after their interests.

Tyranny and despotism are not the same thing, as noted earlier. It seems from this passage that tyrants can maintain a dynasty without the use of mercenaries; this was not the attitude of the Pisistratids in Athens, however. Pisistratus began his reign in Athens in the sixth century with a bodyguard that was voted to him of citizen club-bearers only. Even after his return from the first period of exile the situation changes little.[20] After his second exile, enforced because of a scandal between himself and his wife, the daughter of Megacles, his return to power was a different affair. Herodotus tells us:[21]

> Pisistratus, learning what was going on, went alone away from the country altogether, and came to Eretria, where he deliberated with his sons. The opinion of Hippias prevailing, that they should recover the sovereignty, they set out collecting contributions from all the cities that owed them anything. Many of these gave great amounts, the Thebans more than any and in course of time, not to make a long story, every-thing was ready for their return: for they brought Argive mercenaries from the Peloponnese, and there joined them on his own initiative a man of Naxos called Lygdamis, who was most keen in their cause and brought them money and men. So after ten years they set out from Eretria and returned home.

Pisistratus returned to Athens as commander of a significant force of mercenaries, which he used to first seize, and then secure, power. This was a policy continued by his sons during their tyrannies in Athens. The career of Pisistratus is a microcosm of the changing attitude of tyrants, and indeed their attitude to, and use of, mercenaries to prop up their regimes. Pisistratus began his rule by popular consent with a bodyguard of citizens voted to him; after his second period of exile, he ruled as a military dictator at the head of a significant force of mercenaries.

By the end of the sixth century it was commonplace for tyrants to employ a bodyguard, and it became exceptional for them not to do so. The age of tyrants was, however, coming to an end in Greece. This change in political outlook also had a major impact upon the Greek mercenary. The city-states were becoming more prosperous and more stable; they both needed their citizens and could find meaningful employment for them. The hardships that had driven many to seek out the life of the mercenary as (in their eyes perhaps) the only means they had of feeding themselves and their families were now ending. Simply put, mercenary service was less attractive. The city-states themselves were becoming more stable entities too, less in need of relying upon a strong individual for leadership, and less willing to tolerate such individuals when they arose. The end of the sixth century and the beginning of the fifth, therefore, saw both the end of tyranny in Greece and the (temporary) end of mercenary service on the mainland. These political changes were not mirrored in Sicily, however.

Sicily

Sicily was a major area of employment for Greek mercenaries throughout the Classical period. The zenith of recruitment was in the fourth century, but even during the Archaic period the numbers were surprisingly large by comparison to the numbers employed on the mainland. The earliest mention of Greek mercenaries in Sicily has been questioned, largely because the reference is only in Polyaenus (second century AD), and secondly because of his poor use of specific terminology:[22]

> Panaetius first stirred up the poor and the infantry against the wealthy and the horsemen on the grounds that the latter benefited from wars whilst the former lost a great deal ... he had 600 peltasts ready for his attempt to take power.

The first part of the quotation is entirely in line with what we have seen of the early tyrants in Greece. Their bids for power were made using the image of themselves as representatives of the poor against the rich (generally speaking), and in my view this lends a certain credence to the passage as a whole. The main legitimate criticism is of Polyaenus' use of the word πελτασταί (peltasts); Thracian peltasts had not yet reached Sicily, and therefore Polyaenus appears to have been using the incorrect term. This could, however, be nothing more than a later historian not fully appreciating that the term 'peltast' was the incorrect one in this context. He was perhaps using the term in a more generic sense, to refer to light-armed troops. I do not believe that the rejection of this evidence for early tyranny in Sicily is justified solely on the grounds of Polyaenus using an incorrect term in his work.

Other than the potential for the above reference, the first tyrant in Sicily for which we have sound evidence is Hippocrates of Gela.[23] Hippocrates not only employed mercenaries within his bodyguard, but he is the first recorded example of a tyrant employing Sicel mercenaries (the indigenous peoples of Sicily); barbarian mercenaries were to become relatively common in the fourth century in Sicily, but were unknown before Hippocrates. It is not recorded why Hippocrates chose to employ barbarian mercenaries over Greeks; the Greeks employed in Sicily and elsewhere had acquitted themselves adequately over the years and it does not, therefore, appear to have been an issue with quality. There could conceivably have been supply issues, or perhaps the Sicels were a cheaper option to a tyrant who needed significant numbers of mercenaries (given his aim of conquering the whole of Sicily). It is also possible that the Sicels were specialists in some fashion, in the same way that Thracian peltasts or Cretan archers became highly desirable troops in the later fifth and fourth centuries. There were probably two reasons for this. The first is that these Sicel mercenaries would have had inside knowledge of their own city and region, vital for Hippocrates given his intention to campaign against them. The second was that the more Sicels he hired, the fewer he would meet in battle in the coming campaign. The decision to hire these barbarian mercenaries was not, therefore, a cultural or political choice, indicating a change in public opinion in some way, but a deliberate strategic attempt to denude their city of able-bodied warriors as far as he could. Herodotus tells us of Hippocrates' fate:[24]

> Hippocrates was the tyrant of Gela for the same length of time as his brother Cleander (seven years), and died attacking Hybla during a campaign against the Sicels.

The tyranny of Hippocrates, and perhaps tyranny generally, was very unpopular in Gela. Upon the death of the tyrant the people tried to 'throw off the yolk of tyranny' and to install a more popular form of government, but the power of the tyrant was still strong. Hippocrates' two sons, Eucleides and Cleander, gathered together the forces loyal to their father and attempted to crush the popular uprising. Herodotus tells us that neither man succeeded Hippocrates, but that:[25]

> His [Hippocrates'] death gave Gelon his opportunity: masking his real purpose under the pretence of supporting Hippocrates' sons, Eucleides and Cleander, in their struggle against the people of Gela, who were eager to throw off the yolk, he crushed the insurgents by force of arms, and then, robbing the two young men of the fruits of their victory, seized power himself.

Gelon was a man with a significant military reputation, which he gained commanding the cavalry of the former tyrant, and he was evidently hungry for power. Soon after seizing the tyranny of Gela for himself, he also captured Syracuse by taking advantage of internal difficulties in that great city. The slaves (Cyllyrii, as Herodotus calls them) had banded together with the lowest rungs of society in order to expel the wealthy landowners. They succeeded for a time, forcing them to flee to Casmene with only what they could carry. The slaves and the commoners had little to no knowledge of how to run or defend a major city, and they were utterly unprepared for leadership. Gelon took advantage by aligning himself with the exiles and marching on Syracuse at the head of his army of mercenaries. The commoners realized instantly that they had no chance and immediately surrendered the city. We can only imagine the retribution that would have been exacted upon them and their slave allies. Gelon, no doubt by agreement with the wealthy elite, took control of Syracuse as tyrant. This was a far more important and substantial city than Gela, which he quickly lost interest in. He appointed his brother, Hieron, to rule Gela in his name, while he set about fortifying and strengthening Syracuse, also populating it with the inhabitants of local towns, which he razed to the ground.[26]

Herodotus' narrative does not give us any real insight into how Gelon used his undoubtedly large contingent of mercenaries to further his ambitions in Sicily, but his response to the delegation from Sparta (this was in 481/0, when the Persians were on the brink of invading Greece) does give us some clues as to the size of the forces he had at his disposal. Herodotus tells us of the envoys from Greece:[27]

> Envoys from Greece arrived in Syracuse, approached Gelon, and spoke to the following effect: 'We have been sent by the Spartans and their allies to obtain your help against the foreigner. You are, of course, aware of what is coming to Greece; that a Persian is about to bridge the Hellespont and to march against us out of Asia with all the armies of the east at his back, and that his true purpose, which he veils under the pretence of an attack on Athens, is the subjugation of the whole of Greece. Your power is great; as lord of Sicily you possess no inconsiderable portion of the Greek world; we ask you, therefore, to help us, and to add your strength to ours in our struggle to maintain our country's liberty ... Do not imagine that if the Persians defeat us in battle they will not afterwards visit *you*.

Gelon was not impressed by the plea from the Spartan envoy. In response, he noted that when he had been in a similarly difficult situation at the mercy of the Carthaginians he had made a similar plea to the Greeks for assistance, and was ignored. He was left to deal with the foreign invader himself. He also noted that he had been ultimately successful in that endeavour, and that he was now in a very strong position, and further pointed out that the tables had turned.

Gelon was, however, a great political opportunist and said to the envoys:[28]

> Though you treated me with contempt, I will not imitate your conduct. I am willing to help you by a contribution of 200 triremes, 20,000 hoplites, 2,000 cavalry, 2,000 archers, 2,000 slingers and 2,000 light horsemen;

and I undertake to provision the entire Greek army for as long as the war may last. My offer, however, is subject to one condition – that the supreme command of the Greek forces against the Persians shall be mine. On any other terms I will neither come myself nor send troops.

One can imagine the Spartan response; they were singularly unimpressed by the terms of Gelon's offer. They desperately needed the Sicilian troops, but there would be no possibility of the Spartans allowing their own troops to be commanded by a Sicilian tyrant. They did recognize them as fellow Greeks, but the Spartans would certainly not have seen them as equals. The Spartans evidently realized that they were in a very difficult position, but their pride (or arrogance) impelled them to reject Gelon's offer.

It is easy to see why Gelon would have made such an offer; his successes in Sicily were complete, and he was looking for further opportunities. He would have imagined a major military success on the mainland, which would have led to inevitable territorial expansion, but his demand for command was a step too far.

In terms of what Gelon offered, we can safely assume that many of the hoplites would have been mercenaries, although this is not explicitly recorded. We do know that Hippocrates had a large body of mercenaries, and that part of the reward he offered for service was citizenship, also that a number were settled in Gela. Upon seizing the throne, Gelon continued the policy of settling mercenaries after a period of service; Diodorus notes that 10,000 were settled in Syracuse alone. Gelon would also have made good the losses in numbers by hiring many more mercenaries to replace those who were no longer on active duty. Some of those mercenaries would have been amongst those troops promised to the Greek cause, whilst still retaining a greater force than that which he proposed to send to Greece.

With hindsight, it may have been fortuitous for Gelon, and indeed Sicily as a whole, that the Spartans had rejected his offer of assistance against the Persians, as the Carthaginians chose this moment to become more actively involved in the affairs of Sicily, by supporting a northern alliance against a southern alliance of Syracuse and Acragas. The Carthaginian invasion that soon followed this supporting of the northern alliance was a significant one and required every resource Gelon had available to repel it, including an unspecified but presumably significant number of his mercenary troops.

The decisive action came when the Carthaginians were besieging Himera. Gelon marched to the aid of the Himerans with 50,000 infantry and 5,000 cavalry; the size of the Carthaginian force is not recorded.[29] Diodorus tells us:

Gelon, who had likewise held his army in readiness, on learning that the Himerans were in despair set out from Syracuse with all speed, accompanied by not less than fifty thousand foot-soldiers and over five thousand cavalry. He covered the distance swiftly, and as he drew near the city of the Himerans he inspired boldness in the hearts of those who before had been dismayed at the forces of the Carthaginians.

The Carthaginians were caught surprisingly unawares by this move, as many of their force were away from the main army plundering the surrounding countryside for booty. Gelon's cavalry easily rounded them up in droves as they were 'without military order'; more than 10,000 of them according to Diodorus.

The capture of so many Carthaginians gave the Syracusans a great deal of confidence, and led Gelon to attempt a bold act of deception that would end the invasion, if it worked.

Gelon's strategy was to have his cavalry circle round to the far side of the Carthaginian camp, and at a preordained time to ride up to the Carthaginians and act as though they were allies just arrived from Selinus. Once admitted by the guards, they were to find and kill Hamilcar, the Carthaginian general. Most armies in the ancient world struggled to maintain any real cohesion when their general died, and Gelon intended to attack the Carthaginians in force once news of Hamilcar's death was relayed to them.

This was a remarkably simple yet bold strategy, and it is perhaps even more surprising that it succeeded. The cavalry were admitted to the Carthaginian camp as though they were newly arrived allies. They immediately saw and then rode for Hamilcar and killed him whilst he was making a sacrifice of his own. Diodorus describes the events for us:[30]

> At sunrise the cavalrymen rode up to the naval camp of the Carthaginians, and when the guards admitted them, thinking them to be allies, they at once galloped to where Hamilcar was busied with the sacrifice, slew him, and then set fire to the ships; thereupon the scouts raised the signal and Gelon advanced with his entire army in battle order against the Carthaginian camp.

Gelon's victory was total, and further cemented his place as the leading man in Sicily, tyrant or not. Gelon died shortly after this high point of his career, and his successor, Hieron, continued his policy with regard to mercenary recruitment. Afraid for his position, he immediately set about recruiting a bodyguard:[31]

> Hieron, who became tyrant of the Syracusans after the death of Gelon, observing how popular his brother Polyzelus was among the Syracusans and believing that he was waiting to seize the tyranny, was eager to put him out of the way, and so, enlisting foreign soldiers and gathering

about his person an organized body of mercenaries, he thought that by these means he could hold the kingship securely.

Foreign, in this context, can be taken to mean Greek mercenaries. Gelon had offered citizenship to many of his former mercenaries, and many had accepted and settled into civilian life. Even if Hieron had not been wary of his brother he likely would have continued the policy of his predecessor and recruited mercenaries to replace those that had accepted citizenship and the peaceful life.

Hieron's lasting achievement was the founding of Etna, which was likely settled with the aid of significant numbers of former mercenaries.[32] He was succeeded by one of his brothers, Thrasybulus, and the process of a major mercenary recruitment drive was undertaken again. The succession of Sicilian tyrants, and the recruitment of mercenaries that it always brought, was a major source of employment opportunities for Greek mercenaries, as well as offering the possibility of a settled life and citizenship in Sicily after a period of service, although nothing was guaranteed, of course.

Thrasybulus was evidently not like his predecessors and soon proved unpopular. In Syracuse, Gelon had settled 10,000 mercenaries, of whom 7,000 were still alive. They, and the other citizens of Syracuse, led a democratic revolt against Thrasybulus and overthrew his regime. Whilst these mercenaries were a key element of the rule of the tyrants, and vital in defeating the Carthaginians and uniting Sicily, there was an undercurrent of distrust felt towards those former mercenaries by the other citizens. Once the tyranny was overthrown, the 7,000 former mercenaries were banned from taking up any magistracy in the new government.[33] These men refused to accept second-class citizenship and in turn rebelled against the new government, which they expelled from Syracuse. The former mercenaries were in turn besieged by those they had just expelled. Their experience and expertise was superior, but they were outnumbered by the besieging forces. They were ultimately defeated by forces opposing them both on land and at sea.

Syracuse was not the only city in Sicily that had difficulties of this type with former mercenaries, but in most other places peaceful agreements were reached without the need to resort to violence and bloodshed.[34]

The rise of democracy in Sicily saw the end of Greek mercenary service in that region, until it was again threatened by the Sicilian expedition from Athens in 415, a campaign that we will return to later in this work.

Persia

During the Classical period, Persia was perhaps the largest and most significant employer of Greek mercenaries, and although the numbers involved were much lower in the Archaic period, Persia was still a sphere in which Greeks could find occasional employment overseas.

Mercenary service in the Near East did not begin with the advent of the Persian Empire. Some Greek mercenaries were employed in Egypt (as already noted), some were employed by specific Mesopotamian cities as and when they were required, and still others found employment amongst the Lydians and would have seen service against the rising power of Persia, transferring their loyalty to the latter upon the defeat of Lydia.[35]

One of the reasons the Persian Empire rose to dominate was because their great wealth allowed them to hire as many Greek mercenaries as they needed. It was also becuse of the realization that Greek hoplites were simply superior to any heavy infantry that the Persian Great Kings could either train themselves or hire from other sources. It is worth noting, as we will discover later in this work, that when employed on the Greek mainland, mercenaries were almost always lightly armed; in service overseas they were almost exclusively heavily armed hoplites.

In the next chapter, we will examine the mercenaries of the fifth century, including those in Persian service, but for now it is sufficient to note that the Persians employed troops from a wide range of geographical areas; their armies were truly multinational. With this employment of professional mercenary soldiers, the Persian army gradually lost its militia origins and became a more professional force itself. Indeed, it is true to argue that the very history of the mercenary soldier is the history of the rise of professionalism on the battlefield.

After the defeat of the Medes in 550/49, Cyrus the Great, the first Great King of the new Persian Empire, formed a powerful standing army of both Persians and Medes. As has been noted by others, the Medes were allies rather than mercenary soldiers, but as Persian influence spread, the influx of foreign mercenaries into the Persian army grew steadily.[36] Shortly after the fall of the Medes to the Persians, Croesus of Lydia launched a pre-emptive war against Cyrus. The Lydian king was evidently worried about the growing strength and unpredictability of the new power to his east.[37]

The Lydian army consisted largely of heavy infantry, which included Ionian Greek mercenaries from the Aegean.[38] There were, however, a significant number of heavy cavalry too; these were of excellent quality and probably were the major threat to the Persian forces. The war began with Croesus invading Cappadocia; from there, Croesus could attack the Iranian plateau or modern Azerbaijan with relative ease.[39] Cyrus did not wish to wait for the Lydian king to capture any more of his newly won territory and marched out to meet the invader shortly after news of the invasion was received; one of the benefits of maintaining a large standing army is that they can be mobilized quickly when the need arises. The Persian army crossed the Tigris near the small town of Arbela, close to the site of the decisive battle in 331 between Alexander and Darius at Gaugamela. Once safely across the Tigris, Cyrus marched into the Pteria region of Cappadocia. A battle quickly ensued, which was apparently inconclusive. Cyrus' army outnumbered that of Croesus, and the latter attributed his lack of victory to that fact alone. Unwilling to risk a further engagement because of his numerical disadvantage, Croesus retired to the relative safety of Sardis the day after the battle.

Once he arrived in Sardis, Croesus thought he had reached safety and disbanded a significant part of his army with the intention of re-forming it some months later when he expected Cyrus to advance. This act would both save him money and reduce the strain on his logistical systems. We can likely assume that at least some of those disbanded would have been mercenary troops. It was probably standard practice to disband mercenaries and allies outside of the campaigning season with the intention of recruiting again when they were needed the following year. If that is what Croesus intended, to resume the campaign after a break, then he severely underestimated the aggressive expansionism of Cyrus. Cyrus followed Croesus back to Sardis, presumably after enough of a pause to allow for the disbanding of part of Croesus' army. Cyrus' arrival at Sardis took Croesus completely by surprise. Despite now being heavily outnumbered by Cyrus, he chose to fight an open-field battle rather than remain within the walls and attempt to withstand a siege.

Cyrus' stratagem was extremely interesting and unique to this point in history. He needed a tactic that would defeat the dangerous Lydian cavalry, and he found it within his baggage train. The camels that were hauling food were pressed, temporarily, into active service. They were stationed in front of an infantry unit and advanced towards the Lydian cavalry. The sight, and in particular the smell, of the camels was too much for the horses of the Lydians and they whinnied and reared, forcing their riders to dismount and fight on foot, which they were poorly equipped to do. Cyrus' tactic with the camels had worked perfectly. Along with this tactic, Cyrus launched a barrage of missiles from archers and slingers at the Lydian lines, causing many casualties. With the Lydians thusly softened up, the Persians attacked.[40]

Croesus was quickly pushed back and took refuge within Sardis with the remnants of his once-powerful army. Cyrus immediately began what was to become a brief siege, lasting only fourteen days. After the fall of Sardis, Cyrus annexed the whole of the former Lydian kingdom, thus massively expanding his burgeoning empire. His victory was not due entirely to his employment of Greek mercenaries, but they were certainly a part of the victory, as was, conversely, the disbanding of the mercenaries by Croesus.

This act robbed him of a number of professional, highly trained soldiers when he needed them most.

The Lydian Empire had made good use of mercenary troops from several different regions, Egypt and Greece being perhaps the most important. With its fall, Persia became the dominant player in the Near East and therefore became a major paymaster for mercenaries too. Following the conquest of Lydia, Babylon soon followed, as did Parthia, Bactria, Sogdiana, Arachosia, Armenia and Assyria.[41] The Ionian Greek cities of Asia Minor also followed, over a period of ten years. All of the members of the newly expanded empire were required to furnish the Great King with troops upon request, although for the purposes of this work we should consider these troops to have been allies rather than mercenaries because of the political imperative on their home cities.

Cyrus was killed before he could attempt to claim the great prize of Egypt. This was accomplished by his successor, Cambyses, who employed Ionian and Aeolian Greek mercenaries, as well as Armenian and Jewish mercenary troops, on the campaign that finally brought Egypt within the Persian sphere of influence.

The final campaign we need to look at in terms of Persian activity in the Archaic period is the invasion of Thrace and Scythia by Darius in 513.[42] It is difficult to know what Darius was intending with this campaign; he could have been preparing the ground for a later invasion of Greece by securing Thrace as a base of operations and ensuring the security of what would be his northern flank. It could equally be that the campaign was the aim in and of itself, simply to expand Persian rule into Thrace and across the Danube. Either way, he invaded Europe by crossing the Bosporus on a bridge constructed by the Greek mercenaries he had hired from Asia Minor, who created the structure by lashing triremes together, thus demonstrating that they were capable of more than just fighting and dying for the highest bidder, but that they were skilled engineers also.

Once across the pontoon bridge Darius had no difficulty in suppressing Thrace. The Thracians were a proud and resilient warrior society, but their tribes were small and disparate and therefore easily fell prey to the invading Persians. Thrace was also a major source of mercenary peltasts *within* Greece in the fourth century.[43] Darius wasted no time in beginning the campaign against the Scythians and marched straight towards the Danube, where he crossed another pontoon bridge, this time built by his Ionian Greeks.

Darius had originally ordered the pontoon bridge to be destroyed once he had crossed, and for the Ionian Greeks to join him on the campaign, but one of the Greek commanders persuaded him of the wisdom of keeping the bridge intact, and also indicated that the Scythians were unlikely to offer battle but would use guerrilla tactics, which in the end is exactly what happened. Darius evidently trusted his Ionian Greeks as he rescinded the order to destroy the bridge, and left a force of Ionian Greeks to guard it when he marched north of the Danube.[44]

The campaign went as predicted, with the Scythians refusing to offer battle. The major issue to note is that the Scythians evidently approached the Greek allied troops guarding the bridge with a proposal to destroy the bridge, stranding Darius in Scythia, where he would surely be defeated through attrition. In a noteworthy act of loyalty, or more likely self-interest, the Greeks refused. Darius eventually made his way back across the bridge, having failed in his goal of conquering the lands of the Scythians. Darius discovered quickly that conquering territory with no settlements of any kind, and populated by a nomadic people who refuse to offer battle, is all but impossible.

The Persian failure north of the Danube emboldened the Ionian Greek cities of Asia Minor to revolt against Persian rule. They received assistance from Athens in their attempt, but were ultimately crushed one by one and brought back into the Persian fold. Whether this act of rebellion, and Athenian support for it, more importantly, led Darius to consider an invasion of Greece seems unlikely, but, whatever the reason, Greece was to be the next target of Persian expansionist policies. The newly re-conquered Ionian Greek cities would again soon be required to provide large numbers of mercenaries and allied troops for the campaign.

The Archaic period saw the rise of the Greek mercenary soldier; his professionalism was welcomed on the battlefield by tyrants and pharaohs to the east, west and south of the mainland, and to a much lesser extent in Greece itself. The fall of these tyrants in many cities, and the rise of democracy, briefly saw a major decline in potential areas of employment, and thus a decline in the numbers seeking such service. This decline in demand would start to be reversed towards the end of the fifth century, and we will see an explosion in the fourth century.

Chapter 3

The Fifth Century

Moving from the Archaic period, with its fairly frequent references to mercenaries in the sources, and into the fifth century, the most immediate and noticeable thing is the lack of source references to mercenaries in the first half of that century. This is not, however, an indication of a deficiency in our surviving sources, but a reflection of the reality. The development of democracies in Greece corresponded to an increase in the general level of prosperity. This prosperity meant that the city-states needed their citizens and could occupy them in the pursuit of necessary tasks and duties. The potential 'push' factor in the creation of mercenary soldiers, that of the economic weakness that existed in the Archaic period, was far less of an issue in the early fifth century. There was, therefore, a lack of supply of mercenaries from Greece, but that is not to say there was zero supply. The fifth century saw the rise of the dominance of Arcadia as a source of mercenaries. There was a seemingly constant stream of mercenaries from that region, although until the Peloponnesian War, towards the end of the fifth century, the majority found employment in Persia.

Persian Wars

The first major campaign of the fifth century, and the first evidence for the employment of mercenaries in that century, was the massive Persian invasion of Greece. It was noted in the previous chapter that this may have been an effort to punish Athens for her support of the rebelling Ionian Greek city-states in Asia Minor. It is just as likely that Persian attention had turned to the west anyway, and that the Athenian attempt to help the Ionians was in fact a sensible strategy of trying to move the potential front line away from the Greek mainland.

In 490, the Persians launched their first major effort to extend their empire against the mainland Greeks. In all likelihood, the Greeks expected an invasion, but the location of the first contact was something that they did not know. The Persians had chosen to strike straight for Athens and landed virtually at their back door, at Marathon.[1] The Athenians sent messengers to a number of city-states asking for help, but only Sparta and the ever-loyal Plataea offered any real support. Sparta was 150 miles from Athens and their support was not sent in time for the battle. Plataea was much closer, but was also considerably smaller; it did send help, but a relatively small amount, likely less than 1,000 troops.[2]

The Persians landed with perhaps 25,000 infantry. These would have consisted of a large body of native Persians, as well as contingents from the western empire and the reluctant Ionian Greeks, although the latter would have been fighting as allied troops sent by their city-states rather than as true mercenaries. This force was eventually opposed by perhaps 10,000 Athenians, of which 9,000 were hoplites and 1,000 lightly armed, and at most 1,000 Plataeans. Callimachus was in overall command of the Athenian forces, whilst his most significant general was Miltiades; in terms of a discussion on mercenaries, Miltiades is the most interesting character on the Athenian side.

Miltiades was, until recently, a tyrant in the Chersonnese and had commanded a personal bodyguard of some 500 mercenaries, largely comprising Greeks and Thracians. Miltiades was one of the Thracian leaders who had medized (gone over to the Persian side), and as a result was part of Darius' Scythian expedition described above. Miltiades, according to his own defence at his trial in Athens before Marathon, apparently wanted to destroy the pontoon bridge over the Danube and strand Darius in Scythia, but he was opposed and ultimately outvoted by the other allied commanders there. At Marathon, Miltiades' first-hand experience of the Persians and of their tactics was a vital factor in his acquittal in Athens, and would have been important in the coming battle.

The battle is one that has been examined many times, and this is not the place for a full discussion, but, in brief, the Athenian order of battle had a weak centre that gave way once the Persians attacked. Conversely, however, they had reinforced wings, which defeated the Ionian Greeks and other allied Persian contingents that had been sent against them. The result was that the Persian centre pushed forwards and was surrounded on three sides: in front by the weak Athenian centre, and to left and right by the Athenian wings.

Whether this was luck or good generalship remains unresolved, although I would tend to favour the latter, but it is interesting to note that the Ionian Greeks on the Persian wings do not appear to have fought terribly hard, their resistance collapsing quite quickly and fairly easily. They evidently had no real desire to fight for Persia, suggesting that they had been forced into reluctant service as allies, rather than being enthusiastic volunteer mercenaries.

Victory at Marathon was important to the Greeks. It demonstrated that they were capable of defeating the Great King, and gave encouragement to those who might try in the future. It was not, however, a decisive victory. The Persians had been driven off, but both their army and navy were largely intact. The Persians withdrew to safety, but it would have seemed evident in Greece that this was simply the opening engagement in what would become a much longer war. Hindsight suggests that Marathon, although important in itself to the Greeks, was little more than an opening salvo from the Persians. In 480, ten years later, they were to return to the Greek mainland with vastly greater numbers in a concerted effort to conquer their western neighbour.

Darius, the defeated Persian king, had died before he could resume his attempt to conquer Greece. This fact, and the succession of Xerxes, was likely the main reason the second invasion was delayed as long as it was. That second invasion began in 480 with the Persians again marching through Thrace, as they had done before their failed invasion of Scythian territory north of the Danube. This time, however, their army was far superior in size to any the Greeks had seen before. Herodotus tells us that:[3]

> my final estimate ... is that Xerxes, the son of Darius, reached Sepias and Thermopylae at the head of an army consisting of, in all, 5,283,220 men.

Half of that figure Herodotus attributes to sailors and camp followers, but even so it hardly needs saying that it is a preposterous overestimate. Many ancient armies are overestimated in terms of their size, but none more so than this estimate of Xerxes' army. Modern scholars admit that there is no way to know for certain the actual size of the invading force, but modern estimates range between 100,000 and 300,000.[4]

Whatever its size, we know it was significantly larger than anything the Greeks could put into the field, hence the request for aid from Greek regions like Sicily. We also know that Xerxes had taken his time in raising and training the army. It consisted of contingents from across the Persian Empire, and also contained an unspecified number of mercenaries from beyond the empire, presumably from mainland Greece.

Once again, the northern states were faced with the choice of collaboration or conquest, and many chose collaboration as they could not possibly stand against such a host. The southern Greeks, seeing the capitulation in the north, resolved to resist the invasion at the Vale of Tempe. Upon arrival, however, they discovered that there were at least three other mountain passes in the vicinity that could be used to turn their position, and they retired without engaging the Persians.

The Greek coalition resolved on a joint land and sea defence at Thermopylae and Artemisium. The defence was not in force and rather suggests that some factions were not fully behind such a proposal, Sparta for one. Both battles were hard fought, and after two days the band of 7,000 hoplites, including the famous 300 Spartans, fought the Persians to a standstill. They were only defeated when a Greek, Ephialtes, showed the Persians a second pass that would allow them to turn the Spartan position. Once the army had been defeated, the Greek navy withdrew from Artemisium after inflicting heavy losses on the Persian navy.[5]

After the battle, Herodotus tells us, in regard to the Persians:[6]

A few Arcadian deserters came in – men who had nothing to live on and wanted employment; they were taken to Xerxes and questioned about what the Greeks were doing.

This is one of the first references to mercenaries in the fifth century. It also appears to be the first that refers specifically to Arcadian mercenaries, and is an indication of how some recruitment would have occurred. The incident also provides an insight into intelligence gathering processes, specifically the questioning of prisoners and deserters.

The Thebans of central Greece were a long-time enemy of Athens, and were one of the many states that had chosen collaboration over opposition to Xerxes. Exactly when that occurred (before or immediately after Thermopylae) is unknown. Accusations of medizing were a common tool used by Athenian orators against the Thebans in the fifth and fourth centuries. After the Greek defeat at Thermopylae, the Thebans no doubt urged Xerxes to march on Athens, although this would likely have been his strategy even without their prompting. The Persians arrived to find a city virtually empty, save for a small band of defenders on the Acropolis; but they were slaughtered after two weeks of dogged resistance. Athens was plundered by the Persians, and much of it was razed to the ground.

The Persians were now in possession of much of Greece, north of the Peloponnese. They still needed to defeat the powerful allied Greek navy (of which the Athenians were the largest faction), and to defeat the Greek land forces at the Isthmus of Corinth. It was the Allied Greek navy that was to be Xerxes' next target. If he could eliminate this, he could land troops anywhere along the Peloponnesian coast and easily outflank the allied Greek land army.

The decisive naval battle was to occur at Salamis, where the Greeks lured the Persians into an area of sea where their superiority in numbers was a liability, and delivered a decisive victory for the Greek coalition, sinking 200 Persian ships for the loss of only 40 of their own.[7] The Ionian contingents fought with considerable vigour; perhaps they feared the consequences if they did not. The Phoenician fleet suffered more than any of the other Persian contingents. They took the lead in the battle and suffered the worst of the casualties. Xerxes was unimpressed and executed a number of Phoenician naval captains. This caused a greater loss to the operational effectiveness of his fleet by further reducing the number of skilled captains he had available. The act also increased the number of desertions in his fleet, as fear spread that further executions might follow.

Each Persian ship, like each Greek ship, carried marines onboard. Many of the Phoenician ships carried Saka mercenaries from the Central Asian region. The significant loss of Phoenician ships also led to a major loss of these mercenaries.[8] Many drowned or were killed in hand-to-hand combat. Xerxes still had a number of mercenaries in his employ, although probably not great numbers; he always had the potential to hire more as required.

Xerxes was now in a very difficult position; he still commanded a very powerful land army, but he did not posses enough of a fleet to keep it supplied or to defend his flanks and prevent the Greeks from landing troops behind any position he was to take up. Further to this, there was the potential for unrest, particularly in Asia Minor, as a result of the defeat. If rebellion did occur in Asia Minor, his only remaining supply line would be compromised.

Xerxes' response was to divide his forces. A large force was left in central Greece under the command of Mardonius, while he marched back through northern Greece and into Asia Minor, where he acted to restore order after news of Salamis reached that region. The troops left behind consisted of contingents from most of the Persian Empire, as well as some Phrygian and Greek mercenaries and Greek allied troops from those areas that had supported Xerxes.

Whilst Xerxes was pacifying the Asia Minor region, Mardonius took up a defensive posture and stationed himself in Thessaly. Once Xerxes had completed his campaign, he sent back to Greece some of his elite units to bolster Mardonius' forces. In order to maintain his army at a manageable size, Mardonius then dismissed some of his lesser-quality central Asian mercenaries. The reorganization of Mardonius' army made it a little smaller, but more effective, as it retained the best-quality troops that were available. The Central Asian mercenaries were gone, but there were still some Greek mercenaries, and particularly Greek allied troops from the city-states of central and northern Greece. Overall, the numbers of mercenaries with Mardonius was probably not terribly large.

Once Mardonius was prepared and his army at full strength (and quality, more importantly) he resolved to force a conclusion with the allied Greeks. He was still in a relatively weak position strategically. He certainly possessed the larger army, but he was in territory with which he was not wholly familiar. Added to which, his supply lines back to Persia through Macedonia and Thrace were vulnerable, and his army was simply too large to live off the land for long. He also recognized the dangers inherent in his not possessing a fleet; he could not defend the coastline from the possibility of the Allies landing troops behind him, severing his lines of supply. If he could win over the Athenians, and their fleet, then he could reasonably assume the Peloponnese would follow either through cooperation or conquest. Mardonius made overtures to Athens in this regard, but was rebuffed. In revenge, he again marched to Athens and sacked what remained of the city after Xerxes' destruction the previous year.

It seems that this aggressive move by Mardonius persuaded the Spartans to put their full levy in the field to join the Athenians. The Spartans knew full well the consequence to them and the Peloponnese if the Athenians medised. The mobilization from Sparta was as much about maintaining the morale of the Athenians and the rest of the allied contingents as anything else. Once the full Spartan levy arrived at the Isthmus of Corinth, the total Greek force was perhaps 70,000 to 80,000, still outnumbered by the force of 100,000 to 120,000 commanded by Mardonius.[9]

Once the Greek army was fully assembled, it began its lumbering advance towards the Persians. The Greeks were an allied army, but they were far from unified. Various contingents evidently found it difficult to overcome decades of political unrest or hostility in order to fight on the same side. The worst offenders, of course, were the Athenians and Spartans. The Greek advance was not cohesive or coherent; different contingents marched at different rates and perhaps via slightly different routes into central Greece. Upon seeing the Greeks begin their advance, Mardonius withdrew to Boeotia, which possessed terrain that was more suitable to his massive superiority in cavalry (the Greeks had none to speak of). To cover his movements, and to harass the Greeks as much as possible, Mardonius left his cavalry behind to operate semi-independently. They were successful in this regard and we know that they caught a 3,000-strong Megarian contingent on open ground and mauled them quite badly before being driven off by a detachment of Athenian light armed.[10] They could not stay to harass the Greek troops indefinitely, however, and as the Allies approached Plataea the Persian cavalry returned to their army to prepare for the coming battle.

This movement by Mardonius demonstrated tremendous tactical awareness. His army was superior in total numbers, and massively superior in cavalry, but he did not seek the first battle that he was offered as a lesser general may have done. He sought to increase his chances of victory by luring the Greeks into terrain of his choosing. The Greeks, however, regained the initiative by moving to a location that was flat enough to tempt the Persians into attacking, but not so flat as to give them the advantage their numbers could have brought. The Greeks then withdrew from that position and the Persians followed them, and the battle ensued.

When the battle came, the disorganized Greeks proved the better soldiers, and the Persians were defeated. Mardonius simply did not have enough good quality infantry to oppose the Spartans in particular, and he was unable to make his cavalry the decisive weapon that he hoped they would be. The Persian defeat was complete and included the death of Mardonius himself. After the battle, the remnants of the Persian army marched back towards Asia Minor via the land route through Thrace, harried all the way by the Greeks.

When considering mercenaries, the Persian Wars are very interesting. There appear to have been very few mercenaries fighting on the Greek side, and not huge numbers on the Persian side either, perhaps the Saka marines being the most numerous. Athens was perhaps the only city-state in the Greek alliance to employ mercenaries, and even then perhaps only 1,000 Cretan and Scythian archers, the latter of which were employed in a quasi-police role in Athens when not at war.[11] The Scythians were obviously mercenaries, since there was no requirement for the nomads to send troops to Athens, but it seems the Cretans were too, given their official refusal to support resistance to Persia. Cretan archers were to become a major part of mercenary recruitment; Alexander consistently employed around 1,000 and they were to become common in the mercenary armies of the Hellenistic period.

On the Persian side, we know of the Saka mercenaries who fought as marines at Salamis and presumably Artemisium, although this does seem a strange choice given that their homeland did not afford them opportunities to learn how to swim, with the fatal consequences that brought when their ships were sunk by the Greeks. We know of the central Asian mercenaries that were dismissed by Mardonius as soon as he was able, suggesting their lack of quality. The Persians did have numbers of Greek mercenaries from the mainland, but exactly how many is unknown, and they were not decisive in the battle and perhaps not significant in number. They also commanded contingents from the Ionian Greek cities of Asia Minor, although strictly these would have been fighting as allied troops supplied under duress by their home city-states rather than as mercenaries. The most important lesson we can learn from the Persian Wars, and it was a lesson not lost on successive Great Kings, was the primacy of Greek hoplites on the battlefield. It was evident that they were superior in quality to anything the Persians could put in the field, save for their own Greek mercenaries who were equipped with the same weapons and armour. At this time in history, heavy infantry were simply superior to the more lightly armed infantry of the Persians, and they were better able to withstand an infantry battle as a result. This is a trend that was eventually reversed by Alexander the Great, whose *pezhetairoi* were equipped rather like lightly armed peltasts and were more than capable of defeating more heavily armed infantry. Xerxes, however, saw the superiority of Greek heavy infantry, and future Persian kings sought to employ them as mercenaries in ever-increasing numbers.

After Salamis and Plataea, it was far from certain that the Persians would not simply withdraw to friendly territory, rebuild their army and particularly their navy, and attempt another invasion when they were ready. There was great debate amongst the Greeks regarding what to do next, but ultimately it seems that the coalition sailed to Mycale, where they inflicted another crushing defeat on the surviving Persian forces.[12] In 479, the Athenians were leading the counter-offensive against the Persians, and they were joined by the Spartans in the form of Pausanias in 478. Not long after this, however, the Spartans encountered significant problems in Asia Minor and they adopted a more insular posture, withdrawing from the coalition and into the Peloponnese. Athens, on the other hand, decided to carry on the war with Persia and formed a new alliance, the Delian League, an organization that was ultimately to become the Athenian Empire. The Athenians followed up the success at Plataea and Mycale with a major victory at Eurymedon in 469, although they suffered a major defeat while supporting an Egyptian revolt against Persia between 460 and 454.[13]

During the period between the foundation of the Delian League and the Peloponnesian War, we have very few references to mercenary activity. The main evidence we have for their activity in this period is as hired supporters in rebellions against either Athenian rule or Athenian-backed governments. The rebellion on Samos is a prime example of this.[14] In 440/39 Samos and Miletus were both laying claim to Priene, and when Samos gained the upper hand, Miletus, with the help of some dissident Samians, appealed to Athens. Athens intervened directly on Samos, taking hostages, installing a garrison and setting up a democracy. The deposed Samians gained the support of Pissuthnes, satrap of Sardis, and gathered together a force of 700 mercenaries, overthrowing the democracy that had been recently installed by Athens, as well as capturing the leading democrats and the Athenian garrison.[15] Mercenaries were perfect for this kind of action, as they could be raised in appropriate numbers relatively quickly, and dismissed easily after the action was successful, or perhaps retained as a bodyguard to the reinstated oligarchs. We also have, scattered throughout the surviving sources, minor references to mercenary service in the Near East, and in the employ of native tyrants in the Crimea, but the turning point in terms of mercenary activity in the fifth century was the Peloponnesian War.

Peloponnesian War

In the fifth century, the mercenaries used by the Greek states were mostly specialists, e.g. Cretan archers, while for hoplites Athens and other states automatically relied on their own citizens. One feature of the Peloponnesian War, as we will see, was the growing realization that hoplites were not the best or most appropriate type of infantry in every situation.

There is no question that the Peloponnesian War represented a shift in the nature of warfare in the ancient world. It was not only far longer than any previous conflict; it was also constant and more violent, and it ultimately changed the reliance among the Greeks upon the heavily armed hoplite. Not only did the Peloponnesian War represent a change in style but also a change in the use of mercenaries on the mainland. We saw during the early part of this chapter that the allied Greeks employed very few mercenaries during the Persian Wars. Before the Peloponnesian War, Greek mercenaries were largely employed outside of Greece, notably by Persia, Egypt and the Sicilian tyrants, but that quickly changed after the outbreak of hostilities.

Sparta was the first amongst the protagonists to hire mercenary hoplites in any quantity. The Athenians did not do so in great numbers until the Sicilian expedition (the attempt by Athens and her allies to conquer Sicily, from 415 to 413), although they did hire mercenaries to sail in the fleet. There were three main reasons for this: strategy, finances and location.[16] At the start of the war the Athenians realized that the Spartans were the stronger on land (how could they not?), and thus Pericles' strategy during the opening years of the war was to avoid a land battle that they were far from certain to win, and to try to exploit their naval superiority. In some ways this was a sound strategy as it meant Athens was unlikely to lose the war, but was it a strategy that would bring victory? Perhaps so, but only by attrition.

The second reason why Athens did not hire Greek mercenaries in numbers was the cost. Athens was wealthy, with a major annual income from the Athenian Empire, but its resources were not limitless.[17] In the years since the end of the Persian Wars and the beginning of the Peloponnesian War, Pericles had undertaken a massive building programme, which resulted in the Parthenon and many other now famous buildings. Athens' chosen strategy was also expensive. Manning, for example, 200 ships for a few months was remarkably expensive, and if they had attempted to do this for several years and still hired a mercenary land army it would have bankrupted them.

The third reason was location. Due to the relative geographical positions of Athens and Sparta, Athens did not have easy or obvious access to the major recruiting grounds of Arcadia or Achaea, and thus recruiting large numbers of mercenary hoplites would have been difficult, even if it had been desirable. This point could also help explain the increasing reliance upon lightly armed Thracian peltasts later in the war.

Pericles, quite reasonably given the strategy adopted by Athens, reasoned that any land forces that would be required could be supplied by citizen hoplites, or perhaps allied troops supplied by subject states, but given the reluctance to offer battle the numbers required would likely be small. For the Spartans, however, mercenary hoplites were vital. For some time the Spartans were reluctant to have large numbers of Spartiates campaigning a great distance from the Peloponnese, partly because of an innate reluctance and partly for fear of a helot revolt. Mercenaries could be employed for long periods on foreign campaigns, which Spartan citizens were not capable of undertaking themselves, for fear that the helots might revolt if they were away from the Peloponnese for too long.

The first example we have of mercenaries being employed in this way during the war, on campaign at a distance, was not from Sparta, but from Corinth. Potidaea had rebelled from the Athenian league after sending representatives to Athens, Sparta and Corinth. The delegation in Athens entered negotiations with them, but they were protracted and fruitless. The Spartans, on the other hand, had offered to invade Attica if Potidaea rebelled and the Athenians moved against them. By this means, the Spartans hoped to pin the Athenian navy in Athens and allow Potidaea to leave the Athenian Empire without a fight. An Athenian fleet was dispatched to the Macedonia region before news of the Potidaean revolt arrived at Athens. When the fleet of thirty ships arrived, it was deemed too weak to attack Potidaea directly, so they resumed operations in Macedonia as per the original plan. Thucydides tells us:[18]

> With Potidaea revolted and the Athenian ships off Macedonia, the Corinthians now feared for the place and saw this as a crisis which struck at their own interests. They therefore sent out a force of volunteers from Corinth itself and mercenaries from the rest of the Peloponnese, a total of sixteen hundred hoplites and four hundred light troops. In command was Aristeus ...

The formula 'volunteers and mercenaries' was to become common enough for campaigns conducted at a distance from the Peloponnese for the reasons noted above.

The Athenians reinforced their troops in the north and began a siege of Potidaea. The Spartans, true to their word, invaded Attica (although not until 431), but this was not enough to persuade the Athenians to withdraw, and the siege dragged on. Over the winter of 430/29, the Potidaeans, the Corinthians and the mercenaries hired by that city were exhausted of their ability to resist any further, and sought terms with Athens. After a siege that cost the Athenians 2,000 talents, the generals at Potidaea agreed to terms with the defenders.[19] The inhabitants, including the mercenaries, were allowed free passage out of the city with minimal possessions, and the Athenians sent colonists to occupy the city. The mercenary troops were disbanded after their failure to resist the Athenians. Exactly how many of the 2,000 troops sent by Corinth were mercenaries is not recorded, but their employment on these kinds of campaign was to become commonplace, as was their dismissal from service immediately after the campaign was concluded, either successfully or otherwise, as in this case.

Brasidas' expedition to the region of Chalcidice in the summer of 424 was recruited along similar lines to that of Aristeus noted above.[20] Brasidas raised a force comprising:[21]

> Seven hundred helots ... to serve as hoplites. He hired the rest of his expeditionary force from the Peloponnese.

Brasidas' total force was 1,700 strong, 1,000 of which were mercenaries. Even at the start of the war, Sparta had not been wealthy, certainly not when compared to the economic might of Athens, but by 424 she was seriously lacking funds. This expeditionary force was not huge, but it still had to be paid for, and Sparta could not afford it. The cost, therefore, was born half by Perdiccas and half by the Chalcidean League. This was almost bound to lead to a situation in which Brasidas was, to an extent, compromised. He was not fully in a position to act in Spartan interests, but needed to keep his local paymasters happy lest they withdraw their support and his expeditionary force be disbanded through lack of funds. Brasidas needed to be a diplomat as well as a general, something Spartan generals overseas were not famed for.

Brasidas campaigned in the Thraceward region from the summer of 424, and he almost immediately upset one of his paymasters. As soon as Brasidas arrived he was asked to accompany Perdiccas' forces on a campaign against Arrhabaeus of Lyncestis. Brasidas agreed at first, but as the combined forces approached Lyncestis, Brasidas informed Perdiccas that he wished to proceed alone in the hope of bringing Arrhabaeus into independent alliance with Sparta. This was, of course, utterly unacceptable to Perdiccas as he had been eyeing territorial expansion rather than having another Spartan ally as a neighbour. Perdiccas refused to countenance such a proposal, although Brasidas went ahead and contacted Arrhabaeus anyway via envoys, and eventually came to some form of agreement that averted an invasion of Arrhabaeus territory. Perdiccas was less than happy and immediately reduced the maintenance payments he was making from half of the total cost of Brasidas' mercenary army to one third.[22] This did not have the feared consequence on Brasidas of having to disband parts of the army, although it is unclear how he made up the shortfall; perhaps payments from Arrhabaeus were part of the deal he struck. Brasidas' actions on this occasion did, however, expand Sparta's sphere of influence to Lyncestis without alienating Perdiccas too badly (i.e. without forcing him to withdraw support completely), and without any need for battle.

Brasidas again proved the value of diplomacy, backed up by the threat of a mercenary army, later that summer at Acanthus. The city had made an alliance with Athens at some point before Brasidas' arrival.[23] The Spartan arrived in late summer 424 to find the gates barred against him. He was able to persuade the ruling council to allow him to speak to them and put forward the Spartan case. Thucydides records a lengthy and impassioned speech and noted that he 'was not a bad speaker, for a Spartan.'[24] The Acanthians listened intently to Brasidas and then debated his proposal. Their main fear, it seems, was the potentially hostile mercenary army outside of their gates and the potential damage they could do to the crops that were due for harvest. The debate likely came down to which was the bigger threat, the army outside the walls or the one some distance to the south in Attica. In a secret vote they elected to secede from the Athenian Empire and save their crops.

In the winter of 424/3, after Brasidas had demonstrated that diplomacy backed by the threat of force could be just as effective as actual military action, the Spartan general moved to Amphipolis, the Athenian colony on the River Strymon. Brasidas' diplomatic efforts preceded him here too. Not all of the inhabitants of Amphipolis were Athenian settlers; some were from the nearby town of Argilus, and these had resolved to betray the city to Brasidas. Historically, winter campaigns in Greece, particularly northern Greece, were not common, but that is one of the things the Peloponnesian War changed; not everyone was prepared for them, however. Brasidas advanced upon the city and caught them unawares and unprepared. The countryside fell into his hands with little loss of life, but the defenders inside the walls recovered fast enough to prevent the traitors from betraying the city to the Spartan.[25] Thucydides notes the possibility that the inner city could potentially have been taken too, but Brasidas preferred to allow his troops to plunder the surrounding area rather than push his advantage. Perhaps this was necessary to make up the deficit in wages once Pausanias cut his contributions.

Eucles, the Athenian general, was stationed in Amphipolis at the time, and Thucydides was in command of a small fleet of seven ships, and was stationed around half a day's sail from Amphipolis at Thasos.[26] According to Thucydides, Brasidas feared his arrival, not because of the seven ships he commanded, but because of the many friends and the great influence he exerted in the region. Brasidas apparently believed that Thucydides had the ability to raise a significant force against him in a relatively short time, and that he therefore did not have the opportunity that time would have afforded him to besiege Amphipolis and attempt to take it by force.

Brasidas again resolved, therefore, to attempt to capture the city by diplomatic means, and he sent messengers to the defenders inside the walls offering them terms. His offer was that:[27]

> ... any of the Amphipolitans or Athenians in the city who wished to stay could do so in possession of their property and retention of fair and equal rights; any who did not wish to stay could take their effects with them, but must leave within five days.

The defenders, who had been initially resolved to resist Brasidas, were shaken by the generosity of this offer. Many of the defenders inside the walls had relatives who had been captured by Brasidas in the surrounding countryside, and they feared for their safety. They also feared the potential consequence to themselves of resistance, and the Athenians in particular were drawn by the opportunity to return to Athens safely with all of their possessions. During the public debate, those who had attempted to betray the city to Brasidas spoke up in his favour. One can only imagine how heated the debate would have been on both sides, but eventually a consensus was reached and the inhabitants agreed to Brasidas' terms; thus Amphipolis became another city that fell by diplomacy to Brasidas' mercenary army.

Brasidas' willingness and ability to use diplomacy as his main strategy was paying dividends for Sparta. Thucydides tells us:[28]

> When the cities subject to Athens heard of his taking of Amphipolis, of the offer he had made, and of the mild disposition of the man himself, they were more than ever excited by the prospect of revolt, and began secret negotiations with him, inviting him to come and help them, each of them keen to be the first to defect.

While Brasidas was extending the reach of the Spartans, Athens sent extra garrisons to those cities that remained loyal (or were wavering), as best they could in the winter anyway. Brasidas also sent messengers to Sparta asking for reinforcements; this request was refused because of:[29]

> ... jealousy of their leading men, and also the greater desire to recover their men taken prisoner on the island and to bring an end to the war.

The Spartan rejection did not dim Brasidas' desire for territorial expansion, and in the winter of 424/3 he first began constructing a fleet at the mouth of the Strymon. When work was underway on this he began a minor campaign in the Acte peninsula (the location of Mount Athos), where most towns came over to him willingly; those that did not had their land ravaged by his mercenaries. Brasidas also campaigned against Torone, where there were again dissidents inside who were prepared to surrender the city to him. They were few in number and evidently incapable of achieving this goal themselves, however. Brasidas sent seven volunteers, lightly armed and in disguise, into the city to help break open one of the postern gates. At this, some of the mercenary peltasts entered the city and forced yet more gates open. This led to a general assault on the populace and apparently the Athenian garrison of fifty hoplites, both of whom were taken completely by surprise. Some of the Athenians were killed in the confusion, but the majority, along with some civilians, escaped in two triremes to the nearby fortress of Lecythus, located on a headland connected to the mainland by a narrow isthmus.[30] Brasidas then offered the civilians safe passage and the restoration of their positions if they returned, and demanded the surrender of the Athenians, who refused. Two days later, after a brief truce for the Athenians to recover their dead, Brasidas began his assault. With the aid of some kind of flame-throwing device, Brasidas captured the citadel quickly and many of the defending Athenians were killed. After an active winter campaign, he spent what remained consolidating his gains and awaiting spring.

When the spring of 423 arrived, Brasidas was prepared to continue his activities in winning over former Athenian territory, but he was prevented from doing so by a one-year treaty signed by Athens and Sparta. Thucydides tells us:[31]

> The Athenian thinking was that this would prevent Brasidas securing any further defections among their allies before they had time for counter-measures: and, if the circumstances were right, they could make a more general agreement. The Spartans had accurately identified the Athenians' fears, and thought that a period of relief from setbacks and pressure would make them more inclined to try for reconciliation and, with the return of the Spartan captives, a longer-lasting peace.

This is the first indication we have that the Athenians were really interested in a long-term peace, although we do have earlier references that the Spartans were.[32] Although this peace was now in Brasidas' interests, it does appear to have been in the interests of both Athens and Sparta and may well have been the beginnings of what could have been a genuine attempt to end the war.

Brasidas' efforts in the Thraceward region demonstrated that even a small mercenary army of less than 2,000 troops could be very effective when backed by sound diplomacy. He also demonstrated that it need not necessarily cost the home state anything at all, given that the cost was borne by local allies and through the acquisition of booty at various points. It would have been interesting to see how Brasidas' mercenaries would have fared if seriously opposed by a body of Athenian hoplites.

On the Athenian side, the first evidence we have for the use of mercenaries during the Peloponnesian War is on the ill-fated Sicilian expedition of 415. Along with the contingent from Athens, there were '250 Mantinean and other mercenaries' as well as allied units from Argos, Crete, Rhodes, Megara and other allied states.[33] Reinforcements of allied and mercenary troops were sent to the Sicilians from Corinth in 413. These mercenaries were again from Arcadia, but their numbers were unspecified.[34] Thucydides admits that some of the allied troops were motivated by the prospect of gain alongside their obligations under the alliance with Athens, but it was the mercenaries alone who fought only for financial gain; for example, at the outset of the Sicilian expedition:[35]

> The older men looked forward to conquest at their destination, or at least no reversal for such a large armament; the young men of military age longed for foreign travel and the sights abroad, quite confident of a safe return; and the general mass of troops saw immediate pay and the prospect of further resources to fund a lifetime of public benefits.

We cannot tell what these mercenaries did to aid the Athenian cause, as they are not mentioned in any of the battle narratives or sieges of the whole expedition. We can reasonably infer, therefore, that they were of little military importance to Athens. This would be supported by their small numbers. The important thing about these mercenaries, as already noted, is that they were the first of what was to become an increasing trend in mercenary usage by Athens.

After the disaster of the Sicilian expedition, Athens was on the back foot. If Sparta truly wanted to end the war that would have been an opportune moment, but, as so often when one side believes it has the upper hand, they chose that moment, in 413, to declare war again on the Athenians and to press their advantage. So began the Ionian War, essentially the second phase of the Peloponnesian War.

Although this phase of the war began with a Spartan invasion of Attica and occupation of Decelea, the Ionian War was characterized largely by naval action and the employment of mercenaries in that sphere. Mercenaries do not appear at all on the Athenian side on land for the remainder of the war; their overall usage of land-based mercenaries for the whole of the Peloponnesian War was surprisingly limited to those employed on the Sicilian expedition, and the reinforcements to that expedition. We do have an interesting passage of Thucydides here about some mercenaries that arrived too late to go to Sicily:[36]

> In this same summer thirteen hundred Thracian Peltasts arrived at Athens from the dagger-carrying tribe known as the Dians. They had been due to sail with Demosthenes to Sicily, but had come too late, and the Athenians decided to send them back to where they came from in Thrace. They thought it too expensive to retain them (each earned a drachma a day) in view of the hostilities from Decelea.

During this phase of the war, the Athenians relied heavily on their fleet, but they did not have the manpower, either in citizens or slaves, to fully man the ships. Mercenaries were employed in significant numbers to make up the shortfall.

Athens was not as wealthy in 413 as she had been in 431, at the start of the war. Both the length and the cost of the war could not have been predicted by Pericles or anyone else when hostilities began. This meant that she could pay no more than the going rate for her mercenary sailors. Sparta was backed by Persian gold by this point and spent several years hiring mercenary sailors at a higher rate of pay than the Athenians were capable of paying, in an attempt to ferment rebellion amongst the Athenian fleet.

As mentioned, mercenaries switching allegiance from one side to another was a rare occurrence. If they were to engage in such treachery on a regular basis, employers would lose trust in them and their employment prospects would decline rapidly. One of the few instances of this occurring was in 412 when a Peloponnesian fleet assisted with the suppression of a rebellion from Persian rule in Asia Minor. Amorges, an opponent of Tissaphernes, the Persian satrap, had taken up a position at Iasus, aided by the citizens and an unspecified number of Peloponnesian mercenaries. The Peloponnesian fleet was mistaken for their Athenian counterparts and was allowed to land. Immediately upon doing so, the Spartans attacked, captured Amorges and handed him (and the town) over to Tissaphernes. The Spartans then plundered the town and appropriated large quantities of booty, as the area was traditionally wealthy. Of Amorges' mercenaries, the Spartans:

> ... did no harm to the mercenaries of Amorges, but took them over and conscripted them into their own ranks, since most of them came from the Peloponnese.[37]

Although the Peloponnesian War represented a major change in the nature of warfare in Greece, and it certainly represented a rise in the use of mercenary forces on the mainland, their overall use was still very limited. We have seen that the Athenians only employed mercenary land forces for the Sicilian expedition, and even there, only as a very small percentage of the total troops assigned to that campaign. Proposals were made, as noted in an earlier chapter, to employ a mercenary land army paid for from pillage, but these were never more than proposals, ultimately unpopular ones at that. The Spartans did make greater use of land-based mercenaries, particularly on campaigns such as the one commanded by Brasidas in Thrace. This was ultimately very successful and cost Sparta little in terms of financial outlay. But even given this success, the Peloponnesians preferred to rely largely on allied troops to accompany the Spartan land armies. The reason was probably nothing more sinister than the Spartans having access to enough allied troops to man their armies without resorting to mercenaries. The only area where mercenaries were indispensible during the war was in the Athenian fleet, and even here they proved ultimately unsuccessful, given Athens' defeat in the war. However small an impact they had in the Peloponnesian War, their usage did increase rapidly into the fourth century and beyond.

The end of the Peloponnesian War saw large numbers of men released onto the streets of the various city-states with no other way to make a living than through force of arms. Although very few of these men would have served as mercenaries, we must not forget that large numbers of allied troops fought for both Athens and Sparta. Some of these men would have served for long periods, with the result that they were simply accustomed to earning their living in exactly the same way a mercenary would, through force of arms. The war was long enough that some may not have known any other life.

Some of these unemployed soldiers found work in 403 with both the oligarchs and democrats in Athens. During the rule of the Thirty in Athens, an appeal was made to Sparta by these tyrants for protection from the Athenian citizens. Lysander arranged for a loan of 100 talents, which were to be used to hire Peloponnesian hoplites.[38] The democrats in Athens were also supported with around 300 mercenaries. The democracy was finally permanently restored in 401 as news arrived that the oligarchs were again trying to raise mercenary soldiers in Eleusis. Although the details of the restoration of the democracy are not important here, it should be noted that at the very end of the fifth century Athens' internal political difficulties were an opportunity for employment to some of the mercenaries who survived the Peloponnesian War.[39]

Chapter 4

The Ten Thousand

There is no question that when Cyrus resolved to raise a mercenary army at the end of the fifth century to challenge his brother, Artaxerxes II, for the Persian throne, he changed the face of mercenary service until the Roman conquest. Mercenary activity had existed both during the Archaic period and throughout the fifth century, but mercenary armies and their activities tended to be limited in scope and size. Cyrus' army was the largest of its type, perhaps around the same size as the total force Athens had sent to Sicily, although of course only a very small proportion of the latter forces were mercenaries. The 10,000 were hired for a specific purpose, even though the individual mercenaries were unaware of what that was when they were hired. After the death of their paymaster and the loss of many of their commanders, they were also to become the first roving band of mercenaries.

The creation of the army was not a simple process, and was complicated by the fact that Cyrus did not want anyone – specifically anyone in Persia – to know its true purpose. In order to maintain the charade, the mercenaries themselves were also not told the truth about the overall strategic objective of the planned campaign. In order to maintain the secrecy, the army was recruited in different locations as a number of smaller armies, with none of them being told about the others.

The mercenary army of Cyrus did not come out of nothing, of course. Cyrus already commanded a number of mercenaries on garrison duty in the cities for which he was satrap in Asia Minor. He also had with him a personal bodyguard of 300 Arcadian hoplites since at least the year 405.[1]

The first contingent of any significant size was raised in the Chersonese. Xenophon tells us:

> Clearchus was a Lacedaemonian exile; Cyrus, making his acquaintance, came to admire him, and gave him ten thousand darics. And Clearchus, taking the gold, collected an army by means of this money,

and using the Chersonese as a base of operations, proceeded to make war upon the Thracians who dwell beyond the Hellespont, thereby aiding the Greeks. Consequently, the Hellespontine cities of their own free will sent Clearchus contributions of money for the support of his troops. So it was that this army also was being secretly maintained for Cyrus.

The sum of 10,000 darics would equate to around six months' salary for the 2,000 troops that Clearchus raised. Campaigning against the Thracians with these mercenaries was more than likely an attempt to hide the true goal of these mercenaries, rather than a real and concerted effort to conquer this region.

The next army to be raised was commanded by Aristippus in Larissa. Aristippus appears to have been attempting some kind of oligarchic coup and requested assistance from Cyrus of 2,000 troops and three months' pay. Cyrus, seeing an opportunity, instead sent 4,000 mercenaries and six months' pay to Aristippus. A significant mercenary army in Thessaly at this time would not have raised any eyebrows in Persia and was an excellent place to 'hide' 4,000 troops. When the time came to send the troops to Persia, Aristippus only sent 1,000 hoplites and 500 peltasts under the command of Menon.[2] What happened to the rest of the troops, and to Cyrus' money, is unknown. Perhaps Aristippus, knowing that Cyrus' attentions would not be on him, decided to retain the greater part of the army he was sent in order to strengthen his own position in Thessaly.[3]

Cyrus also sent enough money to the Theban, Proxenus, to raise an army of 2,000, mostly hoplites. These were stationed in southwest Asia Minor with the stated intention of launching an offensive against Pisidia, in southwest Asia Minor, a region the Persians never fully controlled and an area that Cyrus quite reasonably might wish to conquer. They also had the advantage of already being in Asia, and so were easy to divert to a given location at a specified time.

The final two armies were both also raised in Asia Minor, but were small and thus would avoid attention. Socrates the Achaean raised 500 hoplites and Sophaenetus raised a body of 1,000 hoplites. Both forces were raised with the intention of ensuring Tissaphernes did not regain his former satrapy, which would have meant a loss of territory for Cyrus. This was again, of course, another perfectly plausible reason to raise a force of mercenaries.

Along with these major areas of recruitment, Cyrus gathered together small numbers of mercenaries from other sources as and where he could, including 400 deserters from Artaxerxes' army. The final – and one of the most intriguing – elements of the mercenary army, was a force of 700 hoplites commanded by a Spartan named Cheirisophus. Xenophon gives little indication of why the Peloponnesians would send a valuable body of 700 hoplites to the Near East, saying only that they were 'sent for by Cyrus.'[4] Diodorus, however, sheds more light on them; he tells us that Cyrus essentially activated an alliance with Sparta, and these men, along with twenty-five triremes, were put at his disposal as a result.[5] These Peloponnesians were not, therefore, mercenaries, but allies. For the purposes of the campaign, the distinction would hardly have mattered to those involved.

The campaign culminating at Cunaxa (in 401) will forever be remembered for the 10,000 Greek mercenaries, but we must not forget that they were not the only troops commanded by Cyrus; they were not even the majority of troops at his disposal. While the recruiting was underway in various parts of Greece and Asia Minor, Cyrus had mustered his own native troops, as well as some of the mercenaries he had at his command. He had taken up a position at Sardis, ideally suited to maintain the pretence of being about to launch a campaign against the Pisidians, and to keep Tissaphernes in check. He had at his disposal something in the region of 35,000 oriental infantry under the command of a Persian general, Ariaeus. On top of the infantry were 3,200 cavalry, of which 600 can be considered to have been of superior quality, comprising, as they did, Cyrus' personal guard. Before mustering his own forces, he sent a summons to his mercenary commanders for them to meet him at various prearranged rendezvous along his proposed route. Some of them were instructed to meet Cyrus at Sardis, and Xenias, Proxenus, Sophaenetus, Socrates and Pasion met him over a period of some days. The last of these mercenary commanders is something of a mystery; we know little about where he had been stationed, and only that he brought 300 hoplites and 300 peltasts.[6]

Once the mercenary contingents had gathered at Sardis, they maintained the organizational structures that they previously had. Their commanders remained in position and would have become the senior commanders on the expedition, along with selected Persian generals. The mercenary divisions were divided into *lochoi* of varying sizes. Menon's troops, for example, were divided into *lochoi* of 50 troops, whilst most of the other mercenary contingents were divided into *lochoi* of 100 men each.[7] With regard to the light troops, they were divided into *taxeis* and commanded by a *taxiarch*, but we have little other detail than that.

With the majority of his army mustered, Cyrus set off from Sardis towards Phrygia at a slow and deliberate pace, intended to maintain the illusion that his goal was in fact the Pisidians. Tissaphernes had been watching the gathering army with an equal measure of interest and suspicion. In Tissaphernes' eyes, the size of the force gathered by Cyrus was not commensurate with a campaign to crush Pisidia. Once Cyrus marched, Tissaphernes set off for Susa, the seat of Artaxerxes.[8]

Upon arriving at Colossae, near the modern town of Hornaz in Turkey, the host was joined by the troops commanded by Menon, although only 1,500 in total, rather than the 4,000 that Cyrus had paid for. Xenophon described Menon as a liar and a cheat, although this view is rather coloured by Menon's rivalry with Clearchus, the overall commander of the expedition and a good friend of Xenophon. Bias aside, given Menon's failure to arrive with the required troops, the description may not have been entirely off the mark.

After a seven-day stay in Colossae, Cyrus turned northeast and made for Celaenae (the capital of the satrapy of Greater Phrygia, near the source of the Maeander River) where he attempted to again maintain the subterfuge by remaining in the city for a month.[9] He was met there by the contingents of Clearchus and Sosis.[10] The reason for such a lengthy delay at Celaenae is not easy to fathom, and it was to cost Cyrus dear in terms of his finances. After this delay, Cyrus turned his army north, heading away from Pisidia and towards the town of Peltae, where he again delayed for three days. From there he turned east towards the town of Cayster Plain. It was here, during a five-day stay, that Cyrus encountered his first real difficulty on the campaign. His resources were far from limitless and were raised from taxation on the cities in Asia Minor under his control. However wealthy some of those cities might have been, there was still a limit on the amount of taxation he could demand in a single year. Cyrus had been very liberal with the distribution of this money to his recruiters, and the pay he offered was more generous than was sometimes the case. Perhaps he felt this necessary because he knew the ultimate goal would be unpopular, or perhaps it was an attempt to hire the very best of the available mercenaries, and higher wages would allow this. Either way, he had basically run out of money. The mercenaries in the army, and presumably the regular soldiers too (although this is not specified), demanded the immediate payment of their wages and of all back pay. Cyrus was already three months behind by this point, which makes the one-month delay in Celaenae, during which time he simply cannot have been paying the men, look even more suspect strategically. Xenophon tells us only that:[11]

> ... more than three months' pay was due to the soldiers, they often went up to his tent and demanded it. He had to keep putting them off with promises and was obviously upset about it; indeed it was not like Cyrus to hold back pay if he had it.

Xenophon implies that this discontent had been growing for some time, and one wonders how Cyrus had managed to develop a reputation for paying men if he had the money, given that these mercenaries were all newly recruited and did not have a lengthy history with the would-be Great King.

Perhaps Cyrus' slow and deliberate pace was connected with the arrival of Epyaxa, wife of Syennesis, king of Cilicia, who offered to pay the mercenaries' back pay and to ensure that they did not fall behind again. At this time the army received four months' pay and the immediate financial difficulty passed. It is a reasonable assumption that Cyrus had been in secret negotiations with Syennesis for some time, and the arrival of Epyaxa with a large amount of money was the culmination of those discussions. Syennesis was a man who was not entirely to be trusted, however, and his subjective loyalties were something that Cyrus had exploited brilliantly. Syennesis was determined to maintain his position as king, and during a potential civil war the only way to do that was to be on the winning side. Syennesis' decision was to play both sides: to send his wife with the money Cyrus needed, and to occupy the mountain passes that Cyrus would have to cross in order to reach the Persian heartlands. To say the least, this was a dangerous game to play, but for now it kept Cyrus' army intact.

With the army now satisfied, financially at least, Cyrus set off southwest on a four-day march through Thymbrion to Tyriaeon, where he stayed for three days. If his earlier delays and slow pace were connected with the negotiations with Syennesis and the arrival of Epyaxa, then why he continued to delay here is far less clear. At Tyriaeon, Xenophon recounts a very interesting tale of parade ground drill and martial discipline from the Greek mercenaries, and it is particularly interesting that the main part of the drill was conducted only by the mercenaries, although the native troops were also on display.[12]

After this display, which greatly encouraged Cyrus, he marched for three days to Iconium, where he again inexplicably delayed for three days. From here, Cyrus left Phrygia and entered Lycaonia; from now on the army was in hostile territory: 'This being hostile territory he handed it over to the Greeks to plunder.'[13] This act would also have served to keep the mercenaries happy and distracted from the fact that it must now have been obvious the target could not have been Pisidia. Cyrus' host then marched through Cappadocia towards Dana, where he delayed for three days, perhaps because of an unspecified plot that was uncovered involving at least two high-ranking Persians.[14]

Some time before the arrival of the army at Dana, Menon's mercenaries set off to look for a route through the mountains, taking Epyaxa to act as a guide. The intention was to turn the position occupied by her husband, Syennesis, undoubtedly with his knowledge and approval.[15] Once the main body of the army approached the Cilician Gates where Syennesis had been stationed, he realized his position had been compromised by Menon and his own wife (as previously arranged), who had passed through the mountains. He abandoned the pass without a fight.

By this mechanism he could claim to Artaxerxes that abandoning the pass, and thus allowing Cyrus into Cilicia, was his only option once his position had been turned. After turning the pass, Cyrus headed for Tarsus, the seat of Syennesis and Epyaxa, where he met up again with Menon's mercenary contingents, less two *lochoi* that had been killed whilst on a plundering raid. Xenophon tells us that these mercenaries then sacked Tarsus, including the royal palace, in vengeance for the loss of their comrades.[16] As an interesting counterpoint to the display of parade ground drill and discipline that the Greek mercenaries had demonstrated a couple of short weeks before their arrival at Tarsus, their actions there demonstrated exactly the opposite qualities. Tarsus also saw the second rebellious action by the Greek mercenaries in regard to their pay. They refused to go any further into Persian territory.[17]

> They already suspected that they were marching against the king and said that this was not the job for which they had been engaged.

Contractual disputes of this kind between mercenaries and their employers were rare. It was not uncommon for them to demand payment of what they were due if their employer had been recalcitrant in his duties for any reason, but to rebel in this fashion because the mission was different from what they signed up for was unusual. However, it was perhaps understandable, given that they had signed up for a campaign in western Asia Minor (they believed), and were now being taken into Mesopotamia.

Clearchus first attempted to persuade them by force, but he was met by a volley of rocks and other missiles directed at him and his mount that almost killed him. One can only imagine the shock this would have engendered in both Clearchus and Cyrus, and was a worrying development indeed amongst the latter's prized troops. We hear nothing of the native troops at this time, but they were presumably loyal to Cyrus and would have fought anywhere.

After the shocking and violent reaction from the troops, Clearchus tried another tack. Instead of force, he next attempted persuasion. Xenophon records the speech:[18]

> Fellow-soldiers, do not wonder that I am distressed at the present situation. For Cyrus became my friend and not only honoured me, an exile from my fatherland, in various ways, but gave me ten thousand darics. And I, receiving this money, did not lay it up for my own personal use or squander it in pleasure, but I proceeded to expend it on you. First I went to war with the Thracians, and for the sake of Greece

I inflicted punishment upon them with your aid, driving them out of the Chersonese when they wanted to deprive the Greeks who dwelt there of their land. Then when Cyrus' summons came, I took you with me and set out, in order that, if he had need of me, I might give him aid in return for the benefits I had received from him. But you now do not wish to continue the march with me; so it seems that I must either desert you and continue to enjoy Cyrus' friendship, or prove false to him and remain with you. Whether I shall be doing what is right, I know not, but at any rate I shall choose you and with you shall suffer whatever I must. And never shall any man say that I, after leading Greeks into the land of the barbarians, betrayed the Greeks and chose the friendship of the barbarians; nay, since you do not care to obey me, I shall follow with you and suffer whatever I must. For I consider that you are to me both fatherland and friends and allies; with you I think I shall be honoured wherever I may be, bereft of you I do not think I shall be able either to aid a friend or to ward off a foe. Be sure, therefore, that wherever you go, I shall go also.

This speech of Clearchus was well received by the listeners, and some of the mercenaries immediately took up their arms and possessions and made camp alongside Clearchus. It appeared, from the outside at least, that a split was forming between Clearchus and the mercenaries on the one hand and Cyrus on the other. Xenophon tells us that Cyrus was unhappy with this turn of events and he summoned Clearchus to a meeting, but the latter refused to attend; no doubt making his refusal public knowledge too. Whilst refusing the official summons, Clearchus sent a secret message to Cyrus telling him not to worry, and to ask Cyrus to summon him again. This Cyrus did and again Clearchus refused.[19] By this time the Greeks were thoroughly convinced that Clearchus was leading them in their best interests, when in fact they were being deceived once again. Upon Clearchus' refusal of Cyrus' second summons he again addressed an assembly of the Greeks.[20]

Fellow-soldiers, it is clear that the relation of Cyrus to us is precisely the same as ours to him; that is, we are no longer his soldiers, since we decline to follow him, and likewise he is no longer our paymaster. I know, however, that he considers himself wronged by us. Therefore, although he keeps sending for me, I decline to go, chiefly, it is true, from a feeling of shame, because I am conscious that I have proved utterly false to him, but, besides that, from fear that he may seize me and inflict punishment upon me for the wrongs he thinks he has suffered at my hands. In my opinion, therefore, it is no time for us to be sleeping or unconcerned about ourselves; we should rather be considering what course we ought to follow under the present circumstances. And so long as we remain here we must consider, I think, how we can remain most safely; or, again, if we count it best to depart at once, how we are to depart most safely and how we shall secure provisions – for without provisions neither general nor private is of any use. And remember that while this Cyrus is a valuable friend when he is your friend, he is a most dangerous foe when he is your enemy; furthermore, he has an armament – infantry and cavalry and fleet – which we all alike see and know about; for I take it that our camp is not very far away from him. It is time, then, to propose whatever plan any one of you deems best.

When he finished his speech, Clearchus simply sat down, inviting others to stand and express their views. A number of soldiers did, but some of these were friends of Clearchus and made speeches that must have been preapproved by the commander. A heated debate ensued in which many (Clearchus-approved) speakers argued that they were better off with Cyrus, whilst others argued for a plundering campaign against Cilicia followed by a return to Greece as wealthy men. At this, Clearchus spoke again and said that he would not lead such a campaign.[21]

After much debate, the assembled Greeks resolved to approach Cyrus directly and demand to know the truth as to where they were going and the truth of who they would ultimately be fighting. Cyrus received this delegation, but again chose to lie in his response, this time more plausibly. Cyrus told the Greek mercenary delegation that their real target was Abrocomas, the satrap of Syria, whom he believed was stationed twelve days' march away on the Euphrates.[22]

The delegates reported this back to the assembled mercenaries and the Greeks were not wholly convinced by the truth of Cyrus' response:

> Upon hearing this reply the deputies reported it to the soldiers, and they, while suspecting that Cyrus was leading them against the King, nevertheless thought it best to follow him. They asked, however, for more pay, and Cyrus promised to give them all half as much again as they had been receiving before, namely, a daric and a half a month to each man instead of a daric; but as regards the suspicion that he was leading them against the King, no one heard it expressed even then – at any rate, not openly.

Thus assured of a generous pay increase, they agreed to continue with Cyrus towards the Euphrates River. After the mercenaries had finally agreed, the army moved to Issus, where the army rendezvoused with a fleet from the Peloponnese. The reasons for this were two-fold: the first was to supply the army; the second was connected with the next obstacle in his path, the pass between Cilicia and Syria. Cyrus knew that he would be unable to capture the two fortresses guarding the gates by frontal assault alone. To turn the gates, Cyrus first marched to Myriandrus, where he paused to rendezvous again with the fleet, his intention being to land a number of hoplites behind the pass and attack the enemy positions from both sides simultaneously. This would have been the first large-sale test for Cyrus' mercenary army, but it did not materialize. Once the commander of the Persian forces, Abrocomas, received news that Cyrus was approaching in force, he abandoned his very defensible position and marched east to join with the host of the Great King.

Myriandrus saw the first desertions from the army. Two of the mercenary commanders, Xenias the Arcadian and Pasion the Megarian, boarded a ship, stowed away their most valuable property and sailed off.[23] They were apparently upset that the troops that had moved their tents next to Clearchus were allowed to join his contingent, weakening their troop strength and perhaps their influence also. Cyrus made a show of allowing them to leave and not pursuing them; given that some in the army probably felt sympathy with their desire to return home, and few still fully trusted the Persian, it was a wise decision not to hunt them down.

Cyrus left Myriandrus and Cilicia and made for the Euphrates. Once reaching the city of Thapsacus on the Euphrates, Cyrus summoned his senior commanders and informed them of the true purpose of the expedition; it cannot have been a great shock given their route. Xenophon tells us that, of the assembled commanders, only Clearchus knew the truth previously.[24] We do not know how the generals reacted to the news, but when they told their soldiers they were less than happy and again demanded an increase in their rate of pay. Cyrus evidently did not argue much about this demand and agreed the pay rise the mercenaries demanded. The Persian was in no position to refuse their demand as his plan was so far advanced he could no longer hide his objective from Artaxerxes. If a major part of his army disintegrated then Artaxerxes would surely hunt him down. Besides this, Cyrus would have reasoned several things. First, that he was spending Syennesis' money rather than his own. Second, that if he were to lose then spending too much on the army would be the least of his problems. Finally, if he were to be victorious, he would inherit the treasuries of the Persian Empire and become richer than he could possibly imagine. Refusing the mercenaries' demands was not an option for Cyrus. One of the interesting things that we do not know is whether the native troops' pay rates were altered at all during the campaign; the sources tell us nothing either way.

Almost immediately after this new financial agreement had been made, Menon, one of the mercenary commanders, left the main body of the army, crossed the Euphrates and headed for Babylon. By doing this, he hoped to win special favour for himself and his men with Cyrus, and apparently the ploy worked, since they received both praise and the promise of rewards from the would-be Great King.

This is a very interesting and enlightening passage. It tells us quite clearly that this was not a coherent army. The Persian troops would have been consistently loyal to Cyrus alone, and would have acted as we would expect. The Greek mercenaries, on the other hand, were a loose confederation of individual armies with individual commanders who felt no compunction to act within an overall leadership structure if they felt it beneficial to themselves to act otherwise. It also speaks of the indiscipline of the Greeks; such a small force as was commanded by Menon would have been slaughtered if it had run into the advancing army of the Great King, and yet they had no compunction in advancing blindly into enemy territory. This did change after the death of Cyrus, at which point the army became much more cohesive; they had little choice but to cooperate by that time if any of them were to see their homes again.

Whatever the motivation, and whatever it tells us about indiscipline and a lack of coordination in the mercenary army, Menon's act did have an impact upon those he left behind. As quickly as he could, Cyrus gathered together the remainder of the army, crossed the Euphrates and followed Menon with not a man being left behind.

Once across the river, the army marched south for eighteen days, all the while keeping the Euphrates on their right.[25] Much of this march was through desert and the army suffered as a result; particularly the baggage train: '... many of the baggage animals died of hunger, for there was no fodder and, in fact, no growing thing of any kind, but the land was absolutely bare.'[26] The slow rate of march with regular pauses was now a thing of the past; Cyrus pushed the army hard in order to come to grips with Artaxerxes, apparently feeling that the sooner he reached the Great King the less prepared the latter would be.

When the army reached the fortress of Charmande, Cyrus did pause briefly to allow the troops to purchase supplies, and here again we see another remarkable example of indiscipline in the Greek army. Xenophon relates the tale:[27]

> There one of Menon's soldiers and one of Clearchus' men had some
> dispute, and Clearchus, deciding that Menon's man was in the wrong,
> gave him a flogging. The man then went to his own army and told

about it, and when his comrades heard of the matter, they took it hard and were exceedingly angry with Clearchus.

Menon took exception to Clearchus disciplining one of his men, further emphasizing the lack of cohesion in the army. Clearchus could rightly consider himself to be the most senior Greek, but neither Menon nor his men saw him in those terms. Xenophon continues:[28]

> On the same day Clearchus, after going to the place where they crossed the river and there inspecting the market, was riding back to his own tent through Menon's army, having only a few men with him; and Cyrus had not yet arrived, but was still on the march toward the place; and one of Menon's soldiers who was splitting wood threw his axe at Clearchus when he saw him riding through the camp. Now this man missed him, but another threw a stone at him, and still another, and then, after an outcry had been raised, many. Clearchus escaped to his own army and at once called his troops to arms; he ordered his hoplites to remain where they were, resting their shields against their knees, while he himself with the Thracians and the horsemen, of which he had in his army more than forty, most of them Thracians, advanced upon Menon's troops; the result was that these and Menon himself were thoroughly frightened and ran to their arms, though there were some who stood stock-still, nonplussed by the situation.

This incident, in all likelihood, would have led to civil war between the two armies had Proxenus and his army not intervened to calm the situation. Cyrus then stepped in to exert his influence on Clearchus and further calm the situation.[29] If the combined army had been much further away from Artaxerxes, back in Cilicia perhaps, it seems probable that it would have disintegrated with internal squabbles. The proximity of the Persians reduced such open displays of hostility to the level of issues bubbling just below the surface.

After this incident, the army continued to march along the Euphrates towards Cunaxa and found that Artaxerxes' cavalry were conducting a scorched-earth policy against him, which was sensible given Cyrus' recent difficulties with supplies. Cyrus dispatched some cavalry in an attempt to stop the Persian cavalry. Given the lack of reference to this policy from then on, they may well have achieved a degree of success. Three days' march into Babylonia, Cyrus conducted a review of his troops, at which he made a speech promising the Greeks a crown of gold each if they were successful in the coming battle. Gaulites, an exile from Samos and a close friend of Cyrus, then replied that the Greeks did not believe that they would receive everything that Cyrus had promised them over the previous few weeks.[30] Cyrus reassured the Greeks once again that the Persian Empire was vast and he would have no difficulties in paying and delivering what he had promised. The mercenaries were reassured by this and caused no further trouble before the crucial battle.

On the following day, Cyrus set up his army on what he believed would be the field of battle, Clearchus on the right and Menon on the left, with the mass of the native Persian troops in the centre. When Artaxerxes did not appear, Cyrus marched nine miles in full battle array, taking much of the day, but still the Great King did not appear. Sometime around noon on the day of the long march, Cyrus came upon a ditch that had been dug by Artaxerxes' troops 'five fathoms across and three fathoms deep'.[31] The ditch apparently extended for 36 miles over the plains as far as the Median wall, but with a 'narrow passage twenty feet wide between the river and the ditch'; a formidable defensive barrier and quite an engineering feat, rather reminiscent of the Maginot Line.[32] Artaxerxes must have planned that spot for his defensive action against Cyrus for some time. When Cyrus reached the ditch, Artaxerxes had already abandoned the position. The reasons are not recorded, but it was perhaps to continue the scorched-earth policy, knowing Cyrus was struggling with his logistics. When Cyrus reached the ditch, he simply went around it; again, rather reminiscent of the Maginot line.

Once around the ditch, Cyrus continued his march for three days, and again we get a picture of indiscipline in Xenophon:[33]

> Hence on the following day Cyrus proceeded more carelessly; and on the third day he was making the march seated in his chariot and with only a small body of troops drawn up in line in front of him, while the greater part of the army was proceeding in disorder and many of the soldiers' arms and accoutrements were being carried in wagons and on pack-animals.

This is hardly the picture of a disciplined fighting unit and stands in stark contrast to the narratives we have of the army of Alexander the Great on the march, or indeed of a Roman legion.

Before midday on the following day, as the army continued its march, one of the scouts returned in great haste, proclaiming that the Great King approached and was already set for battle. This prompted a certain amount of panic within the ranks of Cyrus' army as they rushed to prepare themselves for battle. They managed to set themselves into their prearranged positions relatively quickly, suggesting that the army was in a reasonable condition, although it was somewhat spread out, as later we hear that while they awaited Artaxerxes their ranks were still filling up with those arriving late.[34] They set themselves us as follows:[35]

> Clearchus occupying the right end of the Greek wing, close to the Euphrates River, Proxenus next to him, and the others beyond Proxenus, while Menon and his army took the left end of the Greek wing. As for the barbarians, Paphlagonian horsemen to the number of a thousand took station beside Clearchus on the right wing, as did the Greek peltasts, on the left was Ariaeus, Cyrus' lieutenant, with the rest of the barbarian army and in the centre Cyrus and his horsemen, about six hundred in number. These troopers were armed with breastplates and thigh-pieces and, all of them except Cyrus, with helmets – Cyrus, however, went into the battle with his head unprotected. [In fact, it is said of the Persians in general that they venture all the perils of war with their heads unprotected.] And all their horses [with Cyrus] had frontlets and breast-pieces; and the men carried, besides their other weapons, Greek sabres.

There is little surprising or innovative in Cyrus' dispositions; native Persian infantry in the centre with the detachments of Greek mercenaries to either side, and on the extreme wings, cavalry and light infantry. The only unusual element is Cyrus keeping 600 cavalry of his personal guard with him in the centre where they could be of least use. In all likelihood, these would have been stationed behind a continuous line of Persian infantry.

Cyrus managed to set up quickly and was ready for battle by midday, but Artaxerxes was yet to appear. At some point in the early afternoon Cyrus saw a cloud of dust on the horizon that got progressively larger and more threatening as the Persian host approached.

> As the enemy came nearer and nearer, there were presently flashes of bronze here and there, and spears and the hostile ranks began to come into sight. There were horsemen in white cuirasses on the left wing of the enemy, under the command, it was reported, of Tissaphernes; next to them were troops with wicker shields and, farther on, hoplites with wooden shields which reached to their feet, these latter being Egyptians, people said; and then more horsemen and more bowmen. All these troops were marching in national divisions, each nation in a solid square. In front of them were the so-called scythe-bearing chariots, at some distance from one another; and the scythes they carried reached out sideways from the axles and were also set under the chariot bodies, pointing towards the ground, so as to cut to pieces whatever they met;

the intention, then, was that they should drive into the ranks of the Greeks and cut the troops to pieces.

The Persians advanced in silence at a slow, steady and relentless pace; this would have tested the nerve and discipline of Cyrus' men, particularly given that they were also significantly outnumbered.

Cyrus studied the enemy army as it advanced and rode out to Clearchus' position shouting an order at him to attack the Persian centre where the Great King was stationed, the intention being to kill Artaxerxes and thus end the battle almost before it had begun. Clearchus had also been studying the enemy, and was worried that their army was of such a size that the enemy centre was beyond his flanks. If he were to detach the mercenaries on the left flank (Menon) and send them against Artaxerxes directly, he would open a gap at the end of his line that the Persians could exploit, but he would also allow the enemy to surround the detached mercenaries with ease and slaughter them. Clearchus replied that he 'would see to it that things went well.'[36] Cyrus evidently misread this response as acquiescence to his order and returned to his position in the centre; Clearchus had no intention of obeying Cyrus' order, however.

Not all of the Greeks had yet arrived when the two armies were only '600 to 800 yards apart' but the Greeks could wait no longer. Clearchus ordered forward his mercenaries and a gap quickly formed between themselves and the centre of Cyrus' line. Clearchus was doing what countless Spartan commanders had done before him and, without any guile, was charging towards the enemy. They raised a battle cry, which did as much as anything else to rout their opponents, and the battle of Cunaxa was joined. Clearchus' mercenaries quickly smashed through the Persian left and advanced rather further, cutting down the enemy as they went.[37] Cyrus saw this and was pleased; although less pleased that his orders to attack Artaxerxes directly had been ignored.

Artaxerxes was also studying the progress of the battle, and would have been distressed at how easily his left flank had collapsed. This collapse did present an opportunity for the Persians (essentially the opposite of what had occurred at Marathon, where the Greek centre had collapsed and the Persians had charged into the gap); Clearchus was now separated from the rest of Cyrus' army, and the Persians began to press him on all sides. Artaxerxes also ordered his right wing, which overlapped the Greeks by quite a distance, to encircle Cyrus and outflank his position. If Cyrus allowed this to happen, his army would have been slaughtered, and he knew it. Still believing his tactic to be sound, Cyrus ordered the 600 cavalry of his personal bodyguard that were stationed in the centre of the line to charge directly at Artaxerxes in order to cut the head from the snake.[38] They charged and quickly routed the 6,000 men arrayed in front of the Great King. The battle descended into confusion at that point, with some of the Persians fleeing and some of Cyrus' bodyguard pursuing them. The confusion left Cyrus with very few cavalry under his immediate command. He tried to make one last desperate attempt to reach Artaxerxes but, on the very verge of victory, an unknown assailant struck Cyrus in the face with a javelin and killed him.[39]

> In this way, then, Cyrus came to his end, a man who was the most kingly and the most worthy to rule of all the Persians who have been born since Cyrus the Elder, as all agree who are reputed to have known Cyrus intimately.

While the battle was raging in the centre, Clearchus, realizing he was being outflanked, withdrew from the battle in order to save his troops from destruction. It was only on the following day that he was informed that Cyrus had been killed whilst the Greeks were ensuring their own safety. What remained of the several Greek mercenary armies now stood together in a defensive formation close to the site of battle. They realized that they were in an very precarious position. They were hundreds of miles inside the Persian heartlands with no immediate hope of reaching home. Artaxerxes' army remained largely intact and that of Cyrus had largely disintegrated after the death of the would-be usurper. The Great King demanded that the Greeks lay down their arms, which they steadfastly refused to do. Some of the Greeks 'in a moment of weakness' offered to join the Persians for a prospective invasion of Egypt. Clearchus, on the other hand, was attempting to find another Persian nobleman to lead the remnants of Cyrus' army. He apparently offered the role to Ariaeus (the commander of a detachment of Cyrus' cavalry), but he refused.[40] One wonders why Clearchus did not simply assume command himself, and I think there are a number of very sound reasons for this. Firstly, he did not have the trust of all of the Greek mercenaries; Menon and those he commanded still harboured a grudge for his previous actions. Secondly, the Persian element of the army might not have followed him. Finally, these were mercenaries, and quite simply needed another paymaster; Clearchus could never have performed that role satisfactorily.

The standoff lasted for some time. Artaxerxes did not want to risk any more of his army by attempting to destroy these Greeks, especially after seeing what Clearchus had done to his left wing. The Greeks were marooned, probably surrounded, and had little chance of escape; a defensive square was their safest posture at that moment. During this time, remarkably few

Greeks deserted to the Persian side; 300 Thracians and forty cavalry are all we hear of.[41]

One of the Persian commanders, Tissaphernes, eventually approached the Greeks and informed them that the Great King would allow them all to return to Greece, and that he was to act as their guide. The route would be north along the Tigris rather than back the way they had come. A return journey along this latter route would likely have been impossible, as they would already have pillaged any available supplies. There was some agreement to this proposal amongst the Greek leadership, and they do not appear to have consulted an assembly of the soldiers; they were evidently trusted in such matters to do what was right. The Greeks agreed to this proposal, and they set off north very soon afterwards. The only one among the Greeks who did not trust Clearchus was, of course, Menon, because of their previous feud. The latter secretly approached Tissaphernes, using Ariaeus as an intermediary, with the intention of negotiating some kind of deal with the Persian, along with the added bonus of betraying Clearchus.

When the two armies reached the confluence of the Great Zab and the Tigris, Clearchus asked for an audience with Tissaphernes to clear the air of mutual mistrust that existed between the two sides. Tissaphernes was a man of cunning and guile, whilst Clearchus was a straightforward Spartan warrior. Tissaphernes exploited this by inviting Clearchus, his fellow officers, 20 generals and 200 hoplites to a great banquet in their honour; they accepted without suspicion.[42] Some among the Greeks attempted to dissuade Clearchus from accepting the invitation, stating that Tissaphernes could not be trusted, but Clearchus was insistent, and the offer was accepted.[43]

> When they reached Tissaphernes' doors, the generals were invited in – Proxenus the Boeotian, Menon the Thessalian, Agias the Arcadian, Clearchus the Laconian, and Socrates the Achaean – while the captains waited at the doors. Not long afterward, at the same signal, those within were seized and those outside were cut down. After this, some of the barbarian horsemen rode about over the plain and killed every Greek they met, whether slave or freeman. And the Greeks wondered at this riding about, as they saw it from their camp, and were puzzled to know what the horsemen were doing, until Nicarchus the Arcadian reached the camp in flight, wounded in his belly and holding his bowels in his hands, and told all that had happened. Thereupon the Greeks, one and all, ran to their arms, panic-stricken and believing that the enemy would come at once against the camp.

The Persians did approach the Greeks, but not in great numbers. Ariaeus approached the Greek camp in order to deliver a message from Artaxerxes.

Ariaeus informed the Greeks that Clearchus was dead, but that Proxenus and Menon were not, since they had given information to the Great King regarding Clearchus' treacherous activities. Ariaeus further demanded that the Greeks lay down their arms. The Greeks responded with a predictably negative answer, partly delivered by Xenophon himself.[44]

The Greeks remained belligerent, but they were now utterly leaderless. In most situations throughout history their predicament would have led to surrender, negotiation or simply the dissolution of the army in panic. These mercenaries, for the most part, were veterans of the Peloponnesian War, as well as the many privations of the march to this point; panic did not enter their heads. They gathered together the remnants of the mercenary armies and elected five new generals, including Xenophon. Once these had been elected, the Greeks slipped away from Tissaphernes and continued their march north along the eastern banks of the Tigris.[45]

A few days later, as the Greeks continued their march along the Tigris, they were confronted by Mithridates, formerly a general in Cyrus' army, but along with several others, now supporters of Artaxerxes. He attempted to ascertain their intentions, whilst also trying to induce as many as possible to desert to the side of the Great King. He succeeded, but in a remarkably limited fashion. Nicarchus and twenty hoplites deserted, but no more. The cohesion and sense of collective cause was probably greater now among the Greeks than at any time during the whole campaign, particularly given that Clearchus and Menon were both no longer with the army.[46]

Mithridates retired, only to return several days later with Tisaphernes, and at the head of a small force of cavalry, light-armed infantry and archers. The Greeks formed up into a defensive square with the hoplites on the outside, and their own light-armed troops in the centre. Tissaphernes used his archers and greater mobility to inflict significant casualties on the Greeks, who could not respond; their Thracian cavalry had already rebelled and the enemy were out of range of the archers, as they were in the centre of the square. This incident is a perfect example of how lightly armed troops that are mobile could cause havoc to a heavily armed group of hoplites with little manoeuvrability. The Greeks finally tried to charge the enemy, but did no damage to them other than to cause their withdrawal. Tissaphernes was apparently happy with the level of damage he had caused.[47]

For several days, Tissaphernes shadowed the Greeks as they marched, and harried them at any opportunity, particularly when they broke formation to cross a bridge or a river. The nature of these hit-and-run attacks was to inflict a constant stream of casualties upon the Greeks whilst sustaining almost none themselves. At one point, the Persians used their greater mobility to skirt around the Greeks and to occupy the heights of a pass through which the Greeks would need to march. Xenophon realized the potential difficulty and used the light troops in the army to dislodge the Persians, allowing the mercenary army to cross unhindered. The Greeks, showing frustration and a disrespect to the gods, mutilated the corpses of the enemies they had slain 'in order that the sight of them might inspire the utmost terror in the enemy.'[48]

Once back on the plains, Persians continued to harry the Greeks. They inflicted casualties upon them as they were plundering what they could from the local areas through which they passed, more for food and water than for booty or slaves. The harrying attacks by the Persians were very effective and demonstrated a solid understanding of the relative strengths and weaknesses of each side; they also demonstrated that Tissaphernes had a sound under-standing of infantry tactics.

Earlier in the march, before Cunaxa, we see several acts of insubordination and ill-discipline, but very few after the defeat, when they were united in a common cause of getting home safely. As noted above, they were aided in this by the removal of Clearchus and Menon. The army, however, was to undergo one further act of insubordination, albeit minor, when they were in something of a race to occupy a mountain pass. Xenophon narrates the tale:[49]

> Xenophon, riding along the lines upon his horse, cheered his troops forward: 'My good men,' he said, 'believe that now you are racing for Greece, racing this very hour back to your wives and children, a little toil for this one moment and no more fighting for the rest of our journey.' But Soteridas the Sicyonian said: 'We are not on an equality, Xenophon; you are riding on horseback, while I am desperately tired with carrying my shield.'

This is a minor act of insubordination, but one which needed to be addressed, as, when troops are under stress and in constant danger, one belligerent individual can cause problems beyond what he otherwise would be capable of. Xenophon acted quickly and decisively:[50]

> When Xenophon heard that, he leaped down from his horse and pushed Soteridas out of his place in the line, then took his shield away from him and marched on with it as fast as he could; he had on also, as it happened, his cavalry breastplate, and the result was that he was heavily burdened. And he urged the men in front of him to keep going, while he told those who were behind to pass along by him, for he found it hard to keep up. The rest of the soldiers, however, struck and pelted and abused Soteridas until they forced him to take back his shield and march on. Then Xenophon remounted and, as long as riding was

possible, led the way on horseback, but when the ground became too difficult he left his horse behind and hurried forward on foot. And they reached the summit before the enemy.

Xenophon demonstrates here a knack for leadership and an understanding of the psychology of the military mind that was no doubt invaluable to him throughout the march, probably even before he was elected to a formal position.

After an arduous march through the Armenian Mountains, the bedraggled mercenary army reached 'the sea, the sea!' at Trapezus. Their arrival was something of a surprise to the inhabitants of that city, and not a welcome one. Of the roughly 13,000 Greek mercenaries who had marched to Cunaxa, around 9,000 survived, an impressively high number given the battle, the constant harrying by Tissaphernes and the logistical difficulties they encountered.[51]

Now that they were in touch with the Greek world again, or at least the Black Sea fringes of it, the Greeks set about discussing their next course of action. Their first proposal was to ask the Spartan *navarch*, Anaxibius, to provide transportation for them back to Greece. Cheirisophus, a friend of the Spartan, was dispatched immediately in order to make the request.[52] Once Cheirisophus had been dispatched, the assembly continued, with Xenophon addressing the men in order to formulate a plan B:[53]

> 'Here is still another point to note. If we knew beyond doubt that Cheirisophus would bring back with him an adequate number of ships, there would be no need of what I am about to say; but since in fact that is uncertain, I think we should try to do our part by procuring ships here also. For if he does bring enough, then with those at hand here we shall have a more abundant supply to sail in, while if he does not, we shall use those which we have here. Now I see ships sailing past frequently, and if we can get the Trapezuntians to give us men-of-war and so bring these ships into port and keep them under guard, unshipping their rudders meanwhile, until we get enough to carry us, perhaps we should not lack such means of transport as we need.' This proposal also was adopted.

This plan then, was to 'borrow' a penteconter from the citizens of Trapezus and to engage in some piracy on the Black Sea in order to capture some other ships (and their cargo, of course) with the intention of using them as transports to help move along the coast closer to the Greek mainland. Piracy and mercenary service were not that far removed from each other, so we should not be terribly surprised by this. The Trapezians were no doubt happy to loan them a ship, because the plan, if successful, would see them moving west along the coast and away from their city. After all, one ship was a small price to pay to rid themselves of 9,000 dangerous mercenaries who were taking every opportunity to raid the surrounding countryside in search of booty.[54] Dexippus was entrusted with the captaincy of this penteconter, but he used it to sail himself and his crew out of the Black Sea and back to Greece, abandoning his comrades at the first opportunity.[55] The Greeks still felt the plan was sound and borrowed a triaconter in order to retry the same policy. Selecting the captain and crew more carefully, they did manage to capture a number of smaller vessels, but nowhere near enough to transport the whole army.[56] A third plan was therefore conceived.

Before Dexippus absconded, Xenophon also proposed marching west if the piracy plan failed, but did not press the matter:[57]

> 'Now it seems to me,' he continued, 'that if perchance this plan also shall fail to provide us with enough ships, we must turn to the roads, which we hear are difficult to travel, and direct the cities that are situated along the sea to repair them; for they will obey, not only from fear, but also from the desire to be rid of us.' At this the soldiers set up a shout, saying that they did not want to go by land. And Xenophon, realizing their foolishness, did not put any proposal regarding this matter to vote, but persuaded the cities to repair the roads voluntarily, urging that they would be rid of the army the more quickly if the roads should be made easy to travel.

The failure of the piracy plan left the Greeks with little choice, and they marched west through hostile territory attacking mountain passes and fortresses as and when they needed to, in order to secure their passing.[58] After capturing the outer city of one particularly difficult mountain fortress, Xenophon ordered:[59]

> Tolmides the herald to proclaim that whoever wanted to get any plunder should go in. At that many proceeded to rush into the gates, and the crowd that was pushing in overcame the crowd that was tumbling out and shut up the enemy again in their citadel. So everything outside the citadel was seized and carried off by the Greeks, and the hoplites took up their position, some about the ramparts, others along the road leading up to the citadel.

Xenophon then decided the fortress itself was impregnable, and the march west was resumed. Wherever they went they were not greeted as fellow Greeks, but as brigands; hardly surprising given their tendency to plunder everything in their path.

After passing the city of Sinope, and with the army and its commanders becoming increasingly desperate, Xenophon proposed an idea which he knew would have been unpopular. He suggested founding a colony at some defensible location along the coast and settling there.[60] Seeing an opportunity, two of the Greeks, Timasion and Thorax, secretly sent a message to the neighbouring towns of Sinope and Heraclea telling them of Xenophon's plan. They were not overjoyed at the prospect of the Greeks settling nearby and offered what could be called a bribe to the two Greeks if they could persuade them to move the army away from their territory. There was a heated debate amongst the assembly as they discussed founding a colony, or moving on towards Greece; the debate soon became heated and all semblance of order and discipline disintegrated. A court was set up *ad hoc* and three of the generals were tried and given minor fines. The situation calmed as Cheirisophus returned from his mission to Anaxibius.[61]

The mission had been largely a failure, however. He returned with only one warship and no promise from Anaxibius of more to follow. The only vague hope was that the Spartan had offered to employ the surviving men once they had successfully returned to Greece. This would have been cold comfort given that a return to Greece was their objective, not a step along a longer path. The arrival of the emissary of the 10,000 was an inconvenience to the Spartans. They were temporarily at peace for the first time in years, and hiring thousands of mercenaries would have put some of their neighbours on edge, particularly the Persians; it was not worth the risk. Further to this, of course, they probably did not have the financial means to do so. The vague promise of future employment could easily be rescinded if the mercenary army ever did actually make it back to Greece.

The Greeks had suffered set back after set back, but almost every day they were getting closer to home. The thoughts of some of the mercenaries turned to what they would be taking home by way of booty to show for their privations, and it was very little. There are numerous examples of the mercenaries conducting plundering operations throughout the march, and especially on the route back to the Black Sea, but without a regular paymaster they would have needed that income to purchase supplies. Much of the raiding was probably with the intention of securing food anyway, rather than plunder. The promise and expectations they had at the outset of the campaign had proven utterly unfounded, but that was the risk of mercenary service if you were on the losing side.

To this point on the return journey, the mercenary army had been content to have several generals, and to replace them as and when required. This was no doubt a hangover from the method by which they were recruited, having been raised as several mercenary armies brought together for a specific purpose. That ethos was reduced with the removal of Clearchus and Menon, as suggested earlier, and now the assembly of the army concluded that they would be better off with a single leader, rather than several.[62]

> They came to the conclusion, therefore, that if they should choose one commander, that one man would be able to handle the army better, whether by night or day, than a number of commanders – that if there should be need of concealment, he would be better able to keep matters secret, or again, if there should be need of getting ahead of an adversary, he would be less likely to be too late; for, thought the soldiers, there would be no need of conferences of generals with one another, but the plan resolved upon by the one man would be carried through, whereas in the past the generals had acted in all matters in accordance with a majority vote.

The army turned to Xenophon to fill that role, and he was officially approached by a group of junior commanders with the proposal. Xenophon was at first inclined to accept, and notes the personal glory and prestige that it could bring:[63]

> As for Xenophon, he was inclined on some accounts to accept the command, for he thought that if he did so the greater would be the honour he would enjoy among his friends and the greater his name when it should reach his city, while, furthermore, it might chance that he could be the means of accomplishing some good thing for the army.

He also considered the possible negative impact on the reputation he had already gained if he assumed command and was unsuccessful. To help him decide, he made sacrifice to Zeus, and then addressed the assembly to reject the proposal. He did, however, recommend that they elect Cheirisophus to the position.[64] Cheirisophus was what might be called a typical Spartan, and one of the worst choices that the assembly could make. Clearchus had been unpopular, but that was as nothing next to Cheirisophus. The assembly initially rejected the idea, but they were persuaded by Xenophon, and he was duly elected.[65]

After Cheirisophus addressed the assembly, allaying their fears somewhat, the army set off in the direction of Heraclea, a Greek city and a colony of Megara. 'Here the Heracleots sent to the Greeks, as gifts of hospitality, three thousand medimni of barley meal, two thousand jars of wine, twenty cattle, and a hundred sheep.'[66] The gift was accepted, but a proposal was made by one of the mercenaries that they should try to extort 3,000 Cyzicene staters (the local currency) from the citizenry, while others suggested a figure of 10,000 and nominated some of their captains to carry the threat to the city.

Some of the Greeks in the army were unhappy with any attempt to black-mail or make threats against fellow Greeks, but they were shouted down or ignored, and the attempt was made.[67] The inhabitants listened to the demand and asked for time to consider it. They used this time wisely to gather local citizen farmers into the safety of the walls and to move the marketplace too; protecting as much of their property as they were able and preparing for a siege.[68]

The mercenaries had been outmanoeuvred by the Heracleans, who where, in short order, prepared for a siege. Once the city gates were closed, the mercenaries had little hope of carrying by force a well-defended city; they were utterly devoid of siege equipment and short on supplies, and we can only imagine that their basic equipment was hardly in pristine condition any more. Coupled with this, of course, would have been exhaustion and very low morale. The setback before the walls of Heraclea was the final straw for the army. The nationalist feelings of the Arcadians and Achaeans, contained for months, came to the fore and they:[69]

> proceeded to band themselves together, under the leadership particularly of Callimachus the Parrhasian and Lycon the Achaean. Their words were to this effect, that it was shameful that Peloponnesians should be under the command of an Athenian and a Lacedaemonian who contributed no troops to the army, and that the hardships should fall to themselves and the gains to others, all despite the fact that the preservation of the army was their achievement; for it was, they said, the Arcadians and Achaeans who had achieved this result, and the rest of the army amounted to nothing (in truth more than half the army did consist of Arcadians and Achaeans); if they were wise, therefore, they would band together by themselves, choose generals from their own number, make the journey by themselves, and try to get a little good out of it.

The Arcadians and Achaeans elected ten new generals from among their own men and, with the remaining 4,000 mercenaries from those regions of Greece, they set off themselves to make their own way home. Xenophon made great efforts to keep the remaining 4,100 mercenaries together, but ultimately failed. Thus, 1,400 hoplites and 700 peltasts followed Cheirisophus, and the remaining 1,700 hoplites and 300 peltasts followed Xenophon.[70]

The 4,000 Arcadians reached the area of Bithynia and began plundering the land. The native tribesmen, however, gathered together and counter-attacked the mercenaries and inflicted severe casualties upon them. They were only rescued by the arrival of Xenophon's arms, who were marching along the same road the Arcadians had taken. Soon after the army broke up, Cheirisophus was killed, and his army was almost leaderless. After the difficulties of the Arcadians, the army reunited at Calpes Limen.[71] Here, they were in a difficult position in a no-man's land between Heraclea to the east and Byzantium to the west, and still a full day's journey by trireme from the latter. There were no settlements of any kind in this region, be they native or Greek, and the Bithynian Thracians who occupied the area were notoriously hostile to any Greeks they found.[72]

The army was delighted to be back together as a unit; they had discovered that, however bad their situation, they were stronger together than apart. Xenophon goes to great lengths to describe the surrounding terrain and presents a picture of an area that was not quite paradise, but certainly very palatable. Xenophon evidently tried to push for the founding of a colony, as he had done once before, with similar results. Remaining in hostile territory was not a prospect welcomed by the Greeks; all they wanted was a successful return home with some booty to show for it. Xenophon was insistent and refused to allow the army to progress until the omens were right, evidently hoping they would change their minds; they did not.[73] The delay did allow the mercenaries to conduct raiding missions in the surrounding areas, as was now usual practice.

While the Greeks were delayed and engaged in plundering raids, the Spartan harmost, Cleander, arrived accompanied by two ships, and Dexippus, the man who had abandoned the army at Trapezus.[74]

It so chanced that the army was out foraging when he arrived, while certain individuals had gone in quest of plunder to a different place in the mountains and had secured a large number of sheep; so fearing that they might be deprived of them, they told their story to Dexippus, the man who slipped away from Trapezus with the fifty-oared warship, and urged him to save their sheep for them, with the understanding that he was to get some of the sheep himself and give the rest back to them. So he immediately proceeded to drive away the soldiers who were standing about and declaring that the animals were public property, and then he went and told Cleander that they were attempting robbery. Cleander directed him to bring the robber before him. So he seized a man and tried to take him to Cleander, but Agasias, happening to meet them, rescued the man, for he was one of his company. Then the other soldiers who were at hand set to work to stone Dexippus, calling him 'The traitor.' And many of the sailors from the triremes got frightened and began to flee toward the sea, and Cleander also fled.

This was not the way a Spartan harmost would expect to be treated, and not how he would have expected an army to behave, but these Greeks had been through much together, and they now acted rather differently that they would have done when they were recruited only a few short months before.

After this incident, the army marched west towards Byzantium. As they approached, it became increasingly apparent to them that they were unlikely to receive a warm and welcoming homecoming. Anaxibius, the *navarch* supporting Pharnabazus, was at something of a loss as to what to do with the mercenary army. Pharnabazus instructed Anaxibius to offer the Greeks transport into Thrace; the main justification was to get them off Asian soil, along with an offer of future employment if they accepted.[75] The mercenary generals retired to consider the offer, and apparently Xenophon wanted to leave the army immediately to sail home, but was persuaded to cross into Thrace with the army and only then decide upon his future. Once across the Bosphoros, and as Xenophon had seen all along the route, the Byzantines did not appear to want them anywhere near their city and sought to prevent access.[76] The mercenaries had no money or plunder with which to purchase provisions, and if the Byzantines had been sensible they would have realized the danger a large, hungry and unpredictable mercenary army posed, and provided them with provisions that would take them far enough into Thrace that they would no longer represent a threat. Anaxibius gathered together the Greeks, as it was becoming evident that trouble was brewing, and addressed them as follows:[77]

> Get your provisions from the Thracian villages; there is an abundance there of barley and wheat and other supplies; when you have got them, proceed to the Chersonese, and there Cyniscus will take you into his pay.

While some of the assembled mercenaries were discussing this proposal, and which route they would take on the prospective march, some mercenaries snatched up their arms and charged for the city gates, determined to gain access. The defender of the gates, Eteonicus, along with some of his men, immediately slammed the gates closed and dropped the huge wooden bar into position.[78] The attackers were not put off; they hammered at the gates and demanded entry. Some other troops inspired by their actions:[79]

> ran down to the shore, made their way along the break-water, and thus scaled the wall and got into the city, while still others, who chanced to be within the walls, seeing what was going on at the gates, cut through the bar with their axes and threw the gates open, whereupon the rest rushed in.

The mercenary army rushed through the gates in disorder with the intention of sacking and plundering the city. The citizens made for the harbour with the intention of boarding any ships they could, believing their city lost. Xenophon claims much of the credit for stopping the plundering and saving the city, but this makes little sense. Generals typically could not stop their troops from sacking a city once the frenzy had begun. Communication in the ancient world simply was not sufficient to stop groups of soldiers that were spread out over the greater part of the city. Coupled with that, and in this specific case, the mercenary army was tired, hungry, desperate for plunder, and had demonstrated many times that they were often undisciplined. One must conclude that either fewer soldiers had broken through the gates, and these were tracked down and stopped quickly, or there was rather more of the city sacked than Xenophon implies.

Whilst the discussions were underway that apparently saved the city, and in which the mercenaries were again debating what to do next, a certain Coeratidas arrived in camp:[80]

> While the soldiers were still in session Coeratidas the Theban came in, a man who was going up and down Greece, not in exile, but because he was afflicted with a desire to be a general, and he was offering his services to any city or people that might be wanting a general; so at this time he came to the troops and said that he was ready to lead them to the [Danube] Delta, as it is called, of Thrace, where they could get plenty of good things; and until they should reach there, he said he would supply them with food and drink in abundance.

Wandering generals were not a particularly common phenomenon, and one wonders if they were ever terribly successful in wandering into a city in need of a general. In this case, Coeratidas must have sought out the mercenary army with a specific goal in mind, although we never discover what that was. The Theban's offer to feed the army at first implies that he was a man of considerable independent means, and it was undoubtedly the promise of food and plunder that led the assembly to elect him as their new general. Almost as soon as they did, they withdrew from Byzantium and headed for the Danube Delta. Only one day into the journey, however, twenty of his followers brought food to the army, but there was not enough to go round and he was swiftly removed from his position.

The army left the environs of Byzantium without any real direction or purpose. The senior commanders continued to squabble amongst themselves as to what their true purpose and destination should be, and the army again began to fracture. Around 5,000, including Xenophon himself, took up service with Seuthes, the first time Greek mercenaries had been employed by a Thracian warlord.[81] Their actions were limited to border raids into neighbouring territory, with little gain for the mercenaries themselves. Eight hundred others broke away under Neon and marched to the Chersonese. Others left the army in smaller numbers and presumably made for their homes further afield.

After a short term of employment, during which the mercenaries were becoming increasingly unhappy with Seuthes and his failure to live up to his promises, including those regarding payment, two Spartan ambassadors approached the surviving members of the army and offered them employment under the command of Thibron against the Persian satrap, Tissaphernes, at the standard rate of 1 daric per month. Sparta had finally decided to make open war on the Persians and, given their reluctance to have their own citizens away from the Peloponnese for long periods, a large ready-made mercenary army with experience of fighting the Persians was too good an opportunity to pass up. This represents the first time the Spartans had hired a large group of mercenary hoplites.[82]

The story of the 10,000 has always been a fascinating one, and it can tell us a great deal about Greek mercenaries and their attitudes at the end of the Peloponnesian War.

It is noticeable how many examples of undisciplined behaviour we see. Early in the campaign, before Cunaxa, these examples are surprisingly frequent, given their lack of difficulties during that phase of the march. A certain amount of disorder and undisciplined behaviour was to be expected during the march home, as they were constantly harried, they were hungry, thirsty and constantly betrayed by seemingly everyone they encountered. Some of this was due to the individual nature of their recruitment, in that they were gathered together as a series of individual armies fighting under the same banner, and were therefore not a coherent single entity. It is noticeable, however, that during the battle this individual spirit was overcome to a great extent in order to achieve the greater goal. The arrogance demonstrated by Clearchus at disobeying Cyrus' direct orders during the battle should not reflect badly upon the mercenaries themselves, but upon their Spartan commander.

We also see on the march the political power wielded by a mercenary army. They knew they were the most important part of Cyrus' army, even though they were far from the largest, and Cyrus knew it too; that is why they were hired, after all. The mercenaries were happy to use their position as indispensible troops to demand better financial terms on two occasions, both of which Cyrus had no real option but to acquiesce to. If he had not, and they had deserted, then his rebellion would have been over before it had begun. The march also illustrates the precarious nature of the life of a mercenary. If Cyrus had won at Cunaxa, as he very nearly did, then the mercenaries would have been massively rewarded and would have returned to Greece as wealthy men. As it happens, however, they were on the losing side, which left them without a paymaster, hundreds of miles inside hostile territory, with no obvious means of getting home and no riches to show for their efforts. The almost constant maintenance of democracy within the army, once they were left leaderless, is also an interesting feature of the return journey.

Their final act was to sign on with the Spartan commander, Thibron, for another campaign against Tissaphernes in Asia Minor. In many ways, this is surprising; after their experiences and privations of the previous months, we can imagine that another campaign against Persian opposition would be the very last thing they would want to undertake, and certainly not immediately having escaped. Once these men were shipped across the Bosphoros, they had the opportunity to march home. The march may well have still been a long and difficult one through Thrace, Macedonia and down through central Greece, and a march that would likely have taken many weeks, but the opportunity was there, and we must think why they chose not to do this *en masse*, with very few exceptions. The simple truth was, however, that these men were mercenaries. The only way they had of making a living was through force of arms, and they needed to work for whoever would employ them. Sparta, having recently been victorious over Athens in the Peloponnesian War, looked like a good bet in terms of receiving a regular wage, and if that meant a return to Persian soil then so be it.

Chapter 5

The Fourth Century

In this chapter we will address the issue of mercenary service in roughly the first half of the fourth century. There will be a separate chapter on the rise of Macedon that will largely address the remainder of the century. The fifth century saw limited mercenary employment, although it was growing towards the end of the century with the Peloponnesian War and the march of the 10,000. This increasing trend in mercenary employment continued, and indeed quickened, into the fourth century.[1] We will also continue the chronological theme by first looking at the situation down to, and including, the Corinthian War and then moving progressively to the rise of the Macedonian Empire.[2]

As we noted in the previous chapter, the remainder of the 10,000 had signed up with the Spartan general Thibron in Thrace with the intention of campaigning against Tissaphernes in Asia Minor. Thibron's newly completed army consisted of a remarkably small percentage of 'citizens' when compared to other Spartan armies of the fifth century. There were only 1,000 Neodamodes, 4,000 allies, 2,000 Ionians and 5,000 mercenaries.[3]

Neodamodes in Spartan armies became increasingly common, along with the rise in mercenary forces. They were former helots who had been freed from slavery in return for military service. They became something of a staple in Spartan armies overseas because of the falling numbers of full Spartan citizens.

Xenophon, unsurprisingly, tried to argue that it was only the addition of himself and the 5,000 or so remaining mercenaries that enabled Thibron to attack Tissaphernes at all, but this does not appear to be a realistic statement. What they did do was to allow the Spartan the freedom and flexibility to expand his area of operations wider than he otherwise would have been able.[4] It would appear from Xenophon's narrative that the remnants of the 10,000, although useful militarily in allowing an expansion of operations for

Thibron, probably did more harm than good to the Spartans and their alliance, although, unsurprisingly, Xenophon tries to downplay the difficulties.[5]

> When, in pursuance of his intention to march against Caria, he was already at Ephesus, Dercyllidas arrived to take command of the army, a man who was reputed to be exceedingly resourceful; indeed, he bore the nickname 'Sisyphus'. Thibron accordingly went back home, and was condemned and banished; for the allies accused him of allowing his soldiers to plunder their friends.

The remnants of Cyrus' army were clearly so inured to pillage and plunder that they simply saw it as a way of life; this is not altogether surprising, as it was how they had sustained themselves for months in Persia. It was, however, a shock to the Greeks, and had not yet become an accepted way of life for armies at home.

Part of the problem for the actions of the mercenary contingent of the army was undoubtedly their own ingrained behaviour, but that was not helped by Thibron evidently not understanding their psychology. His successor, Dercyllidas, was a significant improvement. He understood that the wages needed to be paid regularly and promptly, that the army needed to be fed and provisioned, and that during periods when they were not campaigning they should be in enemy territory as far as possible to reduce the risk of friendly populations being brutalized. Xenophon tells us specifically that Thibron had been a burden to friendly cities by wintering his troops close to their population centres, but that Dercyllidas did not do this.[6]

> After Dercyllidas had accomplished these things and gained possession of nine cities in eight days, he set about planning how he might avoid being a burden to his allies, as Thibron had been, by wintering in a friendly country ...

This passage is interesting also because it demonstrates that the mercenaries were employed through at least two consecutive winters. Normally, and before the Peloponnesian War certainly, mercenary armies would tend to be disbanded in the winter and reconstituted the following spring for another campaigning season. This was done partly to save money and partly because campaigns simply were not conducted during the winter. The old rules of warfare had been changed forever.

When King Agesilaus arrived in Asia Minor in 396 to take over command of operations he brought with him 2,000 neodamodes, 6,000 allies and 30 Spartiates.[7] More troops were clearly needed for the campaign in Asia Minor, and it is interesting that emancipated helots and allies were used rather than any attempt being made to hire more mercenaries. This is true as far as infantry were concerned, at least. Agesilaus realized the limitations of an army purely comprised of heavy infantry, or even of an army with some light infantry support. He understood that only cavalry would truly give him mobility and flexibility, both from an offensive and defensive perspective. In order to achieve this, he hired mercenary cavalry locally; the Peloponnese was not traditional cavalry country after all, and neither Sparta nor her allies could supply what was required.

By 395, Agesilaus was evidently concerned by his mercenaries and appointed one of his thirty Spartiates, Herippidas, to their command. The reasons for this are not stated, but we can assume he felt they would be easier to control in that they were commanded by a Spartan rather than by Xenophon; the latter remained with the army until at least 394 in a more junior position.[8] Spartan citizens commanding mercenary soldiers was to become a standard feature of future Spartan campaigns. After the change of command, we hear little of their specific campaigns until Coronea in 394. This battle has the distinction of being the first time that both sides commanded significant numbers of mercenary soldiers.

The year 395 saw the outbreak of the Corinthian War, a war between a coalition of Athens, Corinth, Thebes and Argos set against the forces of the Peloponnesian League. The first encounter was at Corinth in July of that year, but in terms of mercenary activity it was uninteresting. Of the dispositions at Coronea, Xenophon tells us:[9]

> Those who were now drawn up against Agesilaus were the Boeotians, Athenians, Argives, Corinthians, Aenianians, Euboeans, and both the Locrian peoples; while with Agesilaus was a regiment of Lacedaemonians which had crossed over from Corinth, half of the regiment from Orchomenus, furthermore the emancipated Helots from Lacedaemon who had made the expedition with him, besides these the foreign contingent which Herippidas commanded, and, furthermore, the troops from the Greek cities in Asia and from all those cities in Europe which he had brought over as he passed through them; and from the immediate neighbourhood there came to him hoplites of the Orchomenians and Phocians. As for peltasts, those with Agesilaus were far more numerous; on the other hand, the horsemen of either side were about equal in number.

Agesilaus took up a position on the right wing rather than in the centre, which was perhaps the more usual place for the commander-in-chief of a largely hoplite army in the ancient world. This was probably to ensure that he was ranged against the Argive contingent of the coalition army.[10]

Agesilaus occupied the right wing of the army under his command, while the Orchomenians were at the extreme end of his left wing. On the other side, the Thebans themselves were on the right and the Argives occupied their left wing.

The battle was joined when both wings charged each other. The Spartans and their mercenaries charged the Argives from the Spartan right, whereas the Thebans charged the Orchomenians on the Spartan left. Xenophon describes the opening of the battle:[11]

> Now as the opposing armies were coming together, there was deep silence for a time in both lines; but when they were distant from one another about a stadium, the Thebans raised the war-cry and rushed to close quarters on the run. When, however, the distance between the armies was still about three plethra, the troops whom Herippidas commanded, and with them the Ionians, Aeolians, and Hellespontines, ran forth in their turn from the phalanx of Agesilaus, and the whole mass joined in the charge and, when they came within spear thrust, put to flight the force in their front. As for the Argives, they did not await the attack of the forces of Agesilaus, but fled to Mount Helicon.

The Argives retreated without a blow being landed by the advancing mercenaries, whereas on the Spartan left wing the Orchomenians were quickly crushed by the Thebans. When Agesilaus had defeated the Argives, he was celebrating victory in the battle with Herippidas when a messenger arrived with news of the disaster on the Spartan left. The first phase of the battle cannot have lasted long, as it seems there was only a short delay between the mercenary charge, the Argive retreat and news of the Theban victory on the Spartan left. The Orchomenians cannot have put up very much more resistance than the Argives. This first phase ended, then, with both right wings comprehensively defeating both left wings.

Both the Spartans and the Thebans were surprised that their individual victories had not led to a decisive overall victory in the battle, and their next actions demonstrate significant battlefield discipline. Both armies reformed (there must have been some level of disarray after a victorious charge), turned around to face the enemy and marched back towards each other. Their relative positions means that neither had access to its baggage train, and this lent a certain desperation to the second phase of the battle.[12]

> At this point one may unquestionably call Agesilaus courageous; at least he certainly did not choose the safest course. For while he might have let the men pass by who were trying to break through and then have followed them and overcome those in the rear, he did not do this, but

crashed against the Thebans front to front; and setting shields against shields they shoved, fought, killed, and were killed. Finally, some of the Thebans broke through and reached Mount Helicon, but many were killed while making their way thither.

The Thebans broke through the Spartan lines and made for their base camp, from which they retired from the field. The Spartans did not pursue them, but withdrew themselves. Both sides were badly mauled in the second phase of the battle, and neither was keen to repeat the experience straight away. Xenophon presents the battle as a victory for Agesilaus, who was himself wounded in the second phase of the battle, but the reality was that it was a stalemate and resolved nothing. The Spartan mercenaries acquitted themselves admirably in both phases of the battle and demonstrated once again what they were capable of. The coalition mercenaries, of whom we hear little in reality, were probably significant numbers of lightly armed troops who fought alongside the Thebans, but did not form a central element to Xenophon's narrative.

We do not know how many of the original 10,000 were left in Spartan employ by 394, but by that year they had been employed by Sparta for five years and must have undergone a level of attrition during that time. We have very little evidence of any other mercenaries in Spartan service during the early years of the fourth century, and no positive evidence that any of the losses were replaced. Roughly 5,000 were originally recruited, and I think it is feasible that perhaps only half that many remained by the end of the Battle of Coronea. Although this is speculation, the number would certainly have declined from the initial figure.

The Spartan hiring of mercenaries was a little new for them, but the fact that they were hoplites and employed in exactly the same way that Sparta had employed its hoplites for generations demonstrates that tactically they had not changed their basic thinking. The mercenaries were employed because they were a ready-made hoplite force and saved the Spartans from employing their own citizens, or too many allied troops. The Athenians, on the other hand, do demonstrate some tactical innovations, although these may have been enforced. As noted earlier during the discussion on the Peloponnesian War, Athens did not have ready access to the recruiting grounds of Arcadia from which to hire mercenary forces. The innovation was that she began to employ bodies of lightly armed troops, and to begin using them as distinct operational units. For heavy infantry, she continued to rely upon citizen soldiers, as had always been the case.

As the Corinthian War dragged on beyond the two indecisive battles of 394, both sides had the potential to be dragged into another Peloponnesian

War, as neither alliance seemingly had the strength to decisively defeat the other. Warfare was again year-round, and from 392 most of the engagements were fought by bodies of mercenaries who could be maintained in the field for indefinite periods.[13]

The Corinthians built long walls at the Isthmus of Corinth to prevent the Spartans campaigning to the north, and it was defended largely by Athenian mercenary peltasts, an army that was raised by Conon and later commanded by Iphicrates. Agesilaus besieged the fortifications for two years in a campaign that sapped the energy and financial resources of both sides. During the lengthy siege, the peltasts fared poorly in pitched battles with hoplites, but that was not what they were equipped to do. They were also used by Iphicrates on raids into the Peloponnese, where their mobility was particularly beneficial to them. The finest hour of the Athenians during this was the destruction of a force of 600 Spartan hoplites and Lechaeum by a force of mercenary peltasts. On the Spartan side, Agesilaus also employed mercenary troops, rebels from Corinth who had signed up to fight for the Peloponnesians.

The peltasts of Iphicrates were a new innovation in warfare. They were lightly armed and fought in open order, which was entirely normal, but they also fought in formations and could be commanded as cohesive units rather than operating as something of a disorganized rabble. Iphicrates' success during the Corinthian War demonstrated to everyone in Greece that hoplites were not invulnerable; that they suffered from a significant tactical disadvantage when faced with mobile, disciplined and well-commanded light-armed troops.[14]

The Corinthian War was not only fought at the Isthmus of Corinth, however. In 388, Sparta sent her admiral, Anaxibius, to the city of Abydos in the Hellespontine region, the only city to remain loyal to Sparta. Anaxibius was also given enough money to raise a force of 1,000 mercenaries from amongst the local populations.[15] The Spartan *navarch* also commanded 250 hoplites from Abydos and a small number of Peloponnesians. His orders were apparently to attempt to disrupt the Athenian grain shipments coming from the Black Sea. The reliance upon foreign grain, and particularly grain from the Black Sea, had long been an Athenian Achilles heel. A strong navy and control of certain key ports could starve the Athenians, or at least force them to look elsewhere, such as Egypt, for their grain supplies.

Anaxibius raised his mercenary force quickly, and immediately began campaigning in the local area. He had a measure of initial success by winning over a number of local towns and cities from Pharnabazus. Riding high, Anaxibius gathered together his fleet, raised and manned another three ships from Abydos, and attacked the Athenian grain shipments directly, hijacking them and taking them to the harbour at Abydos.[16]

The Athenians were, of course, aware of how vulnerable their food supply was, and were alarmed at Spartan attempts to interfere. Iphicrates was immediately redirected to Asia Minor with eight ships and 1,200 mercenary peltasts to confront Anaxibius.[17] The opening moves on both sides were cautious and restricted to raiding each other's territory, but Iphicrates soon learned that:[18]

> Anaxibius had gone to Antandrus with his mercenaries, the Lacedaemonians who were with him, and two hundred hoplites from Abydos, and heard that he had brought Antandrus into relations of friendship with him. Whereupon, suspecting that after he had also established his garrison there he would return again and bring the troops from Abydos back home, Iphicrates crossed over by night to the most deserted portion of the territory of Abydos, and going up into the mountains, set an ambush. Furthermore, he ordered the triremes which had brought him across the strait to sail at daybreak along the coast of the Chersonese, up the strait, in order that it might seem that he had sailed up the Hellespont to collect money, as he was wont to do.

On his return journey, Anaxibius was informed by the citizens of the friendly cities that he passed that Iphicrates had indeed sailed towards the Hellespont; as a result, Anaxibius took few precautions on his march. Whilst the Spartan was on level ground, Iphicrates kept his troops hidden and waited for the opportune moment to spring the ambush.

> When the troops from Abydos, who were in the van, were now in the plain of Cremaste, where their gold mines are, and the rest of the army as it followed along was on the downward slope, and Anaxibius with his Lacedaemonians was just beginning the descent, at this moment Iphicrates started his men up from their ambush and rushed upon him on the run.

Anaxibius' men were too spread out along a narrow path and there was no hope that those at the front or rear could help any of the others. He had been outmanoeuvred by Iphicrates in a perfectly executed ambush by lightly armed mercenary peltasts. Anaxibius, along with several of the Spartans, fell when making a final stand. Much of the rest of the army did not resist Iphicrates for long but turned and fled towards the city of Abydos. Iphicrates' men followed them and killed as many as they could, fifty hoplites from the city and 200 others.[19] After securing his victory, Iphicrates must have campaigned briefly in the area of Abydos, because the Spartans were again confined to their city alone and all of their diplomatic and military gains of the previous months and years were for nothing. Athens was again in control of the region. Iphicrates then returned to the Chersonese and remained in Thrace until after the King's Peace. Xenophon does not record what happened to the captured Athenian grain ships, but presumably they were released to avoid further difficulties.

With the Corinthian war threatening to turn into another Peloponnesian War, and with the front line having moved from the mainland to Asia Minor, the Spartans and Persians were able to force a resolution. They negotiated that the Persians would switch their allegiance from Athens to Sparta and formulated a treaty between the two.[20] Without Persian gold, and with no empire to support it, Athens was running dangerously low on funds. Coupled with this was a Spartan fleet of eighty ships, commanded by Antalcidas, which had taken up a position to blockade the Hellespontine region; Iphicrates could do nothing about a large navy, despite still being in the Thraceward region. Athens was left with little choice but to agree to the terms of a peace treaty brokered by Artaxerxes. The terms of the Kings Peace meant that Sparta remained the dominant power on the Greek mainland, with Athens being allowed to retain some of its possessions in the northern Aegean. Many cities became nominally independent, and Asia Minor was again handed back to the control of the Great King.

The outbreak of peace in the Greek world was, of course, disastrous for the mercenary soldiers fighting on both sides of the Corinthian War. One of the first acts of both Athens and Sparta was to dismiss all of the mercenary troops in their service; they were expensive and an unaffordable luxury, particularly for Athens.

As was usually the case, however, when one war ended another began. Many of the recently unemployed mercenaries were recruited by Artaxerxes for a campaign against Cyprus.[21] These were Greek hoplites recruited from the mainland rather than lightly armed peltasts; Persia could provide her own perfectly adequate light-armed troops. It is an interesting trend of the fourth century that the Greek city-states tended to hire lightly armed mercenaries whereas the Persians tended to hire heavily armoured hoplites.

Cyprus had been an ally of Athens during the Corinthian War, but the terms of the King's Peace meant Athens was forced to abandon her one-time ally, lest she be considered to be in breach of the terms of the treaty. Chabrias, an Athenian general, had been campaigning alongside Evagoras, the Cyprian king, until the peace was signed. At that point, Chabrias was instructed to stay in Cyprus along with his mercenaries, who essentially became freelancers, but he was no longer there in an official capacity as a representative of Athens. It seems unlikely that this would have fooled Artaxerxes if they had encountered one another, and Chabrias was kept well away from the invading Persian force to avoid difficulties for Athens. Evagoras did not immediately need the peltasts of Chabrias. as he employed 6,000 mercenaries of his own. These included some troops from the Egyptian Pharaoh Achoris, who was himself fighting for independence from Persia.

In 386 Achoris requested of Athens that Chabrias be sent to Egypt to aid them in their struggles, and Athens agreed. Chabrias was quickly given a senior command in the Egyptian army and was enjoying considerable success. Although not a breach of the terms of the King's Peace, the Persians complained to Athens anyway, who recalled their general in response. Chabrias did not have the wealth or personal authority to act independently as a mercenary commander, and returned to Athens, where he was given command of the fleet.

Iphicrates was also not keen to retire to a peaceful life after the end of the Corinthian War. He moved to Thrace, where he continued campaigning for the next fifteen years in the employ of one Thracian warlord or another. From 384 to 382, he entered Persian service as commander of a mercenary army numbering somewhere between 12,000 and 20,000.[22] Pharnabazus had raised a significant army for an offensive against Egypt. Once the campaign had begun, however, the Persian consistently ignored Iphicrates' advice and demonstrated no strategic innovation or tactical guile. In frustration, Iphicrates abandoned the army and returned to Athens.

The King's Peace turned out to be merely an interlude between wars, as was so often the case. Sparta remained the dominant power and was constantly in dispute with Thebes, which wished to reconstitute the Boeotian League, but was still tied to Sparta. Athens, under the peace, had been allowed to retain control of her north Aegean possessions and was keen to expand her influence once again. When war did finally break out, it was not because of a dispute between these traditional rivals, however, but the result of a growing power in the north. Olynthus had formed the Chalcidian League, an alliance based upon trade and legal equality whose influence was growing rapidly. The pretext came in 382, when the Olynthians tried to enrol two local cities into their league (Apollonia and Acanthus), but they resisted and made representations to Sparta for assistance. Ambassadors were sent from both cities, and they made impassioned speeches to the member states of the Peloponnesian League. After hearing the ambassadors, the Spartans invited their allies to speak:[23]

> Thereupon many, especially those who desired to gratify the Lacedaemonians, advocated raising an army, and it was decided that each state should send its proportionate contingent for an army of ten thousand. Proposals were also made that any state which so desired should be allowed to give money instead of men, three Aeginetan obols per day

for each man, while if any state normally furnished horsemen, pay equal to that of four hoplites should be given for each horseman; and if any one of the states should fail to send its contingent to the army, the Lacedaemonians were to be permitted to fine such state a stater per day for each man.

The Acanthian ambassador managed to persuade the Spartans, however, that this force would take too long to assemble and that a smaller force should be gathered and dispatched immediately. The Spartans agreed to this and sent a small force of around 2,000, consisting of emancipated helots, perioeci and Scythians, commanded by Eudamidas.[24] On the way north, they took the opportunity presented to them by a group of disaffected Thebans to take control of the Cadmea; as a result they were able to control that city for three years, until 379, when they were unceremoniously driven out by a faction led by Pelopidas.

The secondary force of 10,000, the vast majority of whom were mercenaries, was also approved and began to assemble but, as predicted by the Acanthian ambassador, this was not a quick process. Eudamidas met with some initial success by accepting the surrender of Potidaea, a city which had been formally loyal to Olynthus, but was to become the Peloponnesian base of operations. Eudamidas' advantage did not last long, however. The forward troops sent by the Peloponnesian League simply were not sufficient in either numbers or quality to oppose those of the Chalcidian League, and suffered significantly. The main force of around 10,000 arrived not too long afterwards with the reasonable expectations that they would quickly win victory, given that they now had a significant numerical superiority. Again, however, the Spartans suffered setbacks. The main issue appears to be that Spartan generals historically had commanded hoplites, and they were not familiar with the operational advantages and disadvantages of peltasts. Simply put, Teneutias (who had replaced Eudamidas when the main body arrived) had not moved with the times in regard to the changing face of warfare in the Greek world. Xenophon illustrates this brilliantly when he narrates a battle before Olynthus where the Spartans use peltasts against cavalry, with no heavy infantry support.[25]

As time went on, however, and Teleutias had led his army up to the city of the Olynthians in order to destroy whatever tree was left or whatever field had been cultivated by the enemy, the Olynthian horsemen issued forth and, proceeding quietly, crossed the river which flows by the city and held on their way towards the opposing army. And when Teleutias saw them, being irritated at their audacity, he immediately ordered Tlemonidas, the leader of the peltasts, to charge against them on the run. Now, when the Olynthians saw the peltasts sallying forth, they turned about, retired quietly, and crossed the river again. The peltasts, on the other hand, followed very rashly and, with the thought that the enemy were in flight, pushed into the river after them to pursue them. Thereupon the Olynthian horsemen, at the moment when they thought that those who had crossed the river were still easy to handle, turned about and dashed upon them, and they not only killed Tlemonidas himself, but more than one hundred of the others.

Teleutias had led the peltasts with what could be described as incompetence. He had made a mistake in allowing the peltasts to chase after the enemy cavalry without providing any sort of support. More than 100 men died as a result, including the commander of the contingent. The sensible thing to have done would have been to withdraw, regroup and consider the next tactical move. Teleutias compounded his mistake by allowing emotions to rule his thinking in his desire to force a victory, and many more died as a result:[26]

But Teleutias, filled with anger when he saw what was going on, snatched up his arms and led the hoplites swiftly forward, while he ordered the peltasts and the horsemen to pursue and not stop pursuing. Now in many other instances those who have pressed a pursuit too close to a city's wall have come off badly in their retreat, and in this case also, when the men were showered with missiles from the towers, they were forced to retire in disorder and to guard themselves against the missiles. At this moment the Olynthians sent out their horsemen to the attack, and the peltasts also came to their support; finally, their hoplites likewise rushed out, and fell upon the Lacedaemonian phalanx when it was already in confusion. There Teleutias fell fighting. And when this happened, the troops about him at once gave way, and in fact no one stood his ground any longer, but all fled, some for Spartolus, others for Acanthus, others to Apollonia, and the majority to Potidaea. As they fled in all directions, so likewise the enemy pursued in all directions, and killed a vast number of men, including the most serviceable part of the army.

Although something of a disaster for the campaign, the Spartans refused to contemplate abandoning the war and organized a third force to march north. This new army was commanded by King Agesipolis. Agesipolis was given a staff of thirty Spartiates, as Agesilaus had before him. The army was recruited from across Spartan society, with many wealthy perioeci volunteering. Along with these was a group of bastard children, the sons of Spartans and helot women, and a body of 'Spartan-trained' (that is, foreigners) who were raised in the Spartan system, as Xenophon's own sons were. On top of these men from Sparta were contingents from some allied states and cavalry from Thessaly.[27] The new army was thoroughly familiar with Spartan society and we can assume that each man was a trained warrior. This army should have been powerful, but it ultimately fared little better, again because of the limitations imposed by leadership. The Spartans lost another commander when Agesipolis died of fever whilst besieging Olynthus. Despite incompetence, defeats and untimely death, the Spartans ultimately starved Olynthus into surrender and the Chalcidian League was dissolved temporarily.

The year 379 saw victory for the Spartan army in the north, supported by the remnants of the defeated mercenary army. It also saw the return of Pelopidas and the loss of Spartan control over Thebes and the Boeotian League. Sparta and Athens were also once again at war following an aborted attack on Piraeus by the Spartan general Sphodrias. For their mutual benefit, Athens and Thebes entered into an alliance shortly before Agesilaus attacked Boeotia with a force of 20,000 troops, many of whom were mercenary peltasts, with the intention of dismantling the Boeotian League permanently.[28]

Agesilaus conducted campaigns in two successive seasons, 378 and 377, although notably he and his army returned to the Peloponnese during the winter. These two campaigns saw a major development in the quality and tactical usage of mercenary peltasts. The 378 offensive began with Agesilaus occupying the high ground, including a number of key mountain passes. This way he could control the terrain and the movement of peoples. When he entered the Boeotian plain he discovered that the Thebans had not been idle. There was an extensive network of ditches and a stockade newly constructed around 20 stades from Thebes to defend it from attack.

When the Athenians heard of Agesilaus' invasion of Boeotia, they sent 5,000 mercenary peltasts and 200 cavalry, under the command of Chabrias, to aid the Thebans.[29] Agesilaus saw the combined Theban and Athenian force in a well prepared defensive position and reasoned that they would not be tempted into the plain. He therefore advanced towards the fortifications. Diodorus brilliantly narrates Chabrias' greatest victory, and is an excellent example of the employment of mercenary peltasts:[30]

> As for Agesilaus, he led out his army in battle array against the Boeotians, and, when he had drawn near, in the first place launched his light-armed troops against his opponents, thus testing their disposition to fight him. But when the Thebans had easily from their higher position thrust his men back, he led the whole army against them closely arrayed to strike them with terror. Chabrias the Athenian, however,

leading his mercenary troops, ordered his men to receive the enemy with a show of contempt, maintaining all the while their battle lines, and, leaning their shields against their knees, to wait with upraised spear. Since they did what they were ordered as at a single word of command, Agesilaus, marvelling at the fine discipline of the enemy and their posture of contempt, judged it inadvisable to force a way against the higher ground and compel his opponents to show their valour in a hand-to-hand contest, and, having learned by trial that they would dare, if forced, to dispute the victory, he challenged them in the plain.

Agesilaus was forced to withdraw to the plain, and Chabrias' men demonstrated superb discipline by not following up their attack and potentially turning a victory into a disastrous defeat. The Spartans, for a while at least, were happy to content themselves with plundering the land that they could easily reach on their side of the fortifications. Over a period of several days the Spartans, after breakfast, moved their forces along the fortifications in one direction or another, and their movements were mirrored by the Theban defenders. After this had gone on for several days (or more likely weeks), Agesilaus roused his men earlier than normal and made sacrifice at dawn; he then attacked the defenders before the Thebans were ready, as they had gotten used to the Spartans taking breakfast at a regular time. The ruse worked, and the Spartans got past the defences and pillaged the land up to Thebes itself.[31]

> But when Agesilaus had noted that it was always after breakfast that the enemy also appeared, he offered sacrifice at daybreak, led his army forward as rapidly as possible, and passed within the stockade at an unguarded point. Then he devastated and burned the region within the enclosure up to the walls of the city. After doing this and withdrawing again to Thespiae, he fortified their city for the Thespians. There he left Phoebidas as governor, while he himself crossed the mountain again to Megara, disbanded the allies, and led his citizen troops back home.

Agesilaus had retired early in the campaigning season, and Phoebidas, feeling confident after seeing a Spartan army devastating Theban lands, maintained the pressure on Thebes by continuing the raids. With the Spartans having withdrawn, the Thebans felt they could free themselves of this quasi-siege. They gathered together their heavy infantry, and a detachment of cavalry, and marched into Thespian territory.[32]

> But when they were within the territory of Thespiae, Phoebidas pressed them close with his peltasts and did not allow them to stray at any point from their phalanx; so that the Thebans in great vexation proceeded to

retreat more rapidly than they had advanced, and their mule-drivers also threw away the produce which they had seized and pushed for home; so dreadful a panic had fallen upon the army.

Xenophon gives an excellent description of the impotence of heavy infantry when faced by light infantry if the hoplites are unsupported and the peltasts are well-commanded and disciplined. The Theban hoplites were too slow to charge the peltasts, and if they tried they likely would expose the flanks of the charging troops and leave themselves vulnerable. Much the same was true of the cavalry; there were likely too few of them to charge the peltasts successfully. The peltasts could not directly engage the hoplites, but could continue to harry them. The vulnerability of unsupported hoplites was becoming a common feature of Greek warfare, and the rise of the peltasts saw the end to exclusively heavy infantry engagements.

Phoebidas pressed his advantage and moved forward, with his peltasts in front and hoplites behind, following the line of retreat of the Thebans. During the retreat the Theban cavalry had become separated from the infantry and found themselves trapped against a ravine. The Thespian peltasts, apparently relatively few in number and well in advance of the hoplites, closed on them. Having little option, the cavalry charged the Thespians, who were quickly routed. They fled in disorder back down the road to their city, many peltasts being killed in the retreat, along with Phoebidas himself. Along the way they encountered the supposedly stout hoplites, but these also turned and fled, thus ending the Thespian ambitions on Thebes, for that year at least. The Thespian forces had fallen into the all-too-common trap of pursuing a seemingly defeated enemy, and doing so without maintaining any discipline or cohesion, the exact opposite of what we saw from the superior troops of Chabrias.

For some time the Spartans had been accepting financial contributions from their allies in lieu of troops. This financial clout allowed Sparta to hire mercenary armies when required, without greatly worrying about the cost; it was recoverable from her allies after all. The year 377 saw another sizeable invasion on Boeotia by Agesilaus and a largely mercenary army, but the actions were on a small scale and indecisive. The main impact of the second invasion was the devastation, once again, of Theban farmland. The result was that for two consecutive years they could gather no crops.

This Boeotian campaign is interesting partly because of Chabrias' brilliant action of 378, and partly because of the increasing reliance upon mercenary forces. Sparta and Thebes hired large numbers of mercenary peltasts for the campaign, as did both Athens and Thespiae. There was seemingly never a shortage of mercenaries available at short notice anywhere in Greece. The increasing demand was easily met by the readily available supply. It is further interesting that even small states like Thespiae could afford to hire mercenaries in reasonable numbers, implying that they were readily available, but also that they were an inexpensive option. Mercenaries were becoming the preferred option when city-states had available finances and did not wish to risk the lives of their own citizens. Their increasing professionalism was also starting to set them apart from the citizen soldier. We can reasonably assume that Athenian citizens would not have had the training or discipline to act as Chabrias' men had done.

By 374, Theban influence was growing; she had regained, by various means, a number of cities that had been former members of the Boeotian League. Athens was also regaining some of her former confidence and was wining over allies. Sparta, on the other hand, was finding it increasingly difficult to maintain her position of pre-eminence in the Greek world. This is amply demonstrated by Athens' attempt at a show of power by sailing her fleet, commanded by Timotheus, around the Peloponnese in order to reach her new western ally, Corcyra. They ensured that they were constantly within view of the land, a demonstration to Sparta if ever there was one.[33]

Sparta was far from a spent force, however, and she quickly manned her own fleet under the command of Nicolochus and sailed out to meet Timotheus. The naval battle that ensued is not described in detail in the sources, but Nicolochus was initially defeated and withdrew. Once he had received reinforcements that arrived too late for the initial engagement, he again sailed to meet Timotheus, who this time elected not to sail out to meet the Spartan admiral. Perhaps the Athenian fleet was more damaged than we realize, and they had no reinforcements to bolster their numbers. Either way, a second naval engagement was avoided.

The following year, the Spartans used a convenient oligarchic pretext to support Zacynthus against the Athenians, and similarly dispatched a fleet to Corcyra in order to liberate it from Athenian control. Diodorus tells us that:[34]

> The Lacedaemonian, aware of the great importance that Corcyra had for the aspirants to sea power, made haste to possess themselves of this city.

Xenophon adds that the Spartans also sent an embassy to Dionysius of Syracuse pointing out that it would not be in his interests for the Athenians to possess Corcyra either, although we have nothing recorded as to his response.

The Spartans appointed Mnasippus as the commander of the fleet and the expedition. He had at his disposal an unspecified number of Peloponnesians (probably allies or emancipated helots) and 'at least' 1,500 mercenaries. They landed on Corcyra unopposed, and apparently had free reign to plunder at will. Xenophon gives an excellent description of the destruction wrought by a mercenary army:[35]

> Now when he had disembarked he was master of the country, laid waste the land, which was most beautifully cultivated and planted, and destroyed magnificent dwellings and wine-cellars with which the farms were furnished; the result was, it was said, that his soldiers became so luxurious that they would not drink any wine unless it had a fine bouquet. Furthermore, very many slaves and cattle were captured on the farms.

Corcyra was a mercenary's paradise; it was wealthy and undefended, and the Spartans seemingly gave their mercenaries free reign. Members of the expedition of the 10,000 dreamed of a situation like this one, rather than what they actually saw in Asia. The Lacaedemonian forces, after pillaging the land and outlying farmsteads and mansion houses, retired to a hill over-looking both the city and the harbour. From that vantage point they could control access to both the city and the island as a whole. The city of Corcyra was effectively under siege without the Spartans needing any special siege equipment, and without any Peloponnesian loss of life.

The Corcyrians were worried, and they evidently possessed no significant army (and did not have the transport capacity to reach a mercenary recruiting ground with any amount of cash). They had to content themselves with being under a state of siege, and as the food began to run out they approached Athens for aid. The Athenians agreed that they needed to pursue the matter vigorously. Ctesicles with a force of 600 mercenaries was sent to the island, landed under cover of darkness and immediately made their way to the city to strengthen the garrison. They were a mixed blessing, since they were extra mouths to feed but were not enough to defeat the Peloponnesians.[36] The Athenians also attempted to man a fleet, but could not find enough sailors in Athens. She sailed some vessels to the islands under her control in a recruitment drive; the result was that the navy was largely manned by mercenaries. The fleet was commanded by Iphicrates.

On Corcyra the Spartan commander, Mnasippus, was on the verge of victory. Every day deserters from the city were approaching the army in the hope of receiving food. Some he captured and treated as slaves, but when the numbers deserting became too high he drove them back to the city with whips. The inhabitants of the city refused to allow them back in, believing them to be little better than slaves themselves, and many died between the two forces. With victory in sight Mnasippus began to treat his mercenaries rather less favourably. He dismissed some from service and withheld payments from the others so that some were owed up to two months' wages. This was not because of a lack of funds; many of the allied states of the Peloponnesian League had offered money rather than troops. Rather, this was an act of greed and an example of remarkably poor generalship.[37]

The mercenaries defending the city, either getting desperate or seeing an opportunity, made a sortie against Mnasippus and killed some of his men, capturing others. The Spartan ordered his men to form up to counter-attack the Athenian mercenaries:[38]

> And when some captains replied that it was not easy to keep men obedient unless they were given provisions, he struck one of them with a staff and another with the spike of his spear. So it was, then, that when his forces issued from the city with him they were all dispirited and hostile to him. There can be no worse state of mind for men going in to battle.

As the Peloponnesians approached the city they formed up into a standard battle line. The Athenians had set up a rear guard to protect their retreat, and Mnasippus attacked these with the troops he had stationed in the centre of his formation and drove them back. This only served to draw the Spartans on towards the walls of the city and into the graveyard where the defenders were occupying the tops of the tallest memorials, hurling stones and javelins down on the attackers. While the Spartans were thus under pressure, more troops came streaming out of the city to attack the end of the Spartan line, where the attackers were only eight ranks deep. Mnasippus could see his flank struggling and he attempted to wheel it around behind the rest of the line. As soon as they began to move, however, the defenders assumed they were retreating and redoubled their attacks. This forced the Peloponnesians to stop their defensive manoeuvre and to stand and fight. What was worse for the Spartans, the troops posted next to those on the wing began to break.[39]

> As for Mnasippus, while he was unable to aid the troops which were hard pressed, because the enemy was attacking him in front, he was left with an ever smaller number of men. Finally, all of the enemy massed themselves together and charged upon Mnasippus and his troops, which were by this time very few. And the citizens, seeing what was going on, came out to join in the attack. Then after they had killed Mnasippus, all straightway joined in the pursuit. And they probably would have captured the very camp, along with its stockade, had not the pursuers turned back upon seeing the crowd of camp-followers, of attendants, and of slaves, imagining that there was some fighting ability in them.

With rumours rife of the impending arrival of Iphicrates, Hypermenes, the second in command of the Peloponnesian forces, gathered up what ships he could, loaded as much booty and as many slaves as they would carry, and abandoned the forces' defensive position in considerable haste and confusion.

Iphicrates proceeded cautiously towards Corcyra, taking possession of a number of cities in Cephalenia along the way. He had been informed of the death of Mnasippus, but was unsure of the validity of the tale, and so constantly sailed in battle order, expecting an ambush at any moment. He reached Corcyra and heard the truth of what had happened. He also heard that ten ships were approaching from Syracuse that were intended to support the troops from Sparta. Iphicrates set sail once again and captured all ten Syracusan ships and their crews, the latter of which he ransomed and returned to their home city.

Iphicrates then hired his troops out, without the permission of Athens, to the Acarnanians for their war against their Thyrian neighbours. He maintained his army by hiring it out, extorting money from allies on the mainland and activities that can only be described as blackmail. The nature of Iphicrates' campaign is indicative of the changing nature of warfare in the fourth century. Generals were now the commanders of largely light-armed mercenary contingents, rather than a body of citizen hoplites as previously. They were also experiencing the same general changes as their troops in that they were becoming increasingly professional. Typically, generals were no longer politicians who had been elected to a position, often one to which they were unsuited. The increasing complexity and variability of warfare in the fourth century meant that specialists were needed to command troops, individuals who understood strategy and tactics, as well as possessing the necessary leadership qualities.[40]

In terms of a study of mercenaries, Iphicrates was not only a fine exponent of their use; he was also a major reformer of light-armed troops. The exact dating of the reforms is not relevant here; it is their nature and consequence that most interest us. The primary sources of information that we have for Iphicrates' reforms are Diodorus and Nepos, both of whose accounts are very similar in reality. Xenophon tells us little that is of value in this regard. According to them, the most significant changes were as follows:[41]

> Iphicrates replaced the large (shield) of the Greeks by the light pelte, which had the advantage that it protected the body while allowing the wearer more freedom of movement; the soldiers who had formerly carried the (large hoplite shield) and who were called hoplites, were henceforth called peltasts after the name of their new shields; their new spears were half as long again or even twice as long as the old ones,

the new swords were also double in length. In addition Iphicrates introduced light and easily untied footwear, and the bronze harness was replaced by a linen covering, which although it was lighter, still protected the body.

Diodorus regards these changes as having been introduced into the existing hoplite troops and in the process discounts the possibility of already existing peltast-style light infantry. Diodorus' failure to recognize the existence of peltast troops before Iphicrates is very striking and a major error. In this omission, Diodorus shows his serious lack of understanding of the military situation of the day. Modern commentators have frequently been struck with the absurdity of this, and have taken up an opposite stance. For them, the change was a trivial one and consisted chiefly of the standardizing of the existing, but rather haphazard, peltast equipment. This argument, however, simply will not do. It assumes that the lightly armed skirmishers of earlier narratives were equipped in the same manner that Diodorus describes. This cannot be the case; lightly armed skirmishers would not have carried a sword and spear twice the length of those carried by hoplites. Earlier narratives also tell of peltasts actually throwing their spears. If Iphicrates had been standardizing that which already existed, then why did he not provide his troops with these throwing spears? We are surely not to believe that they carried these as well. Some other explanation must be sought.

Was Iphicrates actually inventing a new type of peltast, one with specific and specialized equipment? The other extreme view is that Iphicratean peltasts were in no way different from Thracian peltasts.[42] On this interpretation, Iphicrates' reforms were of little significance, as troops of exactly the same type existed already in Thrace. The truth probably lies somewhere between these two extreme positions. There was probably no uniformity of peltast equipment before Iphicrates, with some using primarily throwing spears, some longer spears, still others using swords of various sizes. The size of the shield probably varied too. I suspect, therefore, that Iphicrates studied the light infantry of his day and based his reforms around choosing from the various groups the equipment that best suited the type of soldier that he was trying to create. We may see Iphicrates, therefore, not as creating something entirely new, or as standardizing that which already existed, but as refining the equipment and tactics of the peltasts of his day. Iphicratean peltasts do not appear to have operated as skirmishing troops, as peltasts had traditionally done. Their tactical roles suggest that they were essentially acting as a more mobile and lightly armed hoplite. I have argued elsewhere that Alexander the Great's heavy infantry were essentially this kind of peltast.[43]

The defeat at, and loss of, Corcyra was a disaster for Sparta. She was already struggling to cope with a gradual decline in her influence and military power, and to see a Spartan army defeated so comprehensively, and its commander killed by a relatively small group of lightly armed mercenaries, did nothing to restore confidence or morale. Sparta also suffered several earthquakes at this time, which further weakened them.

Xenophon tells us that in 371, after some kind of summit meeting between the leading powers:[44]

> These speeches by the Athenians won approval and the Spartans also voted for peace. The terms were that governors should be withdrawn from the cities, all forces, both naval and military, should be disbanded, and that the cities should be left independent. It was provided that in any case of violation of these terms, any state which so desired should be free to go to the help of the injured party, but that, if a state did not desire to do this, there should be no legal obligation for it to do so. On these terms the Spartans took the oath for themselves and their allies, and the Athenians and their allies took the oath separately, city by city.

Sparta was struggling at this time and she needed the peace. It is a little harder to see why Athens agreed, although she perhaps feared the consequences of a refusal; she was still in the process of rebuilding herself after prolonged conflicts that started with the Peloponnesian War. Thebes, on the other hand, staunchly refused, as she was determined to reform the Boeotian League, an act the treaty strictly forbade.

Sparta was becoming increasingly fearful of Thebes and her growing influence and ambition, and resolved, once again, to stop her. An army of around 11,000 men was gathered and placed under the command of one of the Spartan kings, Clembrotus (who was already in Phocis). The army had taken no measures at all to conceal itself as it was mustering and training. The Thebans knew well in advance that the invasion was coming and made an attempt to defend the mountain passes that they expected the Spartans to use. The Peloponnesian army advanced into Boeotian territory via less well used routes, however, and avoided potentially difficult mountain combat.

The Thebans seemed somewhat less than confident of their chances of success, sending their wives and children to Athens to ensure their safety, evidently fearing what could happen if the army was defeated. Epaminondas was elected general and he gathered together every Theban citizen of military age, as well as those amongst the allies who were willing to help, and marched to meet the invaders with an army of not more than 6,000, accompanied as they were by unfavourable omens.[45] This number seems remarkably small if it did indeed include 'all Thebans of military age', as Diodorus indicates.

It is also interesting that there were no mercenaries in Theban service at this time, perhaps indicating a lack of funds. It cannot indicate a lack of time to prepare, as they must have realized war with Sparta was highly likely when they rejected the peace treaty and, of course, they could easily have seen the Peloponnesians preparing for the invasion.

The Spartans arrived on the battlefield of Leuctra first; they made camp, rested after their lengthy march and made preparations for battle:[46]

> As the Boeotians neared the enemy in their advance, and then, after surmounting some ridges, suddenly caught sight of the Lacedaemonians covering the entire plain of Leuctra, they were astounded at beholding the great size of the army.

Diodorus here rather overplays the size of the Spartan army; 11,000 was large but was not surprisingly so. The Thebans were worried, however. The troops were well aware of the bad omens at the outset of the campaign and they could see they were heavily outnumbered, almost two to one. The Theban senior commanders debated whether to even engage the Spartans or to retire and seek battle at a different place and time. Epaminondas persuaded the soldiers and his fellow commanders, citing other more positive oracles and omens, and eventually won the argument and with courage in their hearts they stood ready for battle. Epaminondas and the Thebans were further encouraged by the arrival of Jason of Pherae with 1,500 infantry and 500 Thessalian cavalry, so renowned from the campaigns of Alexander later in the fourth century.[47]

After a short and confused period, during which there may or may not have been a brief armistice, both sides drew up in their respective orders of battle. For the Spartans, King Cleombrotus was on one wing and Archidamus, the son of King Agesilaus on the other:[48]

> while on the Boeotian side Epameinondas, by employing an unusual disposition of his own, was enabled through his own strategy to achieve his famous victory.

Diodorus credits the ultimate Theban victory to Epaminondas' tactical innovations. It is an interesting side note that Xenophon does not even mention his presence. He also notes that Archidamus was only sent out after the battle, thus removing him from any blame for the defeat; Archidamus' father, Agesilaus, was a close friend of Xenophon and the historian may have been attempting to exonerate his friend's son.

Epaminondas positioned himself on the wing opposite Cleombrotus, along with the bulk of his finest troops, including the soon-to-be famous Sacred

Band. The Theban forces on this wing were much deeper than those opposing them and the clear intention was to drive through the enemy flank on that side. The Thebans were heavily outnumbered, however, and any strengthening of one area led to the inevitable concomitant weakening of another; this weakened area was the opposite wing of the Theban army. Epaminondas' orders for the battle were simple: his wing was to advance at the double and attempt to smash through the opposing wing. His weaker wing was to withdraw gradually and avoid battle for as long as possible with the Spartans. They would not be able to avoid battle completely, but as long as they wheeled around behind the centre they could delay the battle and avoid allowing the centre to be outflanked, which would likely have happened if they had simply withdrawn straight backwards, opening a gap between their wing and the centre.

The tactic was risky but, given the numbers and the quality of the Lacedaemonian forces arrayed against him, he was forced to take risks. Timing was everything with the proposed tactic. He needed to engage Cleombrotus and defeat his wing as quickly and decisively as possible, as well as probably wheeling on the Spartan centre to outflank them. Whilst this was happening, his other wing would be steadily giving ground and avoiding battle for as long as possible; they did not have the numbers required to hold the Spartans for long if they got themselves into heavy fighting. Diodorus describes the battle:[49]

> When the trumpets on both sides sounded the charge and the armies simultaneously with the first onset raised the battle-cry, the Lacedaemonians attacked both wings with their phalanx in crescent formation, while the Boeotians retreated on one wing, but on the other engaged the enemy in double-quick time. As they met in hand-to-hand combat, at first both fought ardently and the battle was evenly poised; shortly, however, as Epaminondas' men began to derive advantage from their valour and the denseness of their lines, many Peloponnesians began to fall. For they were unable to endure the weight of the courageous fighting of the elite corps; of those who had resisted some fell and others were wounded, taking all the blows in front. Now as long as King Cleombrotus of the Lacedaemonians was alive and had with him many comrades-in-arms who were quite ready to die in his defence, it was uncertain which way the scales of victory inclined; but when, though he shrank from no danger, he proved unable to bear down his opponents, and perished in an heroic resistance after sustaining many wounds, then, as masses of men thronged about his body, there was piled up a great mound of corpses.

The death of King Cleombrotus was the turning point of the battle. Diodorus continues:[50]

There being no one in command of the wing, the heavy column led by Epaminondas bore down upon the Lacedaemonians, and at first by sheer force caused the line of the enemy to buckle somewhat; then, however, the Lacedaemonians, fighting gallantly about their king, got possession of his body, but were not strong enough to achieve victory. For as the corps of elite outdid them in feats of courage, and the valour and exhortations of Epaminondas contributed greatly to its prowess, the Lacedaemonians were with great difficulty forced back; at first, as they gave ground they would not break their formation, but finally, as many fell and the commander who would have rallied them had died, the army turned and fled in utter rout.

The Theban victory was nothing short of stunning. For the Spartans the defeat was bad enough, but of the 700 Spartiates present 400 were killed, along with King Cleombrotus. These losses were irreplaceable in Spartan society. The numbers of full Spartan citizens had been in steady decline since the Persian Wars, and defeats like this only served to speed that trend. One of the most important consequences of the defeat, at least as far as the Peloponnese were concerned, was that almost all of the Arcadian states of the former Peloponnesian League now declared themselves to be openly independent of Sparta, and in order to protect themselves formed into a new league, the Arcadian League, enthusiastically supported by Epaminondas. Only Tegea, Orchomenus and Heraea still remained loyal to Sparta.[51]

In terms of mercenary activity, there were, in reality, relatively few at Leuctra, but its importance to mercenary service was that the Lacedaemonian losses forced the Spartans into a position where they needed to recruit another mercenary army at Corinth to protect the Isthmus from Theban incursions should they feel emboldened enough to try.[52]

Shortly after Sparta had raised her new army and positioned it for a defensive action at the Isthmus of Corinth, the newly formed Arcadian League launched an attack against those three states that had resisted joining. Sparta's mercenaries were withdrawn to garrison Orchomenus against this new anti-Spartan aggression. The attack of the Arcadian League on their neighbours was probably part of a coordinated effort by the Thebans, as it left the Isthmus of Corinth undefended. The Spartan mercenary army, under Polytropus, had intended to meet up with that commanded by Agesilaus to deliver a decisive blow to the new league but, before they were able to achieve this, the Arcadians inflicted a decisive defeat on the Spartan mercenaries outside Orchomenus. The Spartan force was largely composed of peltasts, and they were ineptly led. The peltasts engaged the Arcadians well in advance of any hoplite of cavalry support, and were heavily defeated. Xenophon describes the defeat:[53]

> Meanwhile the Mantineans made an expedition against the Orchome- nians. And they came off very badly from their attack upon the city wall, and some of them were killed; but when in their retreat they had reached Elymia and, although the Orchomenian hoplites now desisted from following them, Polytropus and his troops were very boldly press- ing upon them, then the Mantineans, realizing that if they did not beat them off many of their own number would be struck down by javelins, turned about and charged their assailants. Polytropus fell fighting where he stood; the rest fled, and very many of them would have been killed had not the Phliasian horsemen arrived, and by riding around to the rear of the Mantineans made them desist from their pursuit. The Mantineans, then, after accomplishing these things, went back home.

This was by now a fairly typical defeat for Spartan mercenaries; they pursued a fleeing enemy and found themselves far in advance of any support. The fleeing enemy reformed, turned around and attacked the disorganized and disordered mercenaries, inflicting a heavy defeat. For this to happen so frequently only indicates that Spartan commanders still had not come to terms with the capabilities and limitations of peltasts. These defeated peltasts remained loyal to the Spartan cause, however, and retreated to rejoin with Agesilaus. The Corinthian mercenaries who were also part of the Spartan mercenary army were not cut from the same cloth; they returned to Corinth as soon as their contract was over.

By the time of Epaminondas' invasion, the winter of 370, Sparta was almost bankrupt and was faced with an army invading Laconian soil, some- thing no Spartan had seen in his or her lifetime. At this time the Thebans rebuilt Mantinea and founded Megalopolis, which was intended to serve as the capital of the Arcadian League. After their construction efforts, and after devastating Spartan land, Epaminondas withdrew to Boeotia to consolidate his strength. We do not hear of Sparta hiring mercenaries again for quite some time; she simply could not afford them given the loss of her empire, as well as the loss of Messenia. This does not mean, however, that she was completely without mercenary troops. We do know that some were provided by allied states, and we hear of twenty ships filled with Celtic and Iberian mercenaries, along with fifty cavalry, supplied by Dionysius of Syracuse. Diodorus puts the number at 2,000 and tells us they were paid five months' wages in advance. This is the first reference, incidentally, of Celts operating on the Greek mainland.[54] These mercenaries served the Spartans well in limited actions against the Thebans until they returned to Syracuse in late summer.

The following summer Dionysius sent another similar force of mercenaries to Sparta, this time commanded by Cissidas, the man who had commanded the Syracusan expedition to Corcyra previously. Xenophon tells us:

> ... the second supporting force sent out by Dionysius arrived. And when the Athenians said that it ought to go to Thessaly to oppose the Thebans, while the Lacedaemonians urged that it should go to Laconia, the latter plan carried the day among the allies. Accordingly, after these troops from Dionysius had sailed round to Lacedaemon, Archidamus took them, along with his citizen soldiers, and set out on an expedition. He captured Caryae by storm and put to the sword all whom he took prisoners. From there he marched at once with his united forces against the people of Parrhasia, in Arcadia, and laid waste their land.

This passage illustrates both the different priorities of the Athenians and Spartans, now allied against the Thebans, and the increasing violence of warfare in the fourth century. The death of Dionysius I, however, ended the overseas adventures of mercenaries supplied by Syracuse. As noted above, although Sparta could no longer afford to support her own hired troops, some of her allies took the lead and supplied mercenaries. Just prior to the return to Sicily of the second mercenary army from Syracuse, help arrived from an unlikely source.

In the winter of 369/8 the satrap of Phrygia, Ariobarzanes, sent an ambassador, Philiscus, to Delphi, where he summoned the leading Greek states for a conference with the intention of establishing a lasting peace. This does seem to have been the outward intention, but there is little doubt that the ulterior motive was to stop Greek mercenaries fighting and dying in the seemingly endless Greek civil wars. If he could establish a lasting peace, he would automatically increase the numbers that would be available for a proposed rebellion by Ariobarzanes against the Great King. Philiscus perhaps did not fully understand Greek politics at the time, and he took the position that Messenia should be returned to the possession of Sparta. Even if the Thebans had been nominally in favour of peace, they would never agree to such a proposal. Philiscus saw his only option being to side with the Spartans. Once Philiscus realized this would be his only course, the meeting was dissolved and Philiscus set about hiring a mercenary army with the large amount of gold he had brought with him.[55]

Philiscus raised a large number of mercenaries, of which he left 2,000 in the Peloponnese with their wages paid in advance. We are not told what he did with the rest, but it is a reasonable assumption that he took them with him back to Asia Minor, as was the original intention.[56] These loans of mercenaries from Syracuse and Ariobarzanes, when taken together with the fact that Sparta was not hiring any of her own at this time, only serve to indicate the dire financial situation of the rapidly declining superpower.

The largest employer of Greek mercenaries during these years was Jason of Pherae, who employed a standing force of 6,000. These were nominally on the side of the Thebans, although they may well have arrived too late to assist at Leuctra, and they argued against an all-out assault on the fleeing Spartans after that battle. They could easily have proved far more decisive in Greek history had Jason lived longer. He died an untimely death before he was able to stamp his name and authority indelibly on the Greek world. Jason's death was a huge blow for Thessaly. He had been such an important local figure during his brief life that he had united the cities of that region under the banner of Pherae. As so often with the early and unexpected death of such a charismatic figure, the alliance fell apart. Some states appealed for help from Macedonia against Pherae, but she used this appeal as an opportunity to expand her own influence and annexed them (Larissa and Crannon). Other cities appealed to Thebes, and Pelopidas conducted a major campaign that ultimately repulsed Macedonia, defeated Pherae and brought Thessaly under the sphere of influence of Thebes from 369 to 364.

At this time, similar power struggles were being fought out in the Peloponnese, with the Arcadian League breaking up, the northern states returning to Spartan control (or influence, at least) and the southern states siding with Tegea, and ultimately Thebes. The Thebans had generally been too focussed on their actions in Thessaly and against Macedonia to pay too much attention to the Peloponnese, but the political actions there had undoubtedly strengthened Sparta and weakened Thebes.[57]

In 362, Epaminondas marched into the Peloponnese for a fourth time, this time in order to support Tegea in Arcadia against Mantinea (likely a pretext for another invasion of the Peloponnese). He had at his command '… all the Boeotians, the Euboeans, and many of the Thessalians.'[58] Only the Phocians were not present, citing their alliance with Thebes as being defensive, and there was nothing in their treaty to compel them to take part in this campaign. Epaminondas had at his disposal a large army, despite the absence of the Phocians. He also knew that he would receive support from the Peloponnesian states that were still opposed to Sparta. Xenophon tells us that Epaminondas understood that he would have support from …[59]

… the Argives, the Messenians, and such of the Arcadians as held to their side. These were the Tegeans, the Megalopolitans, the Aseans, the

Pallantians, and whatever cities were constrained to adopt this course for the reason that they were small and surrounded by these others.

Epaminondas set out from Thebes in great haste, hoping to catch the Peloponnesians unprepared. This was strategically sound, and could well have worked but, when he reached Nemea, he paused for what appears to be perhaps a week in the hope of intercepting the Athenians forces as they marched to the Peloponnese to the aid of their allies. He reasoned that if he could catch the Athenians, and defeat them, this would be a major blow to his opponents, whilst simultaneously being a huge morale boost to his own allies in the Peloponnese. Again, this sounds like a perfectly reasonable strategy, but the limitations of military intelligence in the ancient world are manifest in this example as he was unaware that the Athenians had changed their plans and were actually sailing to the Peloponnese rather than marching through the Isthmus of Corinth. To compound this error, his delay at Nemea had allowed the Peloponnesians time to gather their forces together to oppose his invasion. Epaminondas recovered quickly, however, and moved his troops to Tegea. Xenophon's comments on the opening of the campaign are enlightening:[60]

> Now in my view this campaign of his was not a lucky one, but I must say that both for planning and audacity this man cannot possibly be criticized. In the first place, I approve of his decision to make his camp inside the fortifications of Tegea. Here he was in a safer position than he would have been outside, and also the enemy was less able to observe what he was doing. It was easier, too, for him to get whatever he needed from inside the city. And with the enemy camped outside he was able to see whether their dispositions were good ones or whether they were making many mistakes.

Despite Xenophon's assertions of greatness, Epaminondas made a strategic error in trying to intercept the Athenians. The idea was sound, but with the benefit of hindsight his cause would have been better served if he had marched straight into the Peloponnese and attacked the Spartans whilst they were still gathering their forces and organizing themselves. The attack would likely have happened before the Athenians arrived too, thus effectively fulfilling his plan by other means.

Whilst at Tegea, his advanced scouts informed him that the bulk of the Peloponnesian force had formed up at Mantinea, and that Agesilaus with the Spartan muster was quickly advancing towards that city to join with those already there. Epaminondas instructed his troops to partake of their lunch, and then set out on a forced march directly towards Sparta, which he believed to be undefended. By a sheer act of good fortune Xenophon tells us that a Cretan saw what Epaminondas was attempting and managed to reach Agesilaus in time for him to turn his forces around and march back to Sparta.[61] Fortunately, he reached the city before the Thebans, but it must have been a close-run thing.

Epaminondas did not attack the city immediately, but scouted for a weak point. He found it in a hill close to the city, which he believed would give him the advantage of height if he were to attack from that direction.[62]

> As for what happened next, one may either hold the deity responsible, or one may say that nobody could withstand desperate men. For when Archidamus led the advance with not so much as a hundred men and, after crossing the very thing which seemed to present an obstacle, marched uphill against the adversary, at that moment the fire-breathers, the men who had defeated the Lacedaemonians, the men who were altogether superior in numbers and were occupying higher ground besides, did not withstand the attack of the troops under Archidamus, but gave way.

Archidamus' troops saw the Thebans retreating and pressed their advantage, but, as so often, their attempt to drive back the enemy only caused them to expose themselves as they became spread out. The Thebans fought back and both sides suffered badly. A temporary truce was called to recover the dead, and the Thebans withdrew back to Tegea, having failed in their attempt to deliver a decisive blow to Sparta. Once back at Tegea, Epaminondas dispatched his cavalry towards the Mantinea region to plunder the lands of that city as far as they could with a Peloponnesian army just outside the gates. Epaminondas told his cavalry that there were plenty of people and cattle outside of the city as it was harvest time. This may imply that the cavalry were mercenaries and this action was part of ensuring they were receiving the requisite level of payment, or it could mean that the general was planning for what could potentially become a lengthy siege and he wished to deprive the Mantineans of as much as possible while he could.

The Athenian forces, or at the very least the cavalry, reached Mantinea in the late afternoon and immediately retired to their assigned bunks to eat and rest; their forced march had been strenuous in order to reach Mantinea so quickly. Whilst the Athenian cavalry were resting and eating, the Mantinean defenders could see the approaching Theban cavalry and immediately perceived the danger:[63]

> And when the enemy were seen riding toward the city, the Mantineans begged the Athenian horsemen to help them, if in any way they could;

for outside the wall were all their cattle and the labourers, and likewise many children and older men of the free citizens. When the Athenians heard this they sallied forth to the rescue, although they were still without breakfast, they and their horses as well. Here, again, who would not admire the valour of these men also? For although they saw that the enemy were far more numerous, and although a misfortune had befallen the horsemen at Corinth, they took no account of this, nor of the fact that they were about to fight with the Thebans and the Thessalians, who were thought to be the best of horsemen, but rather, being ashamed to be at hand and yet render no service to their allies, just as soon as they saw the enemy they crashed upon them, eagerly desiring to win back their ancestral repute.

The Athenian cavalry fought a very vigorous action against the combined Theban and Thessalian forces and ultimately drove them off, with heavy losses on both sides. We may have assumed the Athenian cavalry would be mercenaries, but the way Xenophon describes them we can probably assume they were Athenians (from the desire to recover their dead, for example). For the Thebans, the cavalry were also nationals and allies from Thessaly.[64]

Epaminondas realized that he would need to depart within a few days, as the time set for the campaign had expired. We don't know exactly what timescale had been agreed, but there are several possibilities. Most likely is that there was a time limit placed upon the campaign by the Theban government, or perhaps in negotiation with the allies, both members of the Boeotian League and the Thessalians. Epaminondas did not want to leave the Peloponnese at this time as the invasion would have been a disaster. He had essentially been defeated at Sparta, his cavalry had been driven back at Mantinea, and if he left now his enemies had a large force already organized that would surely be used against the allies of Thebes in the Peloponnese. Therefore, the invasion would have done nothing more than galvanize his enemies and lose his friends in the region. Given that withdrawal was not an acceptable option, and with time running short, Epaminondas marched his army towards Mantinea. Epaminondas did not march directly at the Lacedaemonians, however:[65]

> But when he had led them forth, thus made ready, it is worth while again to note what he did. In the first place, as was natural, he formed them in line of battle. And by doing this he seemed to make it clear that he was preparing for an engagement; but when his army had been drawn up as he wished it to be, he did not advance by the shortest route towards the enemy, but led the way towards the mountains which lie to

the westward and over against Tegea, so that he gave the enemy the impression that he would not join battle on that day. For as soon as he had arrived at the mountain, and when his battle line had been extended to its full length, he grounded arms at the foot of the heights, so that he seemed like one who was encamping. And by so doing he caused among most of the enemy a relaxation of their mental readiness for fighting, and likewise a relaxation of their readiness as regards their array for battle. It was not until he had moved along successive companies to the wing where he was stationed, and had wheeled them into line thus strengthening the mass formation of this wing, that he gave the order to take up arms and led the advance; and his troops followed.

Epaminondas' movements were a brilliant ruse to lull the Lacedaemonians into thinking that he was attempting to take up a better defensive position in the foothills. The respective dispositions are only described by Diodorus.[66] Of the Lacedaemonians, he tells us that the right wing was occupied by the Mantineans and Arcadians. Next to these, between the wing and the centre, were the Lacedaemonians. In the centre were the Eleians and Achaeans, along with the weaker of the remaining forces. The Athenians occupied the left wing. For the Thebans, Epaminondas and his Theban troops occupied the left wing (which was strengthened before the advance, as noted by Xenophon), with the Arcadians forming the link between the flank and the centre. On the right wing were the troops from Argos. In the centre were the remainder of the Boeotian forces, notably those contingents from Euboea, Locris and Sicyon, along with the Malians and Aenianians. Both opposing armies also stationed detachments of cavalry beyond either wing.

These respective dispositions tell us much about the thinking of each commander. Epaminondas stationed himself and the best of his troops on his left wing, reinforcing this sector. He clearly hoped to break through here and to force a victory by then wheeling on the enemy centre. The Peloponnesians stationed quality troops on their right too, clearly to counter this likely tactic from Epaminondas. That the Lacedaemonians (Spartans) formed a cohesive link between the right and centre also tells us they knew their wing may be pushed back, and they feared the centre being flanked. Both sides appear to have placed their weakest troops in the centre; the battle would evidently not be won and lost there. Exactly which troops among those present were mercenaries is not attested and is difficult to say. We do know that Thebes was not hiring significant numbers of mercenaries at this time, and Sparta could not afford them. If mercenaries were present, it is likely to have been from the smaller states, Arcadia and Achaea. Despite the detailed dispositions given by Diodorus, he hides the fact that, although the Peloponnesians were roughly in the battle order, they were resting, as they did not expect the Thebans to attack.[67]

> Now as soon as the enemy saw them unexpectedly approaching, no one among them was able to keep quiet, but some began running to their posts, others forming into line, others bridling horses, and others putting on breast-plates, while all were like men who were about to suffer, rather than to inflict, harm. Meanwhile Epaminondas led forward his army prow on, like a trireme, believing that if he could strike and cut through anywhere, he would destroy the entire army of his adversaries. For he was preparing to make the contest with the strongest part of his force, and the weakest part he had stationed far back, knowing that if defeated it would cause discouragement to the troops who were with him and give courage to the enemy.

Epaminondas' tactic was simple enough, and much the same as that he used at Leuctra in 371: drive through the enemy wing and wheel on the centre. He also, apparently, like Leuctra, held the weakest parts of his line back from the battle for as long as possible, lest they cause his defeat. Epaminondas also formed his left wing cavalry into a wedge to charge the Peloponnesian right, with infantry support. He also stationed troops in some foothills opposite the Athenians in order to prevent them moving to their right ring to bolster that sector. He planned to win or lose the battle on the Theban left.

Epaminondas' plan worked perfectly; he smashed though the Lacedaemonian right wing, and the rest of the enemy army, still suffering from a measure of confusion after the sudden attack, melted away once the flank had been defeated. Although Epaminondas' left wing won a famous victory, he died during the encounter.[68]

> When, however, he had himself fallen, those who were left proved unable to take full advantage thereafter even of the victory; but although the opposing phalanx had fled before them, their hoplites did not kill a single man or advance beyond the spot where the collision had taken place; and although the cavalry also had fled before them, their cavalry in like manner did not pursue and kill either horsemen or hoplites, but slipped back timorously, like beaten men, through the lines of the flying enemy. Furthermore, while the intermingled footmen and the peltasts, who had shared in the victory of the cavalry, did make their way like victors to the region of the enemy's left wing, most of them were there slain by the Athenians.

Mantinea should have been a stunning victory for the Thebans; the Spartans and their allies were again defeated and, if not for the death of Epaminondas, the Spartans would likely have suffered just as badly as at Leuctra. As it turned out, from the Theban perspective, the battle could be considered a bloody tie at best, a nominal defeat at worst, given the loss of their charismatic general. Xenophon reports that the whole of Greece was on one side or the other and it was widely expected that this climactic battle would settle the issue of who was to rule; the defeated would become subordinate. The indecisive nature of the battle is illustrated by the fact that both sides erected a trophy for victory, and neither side tried to stop the other.

The death of Epaminondas was a huge blow to Thebes, but it did not entirely end their brief period of hegemony in Greece; they were still ambitious into the 350s and were finally exhausted by the Sacred War. Sparta was also profoundly weakened by her two major battles against the Thebans, and the loss of her league and the financial muscle that it brought. Ironically, the Athenians probably came out of the civil war in the best shape, having not suffered badly on land, whilst regaining some of their former Aegean possessions, including in the Hellespontine region. Athens also recaptured Euboea in 357 without much opposition. She did not have it all her own way, however. The maintenance of a large fleet was financially draining, as were the mercenary garrisons that she imposed on her overseas allies/possessions. In order for the mercenaries to remain disciplined, they needed regular payments, and Athens was not able to provide that. She was able to raise contributions from her allies, but some were suspicious of her motives and believed that she was attempting to create another empire. Some of her larger allies, particularly Corcyra, Chios, Rhodes, Byzantium and Cos, abandoned Athens and increased her financial difficulties. Athens tried to increase the taxes on the states that remained loyal, and also resorted to piracy in the Aegean. Her mercenaries stationed as garrisons in allied cities were not paid regularly, with the inevitable result that they started to raid neighbouring states to gain plunder. This obviously led to a spiralling of mistrust of Athens.[69]

However, she did not take the secession of some of her former allies lightly. By gathering together a substantial fleet led by Chabrias, and a mercenary army led by Chares, she began what was to become known as the Social War (357–5). Diodorus tells of the first engagement:[70]

> The two generals on sailing into Chios found that allies had arrived to assist the Chians from Byzantium, Rhodes, and Cos, and also from Mausolus, the tyrant of Caria. They then drew up their forces and began to besiege the city both by land and by sea. Now Chares, who commanded the infantry force, advanced against the walls by land and began a struggle with the enemy who poured out on him from the city;

but Chabrias, sailing up to the harbour, fought a severe naval engagement and was worsted when his ship was shattered by a ramming attack.
While the men on the other ships withdrew in the nick of time and
saved their lives, he, choosing death with glory instead of defeat, fought
on for his ship and died of his wounds.

Chares' mercenaries appear to have held their own for a while at least against
the defenders who were sallying from the city. It should be noted that we
have no idea what type of mercenary these were (peltasts or hoplites), nor
whether they were equipped to undertake a siege. The death of Chabrias
effectively ended the siege prematurely. Some of these mercenaries were
then recalled to Athens where they were dismissed, although some probably
remained with Chares in the Aegean. As noted above, Athens' financial
resources were stretched, to say the least, and the maintenance of a mercenary
army was probably beyond her. The troops commanded by Chares were
probably expected to support themselves from plundering the former allies,
but their defeat at Chios made that impossible, and therefore made their
continued employment impossible. After an excursus on Sicily, Diodorus
returns to his narrative of the Social War in Greece, and there are no further
direct references to mercenary service on either side. Having said this, he
does imply it, with regards to the rebels.[71]

> The Chians, Rhodians, and Byzantians together with their allies manned
> one hundred ships and then sacked Imbros and Lemnos, Athenian
> islands, and having descended on Samos with a large contingent laid
> waste the countryside and besieged the city by land and by sea; and by
> ravaging many other islands that were subject to Athens they collected
> money for the needs of the war.

Of course, these military expenses could have been for the upkeep of ships,
wage payments for national and allied troops, the purchase of provisions and
so on. We do not know with certainty one way or another, but mercenaries
and mercenary service were by now so ubiquitous that it was less worthy of
mention than it had been even just a few decades previously.

The breakup of former alliances was not limited to Athens. Phocis broke
away from the Boeotian League. She had fought on the side of the Spartans
at Leuctra and had been forced to join the League by the victorious Thebans,
but was never a willing member and took the first opportunity to leave.
Thebes feared Phocis potentially bringing either Sparta or Athens into a
war in Central Greece and looked for a pretext to invade; it was not long
in coming. The Phocians had been cultivating land that was claimed by
Delphi, and the Delphic Amphictyony imposed a substantial fine on them

for their sacrilegious actions. The Phocians refused to pay and elected a tyrant, Philomelus, to organize their resistance.[72]

Philomelus apparently travelled to Sparta to appeal directly to King Archidamus for assistance against the Thebans. Diodorus reports that Philomelus told Archidamus of his plan to seize Delphi and annul all of the decrees of the Amphictyony. The Spartans were unwilling (or perhaps unable) to assist directly, but they sent sufficient funds to allow the Phocians to hire 1,000 mercenaries from the local area.[73] Philomelus used these mercenary forces to capture Delphi and he slew a group of Delphians called the Thracidae. The news of the capture of the shrine spread quickly throughout Greece.[74]

> When news of the seizure of the shrine was noised abroad, the Locrians, who lived nearby, straightway took the field against Philomelus. A battle took place near Delphi and the Locrians, having been defeated with the loss of many of their men, fled to their own territory, and Philomelus, being elated by his victory, hacked from the slabs the pronouncements of the Amphictyons, deleted the letters recording their judgements, and personally caused the report to be circulated that he had resolved not to plunder the oracle nor had he purposed to commit any other lawless deed, but that in support of the ancestral claim to the guardianship and because of his desire to annul the unjust decrees of the Amphictyons, he was vindicating the ancestral laws of the Phocians.

The Boeotians voted in an assembly meeting to march to the aid of the oracle, and began to gather appropriate forces. Philomelus expected an attack and built a wall around the already very defensible shrine. The Phocians then used the last of their resources to raise another 4,000 troops from amongst the bravest of the Phocians (their status may have been as mercenaries, but this is far from certain). Rather than waiting for the Thebans, Philomelus launched an attack on the territory of the Locrians, pillaging as they went.[75]

> As he was master of the open country, he sacked a large portion of Locris and returned to Delphi, having given his soldiers their fill of the spoils of war.

By now this was an expected form of payment for a mercenary army. The presence of mercenaries fuelled the cycle of violence that was overtaking Greek warfare. In 355/4 Diodorus tells us that the Locrians and Thebans made an alliance with the intent of waging war on 'behalf of the god upon the Phocians.'[76] Despite this treaty, however, the Thebans were not quick to act against the Phocians, but the Locrians again attempted to dislodge them from Delphi. The battle was fought near the cliffs called Phaedriades, a semi-circular range of rocks on Mount Parnassus facing south. The Locrians were soundly beaten in a bloody and brutal encounter, in which few of them were taken prisoner. Many threw themselves off the cliffs to avoid capture and the consequences at the hands of the Phocians.[77]

The remnants of the Locrian force retreated to Locris and appealed to Thebes for assistance according to the treaty that they had signed. The Thebans again delayed their military response, sending embassies to Thessaly and the other Amphyctyons, demanding that they make war collectively against the Phocians.[78]

> But when the Amphictyons voted the war against the Phocians much confusion and disagreement reigned throughout the length and breadth of Greece. For some decided to stand by the god and punish the Phocians as temple-robbers, while others inclined toward giving the Phocians assistance. As tribes and cities were divided in their choice, the Boeotians, Locrians, Thessalians, and Perrhaebians decided to aid the shrine, and in addition the Dorians and Dolopians, likewise the Athamanians, Achaeans of Phthiotis, and the Magnesians, also the Aenianians and some others; while the Athenians, Lacedaemonians, and some others of the Peloponnesians fought on the side of the Phocians.

Eventually, after seemingly great delay, during which time the Locrians were the only state willing to act against the sacrilege performed by Phocis, the Boeotians began to muster for war. The Phocians, realizing what was happening, decided that a larger force was required, specifically a larger mercenary army. Philomelus increased the basic pay of his mercenaries by 50 per cent and very quickly recruited a large army of mercenaries from the local area and beyond. The fact that the mercenaries were not overly concerned whence their wages came is interesting, although they may have had some minor reservations, hence the need to raise their wages to a suitable level.[79]

> Now no men of honourable character enrolled for the campaign because of their reverence for the gods, but the worst knaves, and those who despised the gods, because of their own greed, eagerly gathered about Philomelus and quickly a strong army was formed out of those whose object it was to plunder the shrine.

Philomelus used his newly raised army to again invade the territory of the Locrians, totalling more than 10,000 infantry and cavalry. They were met by the Locrians and an advance force of Thebans and a fierce cavalry battle ensued, which was ultimately indecisive. The two sides broke away and further reinforcements were received by each: 6,000 Thessalians arrived to aid the Locrians and 1,500 Achaeans arrived to support the Phocians. The Locrians and their allies were camped within the city, and the Phocians close by. The brutality of feeling and action during the Sacred War is illustrated by the actions of the Boeotians.[80]

> After this the Boeotians, who had taken captive on foraging parties a good many mercenaries, brought them out in front of the city and made an announcement by heralds that the Amphictyons were punishing with death these men present who had enlisted with the temple-robbers; and immediately, making the deed follow the word, shot them all down.

The mercenaries in Philomelus' employ were enraged and demanded vengeance in kind. Philomelus ordered detachments of his mercenaries to raid the countryside and take as many Boeotian and Locrian prisoners as possible. These were lined up in sight of the Boeotians and were shot. Both sides eventually came to battle in a nearby forest, with the Phocians heavily outnumbered and defeated with heavy loses to their native and mercenary contingents. Philomelus himself, fearing capture and torture, threw himself off a cliff.[81] Philomelus' successor, Onomarchus, gathered together the survivors and retreated to Delphi. During the winter of 354/3 the Phocians made overtures of peace towards their Locrian and Boeotian enemies. The overtures were convincing, and it looked for a time as if the Scared War would come to an end. In the spring, the Boeotians sent their mercenary army to Asia Minor to fight alongside the rebel satrap, Artabazus. They never would have contemplated such a move if they had any doubt over the likelihood of a peaceful resolution in the near future.

Onomarchus had other ideas, however. He had evidently used his envoys to buy time to ensure his own position (he was elected as sole commander of the Phocian forces) and to reconstitute his mercenary army, again using the temple treasuries to pay his troops. Onomarchus may have justified this action to himself and the Phocians by promising to repay what he took once the national crisis had passed, but his political opponents denounced him.

Along with the war in central Greece, there was also difficulty in the north. There was a popular uprising in Thessaly, supported by Philip of Macedon, against the tyrant of Pherae. The latter appealed for help to his ally Onomarchus at Delphi. Onomarchus, grateful that the Thessalians had kept Philip out of central Greek politics, sent his brother Phayllus and 6,000 mercenaries to prop up the Thessalian regime, but these were quickly and heavily defeated by the growing power that was Philip. Onomarchus marched north with the whole of his army and met Philip twice in Thessaly, defeating him both times and driving the Macedonians out of Thessaly.[82]

> When Onomarchus was deploying against the Macedonians, he put a crescent-shaped mountain in his rear, concealing men on the peaks at both ends with rocks and rock throwing engines, and led his forces forward into the plain below. When the Macedonians came out against them and threw their javelins, the Phocians pretended to flee into the hollow middle of the mountain. As the Macedonians, pursuing with an eager rush, pressed them, the men on the peaks threw rocks and crushed the Macedonian phalanx. Then indeed Onomarchus signalled the Phocians to turn and attack the enemy. The Macedonians, under attack from behind while those up above continued to throw rocks, retreated rapidly in great distress. They say that during this flight the king of the Macedonians, Philip, said 'I do not flee, but retreat like rams do, in order to attack again more violently.'

This is also the first recorded example of catapults being used in a set-piece battle. After the victories against Philip, Onomarchus was riding high. He followed up the victories with the capture, through betrayal, of Coronea, although Aristotle tells us that the citizenry were not happy with their betrayal by a minority of Phocian sympathizers. The capture of Coronea represented the high point of Phocian power and influence, supported as it was by a mercenary army. This was Onomarchus' last real success, however.

In the following summer of 353, Philip again invaded Thessaly and engaged the Phocians in a battle that has been called the Battle of the Crocus Field. Onomarchus commanded 25,000 infantry, many of them mercenaries, and 500 cavalry. Philip, having persuaded the Thessalians to ally with him against the common enemy, fielded an army of 20,000 infantry and 3,000 cavalry.[83]

> A severe battle took place and since the Thessalian cavalry were superior in numbers and valour, Philip won. Because Onomarchus had fled toward the sea and Chares the Athenian was by chance sailing by with many triremes, a great slaughter of the Phocians took place, for the men in their effort to escape would strip off their armour and try to swim out to the triremes, and among them was Onomarchus. Finally more than six thousand of the Phocians and mercenaries were slain, and among them the general himself; and no less than three thousand were taken captives. Philip hanged Onomarchus; the rest he threw into the sea as temple-robbers.

The Sacred War seemed to be at an end; Onomarchus was dead and his mercenary army dispersed and destroyed.[84] The Athenians, fearful of the rising influence and power of Macedonia, had formed an alliance with Phocis and now marched north to block the pass at Thermopylae and prevent Philip from following up his victory in central Greece. With Athenian help, the Sacred War dragged on. Phayllus, the brother of Onomarchus, was elected as his successor, and he managed to reform the mercenary army of his brother. Phayllus was also joined by Lycophron and Peitholaus of Pherae, whom Philip had expelled. These brought a further 2,000 mercenaries.[85] Sparta also sent 1,000 and the Achaeans 2,000; the sacrilege that the Phocians had committed was evidently less of a concern to the southern Greeks than the rise of Philip.

Diodorus records a series of small border engagements between Philip on the one hand and Phocis and her allies on the other, but gives little detail. The nature of small-scale skirmishing or guerrilla warfare was perfectly suited to this type of combat, but it tended to produce indecisive results. Thebes was also engaged with Phocis frequently down to 350 (and again we know little); the drain upon her resources and population was excessive. This drain led to her recruiting more and more mercenaries to take up the slack. The result in central Greece was a continuous state of warfare conducted by mercenaries and fuelled partly by their need for plunder.

In 346, the Thebans invited Philip to march south once more and complete the reduction of Phocis. Phalaecus, the Phocian general, was holding the pass of Thermopylae with 8,000 mercenaries. He refused, however, to attempt to hold the pass against Philip, and he made an arrangement with the Macedonian that he and his mercenaries would surrender their arms and be allowed to withdraw in safety to the Peloponnese.[86] Once the Athenians realized that Thermopylae was lost, they sent a delegation to Philip to sue for peace, and the Peace of Philocrates resulted, although this was not the end of Philip's ambitions in central and southern Greece.

Chapter 6

The Rise of Macedon

The Peace of Philocrates between Athens and Macedonia left Phocis high and dry. The cities under Phocian control were broken up by Philip into their constituent villages. They were also forced to repay what they had taken from Delphi at a rate of 60 talents a year, and Philip took the Phocian seats on the Amphyctyonic council. Philip did not enact any other revenge upon the Phocians, belying the reputation of Macedonians as barbarians from the fringes of Greece. Despite this, the Athenians had felt the peace would protect the Phocians, but Phocis was not formally allied to Athens, and therefore was not included in the peace; the Athenians felt cheated. From Philip's perspective, however, the alliance, he concluded, was between himself and Athens and her allies, and as noted Phocis was not formally allied to Athens, and was therefore fair game.[1]

The peace also meant that the large mercenary armies that had been employed by the Phocians, as well as some employed by Thebes, Sparta and others, were released onto the Greek world without the safety of organized employment. Of some of these mercenaries, Diodorus tells us:[2]

> And the last of all, Phalaecus, who had gathered the remnants of the pillaged property, passed his life for a considerable length of time wandering about in great fear and danger, though it was not Heaven's intent that he should be happier than those who participated with him in the sacrilege, but that by being tortured longer and by becoming known to many for his misfortunes, his sad fate might become notorious. For when he had taken flight with his mercenaries following the agreement, he first sojourned in the Peloponnese, supporting his men on the last remnants of the pillaging, but later he hired in Corinth some large freighters and with four light vessels prepared for the voyage to Italy and Sicily, thinking that in these regions he would either seize some city or obtain service for pay, for a war was in progress, as it chanced,

between the Lucanians and the Tarentines. To his fellow passengers he said that he was making the voyage because he had been summoned by the people of Italy and Sicily.

Before they got far by sea, however, there was something of a mutiny, for these men apparently feared the prospect of campaigning overseas:[3]

> Finally drawing their swords and menacing Phalaecus and the pilot they forced them to reverse their course. And when those who were sailing in the other boats also did the same, they put in again at a Peloponnesian harbour. Then they gathered at the Malean promontory in Laconia and there found Cnossian envoys who had sailed in from Crete to enlist mercenaries. After these envoys had conversed with Phalaecus and the commanders and had offered rather high pay, they all sailed off with them. Having made port at Cnossus in Crete, they immediately took by storm the city called Lyctus. But to the Lyctians, who had been expelled from their native land, there appeared a miraculous and sudden reinforcement. For at about the same time the people of Tarentum were engaged in prosecuting a war against the Lucanians and had sent to the Lacedaemonians, who were the stock of their ancestors, envoys soliciting help, whereupon the Spartans, who were willing to join them because of their relationship, quickly assembled an army and navy and as general in command of it appointed King Archidamus. But as they were about to set sail for Italy, a request came from the Lyctians to help them first. Consenting to this, the Lacedaemonians sailed to Crete, defeated the mercenaries and restored to the Lyctians their native land.

Wandering bands of mercenaries were starting to have an unpredictable and destabilizing effect upon the Greek world.

Between 346, when the Peace of Philocrates was ratified, and 341 when it finally broke down, there was a great deal of political manoeuvring in Greece between Philip, Athens and other leading powers. These included an attempt by Philip to turn the narrow peace between himself and Athens (and her allies) into a broader common peace, which failed, as well as continuous attempts by Demosthenes in particular to have the Athenian assembly throw out the peace and declare war on the Macedonians.

The peace officially came to an end in 341 when Demosthenes travelled to Byzantium to make a treaty of peace with that city, as well as with Abydos, actions that were partly designed to maintain Athens' food supplies through the Black Sea. This triggered Philip's anger, and he complained to Athens, who responded by formally denouncing the terms of the treaty, an act that was essentially a declaration of war.

Philip responded by besieging Byzantium and other cities in the Thrace-ward region, in direct opposition to Athens. The conflict came to a head in 338; Philip was done with Thrace and the north and he marched through the pass of Thermopylae and into central Greece to take part in another Sacred War that started in 340. His army attacked Amphissa, entered Phocis and seized Elateia, where the army camped for some time. As Philip marched south, the Athenians sent Demosthenes to negotiate an anti-Macedonian alliance with the Thebans. This was very much a marriage of convenience, as both feared the rising power of Macedonia and both realized that they were too weak individually to defeat Philip; together they had a chance.[4]

> Now that they had doubled their existing armed forces by the Boeotian alliance, the Athenians recovered their confidence. At once they designated Chares and Lysicles as generals and sent forth their entire army under arms into Boeotia. All their youth reported eager for battle and advanced with forced marches as far as Chaeroneia in Boeotia. Impressed by the promptness of the Athenian arrival and themselves no less ready to act decisively, the Boeotians joined them with their weapons and, brigaded together, all awaited the approach of the enemy.

The Athenians had managed to gather together a force of 10,000 mercenaries; the only reason they could afford this was likely the expectation that it would be a short campaign. Along with the mercenary forces was the whole of the citizen muster; this really was a major undertaking on the part of the Athenians and speaks volumes as to their concerns. The Thebans were heartened by this action of the Athenians and also raised a significant mercenary army, as well as mustering their militia. Troops, mainly mercenaries, also came from Corinth, Megara, Achaea and Boeotia to join the anti-Macedonian coalition.[5]

> He waited for the last of his laggard confederates to arrive, and then marched into Boeotia. His forces came to more than thirty thousand infantry and no less than two thousand cavalry. Both sides were on edge for the battle, high-spirited and eager, and were well matched in courage, but the king had the advantage in numbers and in generalship. He had fought many battles of different sorts and had been victorious in most cases, so that he had a wide experience in military operations. On the Athenian side, the best of their generals were dead – Iphicrates, Chabrias, and Timotheus too – and the best of those who were left, Chares, was no better than any average soldier in the energy and discretion required of a commander.

We might add to Diodorus' bleak assessment of the coalition leadership that the Theban's two greatest generals, Pelopidas and Epaminondas, were also long dead.

On or around 4 August, the two sides took to the field of battle at Chaeronea. For the Macedonians, Alexander was given command of the Companion Cavalry on one wing. He was only 18 years old and had little military experience, but what little he did have had helped him demonstrate his bravery and swiftness of action. Apparently also stationed on Alexander's wing were a number of more senior generals, no doubt there to keep an eye on the future king. Philip 'at the head of picked men' stationed himself on the opposite wing to Alexander. We know nothing of who these picked men were, but they may well have been the hypaspists, 3,000 strong.[6] In the centre was presumably placed the *pezhetairoi*. This became the standard model, and certainly was what Alexander did in every one of his set-piece battles once he became king.

On the coalition side of the battlefield, the troops were divided according to nationality. The Athenian troops occupied one wing (opposite Philip) and the Thebans the other (opposite Alexander). The centre was occupied by the remainder of the allied contingents. Given the sizes of the Theban and Athenian forces compared to those supplied by the other city-states, we must consider some of the Theban and Athenian troops to have also been stationed in the centre, or the wings would have been enormous relative to the size of the centre of the line.

The battle was opened by Alexander, who appears to have charged from his flank before Philip moved, presumably under orders to do so.[7]

> Then Alexander, his heart set on showing his father his prowess and yielding to none in will to win, ably seconded by his men, first succeeded in rupturing the solid front of the enemy line and striking down many he bore heavily on the troops opposite him. As the same success was won by his companions, gaps in the front were constantly opened. Corpses piled up, until finally Alexander forced his way through the line and put his opponents to flight.

When Alexander was heavily engaged on his flank, Philip chose his moment to attack. Why he delayed the charge from his flank is not recorded, and any attempted explanation would only be speculation, but it may be that he hoped some of the troops opposing his side of the line would be withdrawn by the coalition to support the flank under attack by Alexander. It is perhaps more likely, however, that he hoped that Alexander's charge would shatter the Thebans on that wing, which would mean that victory was close. His charge would then be the decisive one, the one that ultimately broke the enemy and forced a general retreat.

More than 1,000 Athenians fell in the battle, and over 2,000 were captured as they tried to flee before Philips forces. The Thebans suffered similar losses in their battle against Alexander, including the annihilation of the whole of the Sacred Band, their elite infantry unit (and the Theban attempt to combine citizen loyalty with the professionalism of the mercenary). Of the coalition troops, those stationed in the centre probably came off least badly. We have no record of fighting in that sector, although there must have been some; the centres probably engaged each other around the time Philip was breaking the wing opposite his position, and therefore would not have been engaged for long.

The victory at Chaeronea effectively gave Philip the control of Greece, outside of the Peloponnese at least. The armies of both Thebes and Athens were destroyed, and neither had the financial means to raise another army of mercenaries, and Sparta had neither the resources nor the will to resist Macedonia on the field of battle.

The army that Philip created and used to gain hegemony over the Greek world was largely a professional force. The majority of those present were Macedonian nationals, or allies from areas like Thessaly. It was professional in the sense that they were a permanent standing army with standard equipment and regular training routines. The army that Philip created, and Alexander perfected, felt a tremendous sense of personal loyalty to the king and a remarkable sense of national pride – this loyalty was tested to the limit by Alexander as he marched them to the very edge of the known world in India.

There were certainly mercenaries present, although their role in set-piece battles was not critical to the victory. Most of the mercenaries that would have been employed by Philip would have been on garrison duties in strategically important cities like Byzantium and Pherae. In terms of numbers, perhaps the most significant use of mercenaries by Philip was on the two main expeditionary missions he sent out. The first of these was to Euboea, where his mercenary army supported one party against another in Porthmus, Oreus, Chalcis and Eretria.[8] The second major expeditionary force was commanded by Parmenio and was sent to Asia Minor in 336, two years after the victory at Chaeronea. Parmenio was sent with 10,000 mercenaries to create a bridgehead, which Philip intended to exploit with a much larger force of Macedonian nationals when he was ready. Parmenio had a fair degree of initial success, but as the Persians became more organized and hired a mercenary army of their own, commanded by Memnon of

Rhodes, they began to retake areas they had lost. Memnon's army was only 5,000 strong, but was commanded brilliantly and fought Parmenio to a standstill before driving him back towards the Hellespont. This demonstrates admirably the advantages of well-led troops over simple superiority in numbers. By the time of Philip's death, and certainly by the time of Alexander's invasion in 334, most of Parmenio's initial gains had been lost.

The use of mercenaries by Philip can be divided into two distinct periods: before and after the year 346. Before this date, only three references are made to mercenaries in the Macedonian army: the first against Chares; the second in the capture of Pharcedon in 353–2; the third instance was when he loaned a contingent of mercenaries to Phocion in 348. During the early part of Philip's reign, his Macedonian national army was in an evolutionary stage of development, during which it was still being trained and organized. I believe it likely that mercenaries played a far greater role in military operations during this period than these sparse references would seem to indicate, because the Macedonian army was not yet the force it was to become. After 346, when Philip had gained control of much of Greece, mercenaries were used to form garrisons at strategic points throughout the Greek world, as already noted. This was a policy that Alexander continued and greatly expanded upon, as we shall see. They also continued to be used in some combat roles, as evidenced by the composition of the expeditionary force sent to Asia Minor by Philip in 336.

Alexander

The majority of the mercenaries employed by Alexander at the beginning of his reign would have accompanied Alexander into Asia, or were already there, having been sent by Philip with the expeditionary force in 336.[9] It is highly unlikely that any would have been left behind with the defensive army left with his regent, Antipater, in Macedonia. If Antipater had need for mercenaries, he could have recruited them as necessary. The example of the Phocians and others rather suggests that, if an employer could pay, finding the requisite troops was not a difficult task. It was also the case that the Macedonian treasury was bare and mercenaries left at home would have been an unnecessary expense. Regarding Macedonian funds, at the outset of the campaign, money was at a premium. We know that Alexander left himself with a huge amount of personal debt before 334, relying upon the conquest of Persia to restore Macedonia's fortunes. Having said this, Alexander had left garrisons at strategic points throughout Greece, and these would have been mercenaries, although Alexander may well have demanded that the city-states pay for their upkeep.[10]

Diodorus gives us a detailed order of battle for the Macedonian army as it crossed the Hellespont and entered Asia in 334.[11]

There were found to be, of infantry, twelve thousand Macedonians, seven thousand allies, and five thousand mercenaries, all of whom were under the command of Parmenion. Odrysians, Triballians, and Illyrians accompanied him to the number of seven thousand; and of archers and the so-called Agrianians one thousand, making up a total of thirty-two thousand foot soldiers. Of cavalry there were eighteen hundred Macedonians, commanded by Philotas son of Parmenion; eighteen hundred Thessalians, commanded by Callas son of Harpalus; six hundred from the rest of Greece under the command of Erigyius; and nine hundred Thracian and Paeonian scouts with Cassander in command, making a total of forty-five hundred cavalry. These were the men who crossed with Alexander to Asia.

This account makes it clear that there were 32,000 infantry in the army of invasion, of which 5,000 were mercenaries. Other sources do give slightly different figures, but Diodorus' account seems reasonable. Five thousand mercenaries seems to be a remarkably small number as a percentage of the total, certainly when compared to other armies of the fourth century and into the Hellenistic period. The mercenaries amounted to only 15.6 per cent.

There are probably four main reasons for this. Firstly, mercenaries had historically not been a major part of Macedonian armies, a trend that Philip did not wholly reverse. The second reason has already been mentioned, and is the almost complete lack of available funds with which to hire or pay mercenaries, although it is worthy of note that we don't really see the type of wanton pillage that had become relatively common in Greece. The third reason is that, in 334, Darius was a competing paymaster. The Great Kings had always been large employers of Greek mercenaries, and 334 was no different. To a mercenary with a choice of employer, Darius probably looked like the better bet; he had wealth almost without limit and a substantially larger army than that commanded by Alexander. The final reason, and this should not be underestimated, is that Alexander simply had very little reason to employ large numbers of mercenaries. His Macedonian army would prove itself to be the most efficient and effective army the Greek world had yet seen; a large force of mercenaries was not a strategic or tactical necessity at the outset of the campaign.

It has long been understood, however, that Diodorus' figure of 5,000 mercenaries carries with it some significant problems. During the first year of the campaign in Asia, up to the battle of Issus in 333, Alexander left behind garrisons at Side, Mytilene, and possibly Ephesus and Miletus. Alexander also left a force of 3,000 mercenary infantry to complete the reduction of Halicarnassus as he left the area to continue the conquest of Asia Minor. After the reduction of that city, those troops remained to act as a garrison for the satrapy of Caria. Our sources do not tell us the size of the garrisons left in Side and Mytilene, or the numbers of casualties in combat to this point, although Alexander did not use mercenaries as front line troops and so their casualty figures were probably small. I think we can safely assume, given that 3,000 were left in Caria, that the total left behind on garrison duty before the battle of Issus would have amounted to in excess of 5,000, more than the number with which Alexander had invaded Asia. To the best of our knowledge, the only additional mercenaries that Alexander received were the 300 that defected to him from the Persian garrison at Miletus. This could be explained by Alexander leaving funds behind with his provincial governors with which to recruit mercenary garrisons. This would have made sense as it would reduce the workload on the army itself; recruiting was probably difficult for an army on the march anyway. After the first few months in Asia Minor, Alexander's financial situation would have improved slightly, and therefore funds would have been available for such an act.

A problem arises when we look at the Battle of Issus. There clearly seem to be two bodies of mercenaries that, I believe, formed a reserve line behind the Macedonian heavy infantry. Arrian's description of the dispositions of Alexander's army is not as detailed as we would like; he does not tell us, for example, the number of mercenaries present.[12] It is probable that such a force, forming a second line, would have been fairly considerable. A figure of somewhere between 5,000 and 8,000 seems a reasonable guess given the length of the front line. If we take the lower of these two figures, this leaves us with a significant shortfall. There are only two possible explanations: either we make up the deficit by suggesting that these troops were the remnants of the expeditionary force, of whose fate we otherwise know nothing, or there was a draft of reinforcements from Greece between 334 and 333, upon which our sources are silent. It would seem that the former explanation is the more plausible, as it is unsafe to invent troops just for our own convenience and to fill a gap in our available evidence.

We can likely assume that with every successful campaign more and more mercenaries would flock to Alexander's banner. A successful general is always a far more attractive paymaster than an unsuccessful one, as Darius discovered. This is demonstrated by the Persian army's employment of mercenaries: Darius had 20,000 Greek mercenary hoplites at the Granicus in 334, and only around 2,000 at Gaugamela three years later. This failure to recruit more was not down to a lack of desire, or a lack of funds on the part of the Persians. The two main reasons were that Alexander could effectively control access to the main recruiting grounds in Greece and, secondly, Alexander was wealthy enough to mop up the available mercenaries for garrison duty in his growing empire.

Given Alexander's increasing need for mercenaries, and my assumption that he employed them in great numbers, is this actually supported by the evidence of the sources? Our sources only record two batches of mercenary reinforcements received by Alexander before Gaugamela, 4,000 from Sidon and 3,000 from Chios.[13] We are also told of a mercenary garrison of 4,000 left behind in Egypt. These must be the reinforcements from Sidon, as they are not mentioned at the Battle of Gaugamela. Although the total number of mercenary troops may have increased slightly during the first three years of the campaign, so did the number of Macedonian troops, so that the proportion of mercenaries to Macedonians would have remained almost constant. Reinforcements were arriving at roughly the same rate as they were required to form garrisons in the newly conquered territory.

After Gaugamela, when there was essentially no competing paymaster, there seems to have been an explosion in the numbers of mercenaries enrolling with Alexander's army, to such an extent that both Arrian and Curtius agree that Alexander had 120,000 men with him for the invasion of India. A significant proportion of those would have been mercenaries, given the lack of Macedonian reinforcements and their continuous losses.[14] Table 1 shows all of the mercenary reinforcements that our sources record as being received by Alexander throughout his career.[15]

The table only contains data for reinforcements that are recorded in the sources; it is highly likely that many more were received by Alexander that we hear nothing about. It is also true that many mercenaries were hired directly by the city or province in which they were to act as garrison, as noted earlier. Thus they would never have been part of the army itself, and would therefore have escaped the attention of our Alexander-centric surviving sources. One thinks of the 20,000 mercenaries recruited by Peucestas, the satrap of Sardis, within one year of the demobilization decree of Alexander in 324, a perfect example of a major mercenary army recruited directly by a satrap. These troops were never part of the field army, and thus are never counted towards troop totals, but they were potentially available for use by Alexander as required.

Organization of the Mercenaries

Throughout Alexander's career there was an almost constant influx of new troops, as existing ones left the grand host to be assigned garrison duties. This trend was particularly prevalent in the later years of his career as the territory he controlled expanded rapidly. The organization of the mercenary

Table 1 Mercenary reinforcements received by Alexander throughout his career

At Miletus	300 infantry	Arrian 1.19.6
From Chios	3,000 infantry (Persian garrison)	Arrian 2.13.5; Curtius 4.5.18
At Sidon	4,000 infantry (Probably left as Egyptian garrison)	Arrian 2.20.5
At Memphis	400 cavalry 500 Thracian cavalry	Arrian 3.5.1
At Susa	4,000 infantry from the Peloponnese 980 cavalry from the Peloponnese 3,500 Trallians 600 Thracian cavalry	Curtius 5.1.41; Diodorus 17.65.1
In Media	5,000 infantry 1,000 cavalry 1,500 infantry (remnants of Darius' mercenaries) X number of infantry and cavalry from among the Greek allies who volunteered to remain with Alexander after their contingents had been demobilized.	Curtius 5.7.12 Arrian 3.23.8; Curtius 6.5.6; Arrian 3.19.6; Diodorus 17.74.4
At Bactra	2,600 infantry 500 cavalry 3,000 Illyrian cavalry 300 cavalry	Curtius 6.6.35
At Zariaspa	16,400 infantry 2,600 cavalry	Curtius 6.10.11; Arrian 4.7.2
In India	7,000 infantry 5,000 cavalry 30,000 infantry 6,000 cavalry	Curtius 9.3.21 Diodorus 17.95.4
In Carmania	5,000 infantry 1,000 cavalry	Curtius 10.1.1
At Babylon	Unknown	Arrian 7.23.1

contingents within Alexander's army was, by necessity, fluid and difficult to pin down. This fluid structure was vital for their operational effectiveness, but makes their study difficult. There does, however, appear to be a terminological distinction preserved by Arrian, who uses the word *xenoi* to refer to mercenaries that had been with the army from the outset, whilst the word *misthophoroi* refers to mercenaries subsequently recruited in Asia.[16] This distinction generally works down to the Battle of Gaugamela, particularly when applied to the mercenary cavalry.

At Gaugamela two bodies of mercenary cavalry are recorded: those who joined the army in Egypt, commanded by Menidas, are called *misthophoroi*, while those under the command of Andromachus are called *xenoi*.[17] We can reasonably assume that these cavalry were originally with the expeditionary force of Parmenio, as no mercenary cavalry are recorded with the army of invasion in Diodorus, and no other reinforcements were recorded beside those in Egypt.[18]

Unfortunately, the distinction in terminology is not universally true, as an examination of the mercenary infantry will demonstrate. *Misthophoroi* infantry are first mentioned just before the Battle of Issus. Parmenio is sent ahead of the main body with a small force, consisting of *misthophoroi*: the Thessalian cavalry and the Thracians. This incident is, however, too early for a significant number of *misthophoroi* to have been present, given that the *misthophoroi* were supposed to be those recruited after the invasion. The only mercenary infantry to have been enlisted with the army to that point were the 300 from the garrison at Miletus – who came over to Alexander when that city surrendered – and this seems far too small a number to be taking part in the expedition that Arrian is describing, especially when compared to the other, significantly larger, contingents being used. It is much more likely that the mercenaries Parmenio took were all the Greek mercenaries with the army, a force of perhaps 5,000 or more. The same problem reoccurs soon after this at the Battle of Issus, where there are two bodies of mercenary infantry mentioned: the *xenoi* can of course be explained as the remnants of the expeditionary force, but the 300 of Miletus are still the only new recruits. Are we to believe that, of these two bodies, one consisted of in excess of 5,000 men, and the other only 300? I think not. It is far more likely that they were of roughly equal size, given that they were assigned to perform a similar tactical function.

The superficially useful terminological distinction encounters another problem with the reinforcements received at Sidon. These were 4,000 in number, and are the only known reinforcements to have reached the army before 331. These troops do not appear, however, in the Greek order of battle at Gaugamela, and therefore must have been left on garrison duty at some unspecified location before that battle. The only logical place for a garrison of this size between Issus and Gaugamela is in Egypt, where, coincidentally enough, we know that Alexander left a garrison, 4,000 strong. Arrian calls the new recruits received at Sidon *misthophoroi*, as he should if the terminological theory is correct; but the troops left behind in Egypt are referred to as *xenoi*.[19] If, however, the Egyptian garrison were original mercenaries, this does not solve the problem, as the Sidonian reinforcements are still not mentioned at Gaugamela. Nor are they known to have been left on garrison duty anywhere else. This scenario would also mean that there were more *xenoi* at Gaugamela than there could possibly have been (as 4,000 of them would have been left behind in Egypt). The simplest answer to the problem of this use of terminology in Arrian is to assume that although the words could indicate a different origin for each batch of mercenaries the distinction does not always hold true. Either it is a misunderstanding on the part of Arrian or his sources; or perhaps the terms originally referred to the two separate bodies of mercenaries, but the distinction between them became confused, or was simply lost, as garrison duty and natural wastage reduced the size of both bodies. New recruits could be assigned to either *misthophoroi* or *xenoi* to keep the numbers at relatively stable levels. This also means that early in the campaign the distinction would be most valid, but would decline in relevance over time; this is exactly the pattern that we see in Arrian's usage of the terms.

Role of the Mercenary
Mercenaries formed a fundamental and immensely important part of Alexander's army throughout the course of his career, despite their seeming lack of involvement in the set-piece battles. Their versatility can be summed up by a consideration of their various roles:

- Secondary columns
- Garrisons
- Frontline troops
- Colonies

Each of these roles was vital to the overall success of the campaign but is generally overlooked by our surviving sources that tend to focus on either Alexander himself, or the exciting narratives of sieges, set-piece battles and other more lurid events, of which there are plenty in the Alexander histories.

Secondary Columns
Before 331, Alexander, with very few exceptions, kept his Macedonian troops with him. If any areas needed to be conquered that were not directly on his marching route, a secondary column would be detached to deal with these threats. These columns were often, although not exclusively, commanded by Parmenio, as with the column sent by Alexander to Magnesia and Tralles when the main body was at Ephesus. This column is particularly interesting as Arrian states that it consisted of:[20]

2,500 allied foot, 2,500 Macedonians, and about 200 Companion Cavalry, giving instructions for a similar force under Alcimachus, son of Agathocles, to proceed to the Aeolian towns and all the Ionian ones still subject to Persia.

The allied foot could easily have been mercenaries; they were used interchangeably on these kinds of mission. This force seems excessively large, as the two cities had already offered their joint surrender, and so this cannot have been an army of conquest, but rather one of occupation. The mercenaries/ allied troops can be explained, as they were probably intended for garrison duty. This does not explain, however, the presence of so many Macedonians. This difficulty is compounded by Arrian a few lines further in his text when he states that a similar force was sent to the Aeolian towns and all the Ionian cities still subject to Persia. This equally powerful force was under the command of Alcimachus. It seems highly unlikely that Alexander would have detached 5,000 Macedonian heavy infantry and 400 Companion Cavalry to conduct these relatively minor operations at the very outset of the campaign; these men were the cream of the army and far too valuable to risk in such a mission when there were plenty of mercenaries and allies who could be sent in their stead. This is especially the case when we consider that he was unsure how swiftly Darius could regroup, or even whether the Persian force at the Granicus was designed to slow his advance in anticipation of Darius' arrival, rather than to defeat him itself. It would seem reasonable for Alexander to have assumed that the Ionian cities would come over to him without a fight, and so sending the elite troops of his army on these expeditions would seem unnecessary. Thus only small numbers of satellite forces were used, supported by small numbers of Macedonians. We hear nothing of pillaging from these troops. Perhaps the land was not wealthy enough, though this is unlikely, or perhaps Alexander had forbidden that particular mercenary activity.

These secondary columns were, however, not always successful in their assigned tasks. When Satibarzanes and Spitamenes revolted in Aria, Alexander sent two expeditions. The first, sent against Satibarzanes, consisted entirely of mercenaries – a fact that we can assume on the basis that both commanders (Erigyius and Andronicus) were mercenaries themselves – and was wholly successful. The expedition sent against Spitamenes, on the other hand, was not. Arrian tells us of the troops used by Alexander on the second mission:[21]

To meet this situation, Andromachus, Menedemus, and Caranus were dispatched with a force consisting of sixty Companions, 800 of Caranus' mercenaries, and some 1,500 mercenary infantry.

They were under the overall command of Pharnuches, a Lydian. This represents a significant break from the norm, in that a non–Macedonian was commanding Macedonian troops, albeit it only sixty cavalry. Curtius and Arrian give different accounts of how the disaster came about, but both represent it as a crushing blow. Neither account apportions any blame to the mercenary troops; it is most likely that the fault lay either with the individual commanders, or more probably with the unsound method of appointing a native civilian to the leadership of a military expedition. One imagines that this latter sentiment would have been felt by the Macedonians; they were always unwilling to accept foreigners, either in command as here, or within their own ranks, as with the Persian cavalry joining the various *ilai* of the Companions.

The very nature of some of these secondary columns also changed after 331. Several times a relatively small group, consisting usually of Macedonians, was detached and led by Alexander himself, whilst the main body of the army, along with the baggage train, proceeded along safer paths. This change likely had more to do with Alexander's ever-present thirst for conquest and personal glory, as well as his crushing boredom when he was not active, rather than any strategic or tactical justifications. An example of this is in 331/0, when Parmenio was given command of the main body of the army with orders to proceed along the main road towards Pasargadae, whilst Alexander campaigned against the Uxii with his Macedonians and Agrianians. See also Alexander's final pursuit of Darius.

Garrisons
One of the most important roles that mercenaries played in Alexander's growing empire was as garrison troops at strategically important locations throughout the conquered territory. Virtually all of the fighting troops in the expanding Macedonian Empire that were not with the immediate entourage of the king were mercenaries. The only exceptions to this general rule were the Macedonians left with Antipater in Greece to defend the Macedonian homeland. Most of the cities that Alexander captured received a garrison of mercenaries; for example, Ephesus, Halicarnassus, Mytilene, Miletus, Egypt (admittedly not a city); the list of garrisoned towns is, of course, as extensive as Alexander's newly forming empire.

The first certain example of a garrison that is of significant size is that of Caria. Alexander left Halicarnassus after only a week-long siege, having captured only one of the three citadels, leaving behind 3,000 troops, under the command of Ptolemy, to complete the reduction of the city. The siege of Halicarnassus was certainly not Alexander's finest hour. It is my belief, however, that he abandoned it so quickly, before its capture was complete, because his newly formulated naval policy made it essential that he capture all the major Persian ports with as little delay as possible. Why Alexander left this major Persian port unconquered, after he stated the policy of defeating the Persian fleet on land, is something of a mystery. It may have been his overwhelming desire to progress further into Asia; a lengthy siege at this stage of his career was simply an unwanted delay to the young king. It could be argued, of course, that he actually had captured the majority of the city and what was left probably could not operate as much of an enemy naval base anyway. We are told nothing more about the organization of a mercenary garrison of Caria, save that Queen Ada was appointed civilian governor of the region. In order to learn more, we must move on to the next great employer of mercenaries: Egypt.

Egypt provides us with the best view of the military organization of a province within Alexander's Empire; it was a model that was to be repeated many times, as we shall see. Alexander appointed two native Egyptian governors, and two members of the Companion Cavalry, to act as commanders of the Macedonian garrisons at Memphis and Pelusium.[22] Lycidas, a Greek, was given command of the mercenary forces throughout the province. Alexander also appointed a 'secretary of foreign troops', these being the mercenaries, and two commissioners. The mercenaries appear to have been rather overstaffed, with four separate officers. A second problem is that Curtius seems to have the view that Aeschylus, one of the commissioners, and Peucestas, the military commander, are of the same status; apparently regarding Aeschylus as the administrative head of Egypt.[23] We cannot be certain, however, that the mercenary troops were 'overstaffed' as we have very little evidence of the organization of any other provinces (this may have been entirely normal), and even less with regard to the organization of mercenaries (or allies) in the main army. This administrative situation may well have been completely normal; there were 4,000 mercenaries after all, and only two small Macedonian garrisons requiring fewer officers. There is a suggestion that the two commissioners – or as he calls them, inspectors of the mercenaries – were in fact there to oversee the civilian governors, and in reality had little to do with the troops. This seems to be an eminently plausible suggestion.[24] This would also parallel the later situation in Eastern Iran, where Tlepolemus and Neiloxenus oversaw the work of the native satraps. If Egypt was assigned a greater number of governors, military officers and so on, then this would simply be an indication of the importance of that satrapy. Egypt had been a source of constant difficulty to the Persians, and Alexander did not want to encounter the same problems. Egypt was also a major source of grain for the Greek world, as it was to become for Rome, and no doubt the same is true for the army too, at least while campaigning in the western Persian Empire. Given that Alexander had almost no difficulty with logistics (other than the Gedrosian Desert disaster), we can assume that the grain supplies from Egypt were never interrupted.

Front Line Troops

The Macedonian elements in the army always played the leading roles in each of Alexander's set-piece battles, but we should not overlook the contributions made by the mercenary troops. At the Battle of the Granicus River, neither the mercenaries nor the allied troops are mentioned at all. This should not worry us too much as the Granicus was a relatively small battle, certainly in comparison to Issus and Gaugamela and the Hydaspes. The question remains, however, what were they doing at the time of the battle? The only answers can be either that they were away from the main body of the army, yet still playing some role in the fighting, or they were away on some secondary mission, or perhaps that they formed a reserve or second line that is not mentioned because it was not called into use. I find this latter argument to be the more likely considering their later tactical roles at Issus and Gaugamela. Their function in these later battles was to prevent the army from being outflanked and to protect the rear of the Macedonian heavy infantry units. The mercenaries were there to ensure Alexander did not lose, rather than to directly aid him in winning the battle. He was evidently a man who re-used successful tactics, albeit adapted to individual circumstances, and the provision of a reserve line would seem a sensible insurance policy against the battle not going entirely as planned.

At Issus the picture is a little clearer; by the time Alexander arrived on the battlefield (which was narrow and wedged between mountains to the east and the sea to the west), Darius had already deployed his troops and was waiting. Darius had evidently studied Alexander's dispositions at the Granicus and expected Alexander to deploy in the same way, and he was broadly speaking correct. To counter the central strength of the Macedonian heavy infantry, he deployed his only quality infantry in the centre, the now-depleted Greek mercenary troops, under the command of Thymondas. The Greek mercenaries were stationed along a stretch of banks between 500m and 1.6km from the coast. The banks were steep in this sector, and an attack from cavalry was highly unlikely. For Darius, deploying Greek mercenary troops in this area was tactically very sound indeed; the steep banks would make an assault by cavalry impossible and would severely disrupt the Macedonian heavy infantry. In order to bolster the defensive strength, he created several abatis, essentially temporary defensive palisades, at the most vulnerable points. Arrian and Curtius, following Callisthenes, both give the strength of the Greek mercenaries in Persian service at 30,000. This simply cannot be possible, given the losses in battle, captives from the Granicus and the inevitable desertions that would have occurred.[25] They were stationed opposite the hypaspists and *pezhetairoi*, which themselves numbered 12,000 and, as they did not seriously overlap the Macedonians, we can assume that there would have been approximately the same number. If their depth was the same as their opponents, their numbers would also have been similar, but that cannot be taken as an argument for assuming similar numbers. It is well known that hoplites could have a depth of fifty or more on occasion, so if the lines were of similar lengths and yet the Persians had much greater numbers then their files would be deeper. We simply cannot know the size of the Persian force, but can safely only assume it was at least as great as Alexander's.

Arrian shows little interest in the Persians, with the exception of the Greek mercenary infantry and of the Cardaces, who he describes as hoplites, clearly believing them to be heavy infantry. Arrian states clearly that the Cardaces were stationed to either side of the Greek mercenaries and numbered 60,000.[26] Given the limitations of space in the plain, and the large mass of cavalry by the sea, it seems highly unlikely that Arrian could be correct that the Cardaces were posted to either side of the Greek mercenaries. The Cardaces are highly likely to be associated with the peltasts of Callisthenes. These peltasts were stationed along the middle section of the Pinarus River, between 1.6km and 3.5km from the coast.

The Persians then deployed their heavy cavalry on the extreme right, commanded by Nabarzanes, screened by a group of slingers and archers. Next to these were the Greek mercenary infantry in their prepared defensive position as mentioned above. Next to these were the Cardaces of an unknown number, perhaps 20,000 strong or slightly more given the size of their frontage, commanded by Aristomedes, a Thessalian mercenary. Next to these were detachments of Hyrcanian and Median cavalry, along with a group of unspecified Persian cavalry and a detachment of javelin men and slingers deployed in front of them. The Persians also employed a reserve line behind the front, 40,000 strong in Curtius. Arrian is cautious about giving the total number of Persian troops at 600,000, reporting it as hearsay, although Plutarch gives the same figure.[27] Diodorus and Justin report 400,000 infantry and 100,000 cavalry, whilst Curtius gives the lowest estimate: 250,000 infantry and 62,000 cavalry.[28] All of these estimates may be too high, but it is likely that Alexander was, as usual, heavily outnumbered.

Alexander drew up his heavy infantry facing the Persians, with the Companion Cavalry to the right of the infantry. A strong flank guard was assigned to the right wing, where the Persian line overlapped his own; on the left it seems that he sent the mercenary troops, along with the Peloponnesians and the rest of the allied cavalry. A curious decision, as they were essentially hoplites assigned to the sandy area next to the sea, terrain most suited to a charge by the Persian cavalry. Alexander seems to have soon realized his error and sent the Thessalian cavalry to the left wing. What then happened to the mercenaries is unclear: they could have occupied a position between the Thessalian cavalry and the Macedonian heavy infantry, similar to the role played by the hypaspists on the right of the line. They may have occupied a position on the far right of the line, equally unlikely, or they were withdrawn from the front to form part of a second line. The sources do not provide us with enough information to answer this directly; the confusion results from Arrian's use of the word *epitasso*, which can mean 'station', either alongside or behind.[29] The context of the passage would seem to make it clear that here it has to mean that the mercenaries were placed behind everybody else. The other interpretation would have the mercenaries, a medium–heavy infantry division, on the extreme left of the whole army, where it was Alexander's practice to put his Thessalian cavalry and some light infantry support. It seems certain then that Alexander used a second line, what some may call a tactical reserve, at the Battle of Issus.

The role of the allied infantry supplied by the League of Corinth, and the Balkan allies, is more difficult to ascertain. They are not mentioned in any of the sources as forming the second line at Issus or Gaugamela, along with the mercenaries. They were surely far too numerous to have been left behind to guard the baggage train, however. Arrian's order of battle is not exhaustive for this campaign; the Odrysian cavalry and Balacrus' javelin men are not mentioned either. The absence is no doubt an omission by Arrian, and not some deeper mystery that could have us inventing another campaign or some elaborate tactic simply to explain away their absence. The mercenaries and allies, therefore, seemed to form a tactically important second line. It should be realized that by 'second line' I mean something distinct from the front line, not simply a group of troops that attached themselves to the back of the heavy infantry *taxeis*, but an entirely separate line with a distinct tactical role.

Gaugamela provides us with the best evidence for the combat role of the mercenary and allied troops. Alexander laid out his heavy infantry, Companion Cavalry and Thessalian cavalry according to his standard plan; which is to say the Thessalians to the extreme left, heavy infantry in the centre, hypaspists to their right and Companion Cavalry to the extreme right of the line. This is the general formation that was adapted at almost every opportunity, where it was appropriate, given the terrain etc. The *prodromoi* and a number of other minor contingents were positioned to the right of the Companions, and Menidas' mercenary cavalry to the extreme right of the formation, with Cleander's mercenary infantry behind them. On the left of the formation were Sitalces' Thracian infantry and three bodies of allied or League cavalry, along with Andromachos' mercenary horse.

A second line of infantry was positioned parallel to the front; it consisted of the allied troops supplied from the League of Corinth and a smaller number of Balkan allies and mercenaries not stationed elsewhere. Closing the gap between the two lines on the right were Cleander's mercenaries, the Agrianians and archers, and the corresponding position on the left. Closing the 'box' that was thus formed were the remainder of the Thracian infantry, those not commanded by Sitalces. The formation that was created was therefore a box with two protrusions to the right and left. It was not a closed formation, however; it would seem that the second line only extended about halfway along the formation, starting from the left wing, resulting in the left-hand half of the front line having no troops positioned behind it. This is suggested by the fact that when a small group of Bactrian cavalry broke through the front line they met no further resistance before reaching Alexander's camp. The mercenary and allied troops at Gaugamela were positioned in order that if Alexander's position were turned, highly likely given the discrepancy in numbers, he would not automatically be defeated. The second line could simply turn around and fight with their backs to the front line. They were there, in short, to ensure that, if the battle did not go well, Alexander could still win. Their ability to perform this function was not seriously tested but that should not detract from the potential importance of this role.

Colonies

After 331 when Alexander began to enter the north-eastern parts of the former Persian Empire, his mercenary and allied troops were to become increasingly important. In this region, Alexander founded a series of colonies, although they were probably rather fewer in number than was believed a few decades ago.[30] This was a move perhaps partly designed to spread Greek culture, although this argument should not be exaggerated, as this was very much a by-product of their presence in these regions and not their primary function. They were primarily designed to help pacify the outer parts of the empire, and to maintain order when the main host had moved on. It was to be hoped that these new foundations, which were, essentially, military colonies, would act as a calming influence on the always potentially rebellious natives. These colonies, then, had a largely strategic rather than a tactical function.

They were also partly forced upon Alexander because he had ever-increasing numbers of troops who were past service and needed to be pensioned off. The best attested evidence for a colony that we have is Alexandria in Caucaso, the modern Bagram in the central Hindu Kush Mountains at the confluence of the Gorband and Panjshir rivers. Here Alexander established a city with a nucleus of 3,000 Graeco-Macedonian settlers, soldiers no longer fit for service, and volunteers from among the mercenaries, together with 7,000 of the local population. This becomes something of a standard pattern, a blend of native and Greek/Macedonian settlers. Alexander no doubt hoped that, if there was a native revolt, these retired troops would act to suppress it, and that as a by-product of their presence they would also spread Greek culture to the furthest reaches of the known world. This later point would be an added bonus that came with the foundation of the cities, rather than a primary purpose. These cities were essentially garrison towns and administrative centres.

Later evidence suggests that these Greeks were far from being the willing settlers that our sources portray them as having been. On two separate occasions, they themselves effectively revolted against Alexander. The first revolt occurred in Bactria when rumour spread that Alexander had died on the Indus. Some of the Greeks revolted under the banner of Athenodorus with the express intent of returning to Greece. This insurrection, however, fell in upon itself, with Athenodorus being assassinated by Biton, who was in turn tortured for such an act by the Greek settlers themselves. Diodorus' account of the fate of these 3,000 rebels is obscure, but Curtius has them eventually getting home.[31] This small revolt was the precursor to a much larger one that occurred after Alexander's death; it seems the Greeks were not at all happy with being left on the edge of the civilized world. They longed for home just as the Macedonians evidently did at the Opis revolt.

Alexander, then, made great use of mercenary troops. This use grew in number and significance as the campaign wore on. In the early years, they were few in number and in reality did little. After 331, and increasingly until his death, mercenaries were a vital part of his empire, and I think it is true to say that Alexander could never have exerted any kind of influence or control on his empire without them. He could not entirely trust the Persian troops to garrison their own cities, not unless he wanted widespread revolts (even more than actually occurred). Nor did he have large enough numbers of native Macedonian troops to garrison the empire. He had no choice but to rely on mercenaries and, by and large, they did a very good job. We hear almost nothing of difficulties from them, nor, interestingly enough, do we hear many stories of wanton looting and pillaging by mercenaries (or anyone else). Alexander was wealthy enough, especially after 331, that he could pay them generously enough that they did not feel the need to supplement their income in a way that would be harmful to the effective governance of an empire.

Persia

In the final section of this chapter, we will look at Persia and the Persian response to the growing power of Macedonia. We have touched on Persia already in the chapter, but here we will examine their employment and deployment of mercenaries in a more systematic way than we did earlier, when the focus was on the Macedonian kings.

Before Macedonia became the great powerhouse of the Greek world, the Persian Empire had been relatively stable for several decades, with only minor satrapal revolts for the Great Kings to manage. Their employment of mercenaries had, therefore, been limited to garrison duty, and parts of the standing armies of the western satraps. The year 340 was a minor watershed for Persian security. In that year, Philip was besieging Perinthus, the final obstacle to his achieving control of the Hellespontine region, and the last buffer between Persia and Macedonia. Artaxerxes could not allow the continued rise of Macedonian power to go unchallenged, and he would not allow Philip to gain control of the corn supply to Greece and create a border with Persia. To prevent this, he ordered his satraps in Asia Minor to send military aid to Perinthus. Diodorus tells us:[32]

> They consequently took counsel and sent off to Perinthus a force of mercenaries, ample funds, and sufficient stocks of food, missiles, and other materials required for operations. Similarly the people of Byzantium also sent them their best officers and soldiers. So the armies were again well matched, and as the fighting was resumed, the siege was waged with supreme determination.

The mercenary force sent by the satraps was commanded by an Athenian, Apollodurus, who was employed by Arsites the satrap of Hellespontine Phrygia.[33] We are not told exactly how large this mercenary relief force was, but it slipped into Perinthus whilst Philip was besieging the city. The arrival of these mercenaries was a shot in the arm to the defenders, who fought on bravely and ultimately successfully, as Philip was forced to withdraw.

The next major deployment of mercenaries against the Macedonians was that which opposed Parmenio and Attalus' expeditionary force in 334. Memnon, with only 5,000 mercenaries – half as many as the Macedonians commanded – succeeded in reversing most of the gains made by Parmenio, so that by the time of Alexander's invasion in 334 the Macedonians only controlled a small area. In many ways, of course, this was enough; all Alexander needed was a bridgehead to provide him with protection whilst his army was most vulnerable, as they disembarked from their ships.

When Alexander landed, Memnon withdrew to Zelea, where he took part in the debate with the satraps as to the best course of action. Memnon offered advice that was, with the benefit of hindsight, perfectly sound:[34]

> Memnon of Rhodes advised against risking an engagement: The Macedonian infantry, he pointed out, were greatly superior in numbers; Alexander was present in person, while Darius was not. It would be better, therefore, to proceed at once to burn all of the crops, trample down and destroy grass and horse-feed, and even gut the towns, to prevent Alexander, from lack of supplies, from remaining in the country.

Memnon was more of a pragmatist than the Persian high command: he could see the potential in Alexander, and more specifically, I think, in the Macedonian army. And as Arrian notes, he was painfully aware that the Persian army was lacking in quality infantry, especially when compared to the Macedonian host. This kind of scorched-earth policy was adopted by the Persians in the run-up to the Battle of Gaugamela in 331, and there it did force Alexander to change direction as he advanced towards Darius, but it did not stop the Macedonians and only barely slowed them down. If it had been attempted here, it may have met with more conclusive results. Alexander was painfully short of funds and needed a quick victory; he would also likely have been short on supplies, and was to an extent living off the land. The Persian satraps, however, would have none of it. They accused Alexander of being a beardless youth, hardly worth running away from, and questioned Memnon's loyalty (he was Greek after all). Arsites, who appears to have been in overall command as the events were occurring in his satrapy, made the decision to oppose Alexander and marched towards the Granicus.

At the battle, the Persians set up their cavalry, 20,000 in number, along the banks of the river with the Greek mercenaries, also 20,000 in number, and the only infantry the Persians had, some distance back from the river on top of a hill. There are a number of competing theories as to how the battle proceeded (Diodorus and Arrian present completely different pictures), but, whatever happened, the mercenaries took little or no part until the Persian cavalry had already retreated.[35] They were too far away from the riverbank to influence events and had orders to maintain their positions. Perhaps Arsites did not want the glory of victory to go to a Greek of dubious loyalty.

When Alexander had routed the Persian cavalry, he did not pursue them for long, and therefore their losses were limited. Arrian tells us:

> About 1,000 were killed – not more, because Alexander soon checked the pursuit of them in order to turn his attention to the foreign mercenaries, who had remained in their original position, shoulder to shoulder – not, indeed, from and deliberate intention of proving their courage, but simply because the suddenness of the disaster had deprived them of their wits. Ordering a combined assault by infantry and cavalry, Alexander quickly had them surrounded and butchered to a man, though one or two may have escaped notice among the heaps of the dead.

Despite Arrian's claim that they were butchered to a man, we know this was not the case, since the survivors that were captured were sent to a hard labour camp in Macedonia, and Memnon with several thousand slipped away to reappear several months later defending Halicarnassus. Alexander felt entirely justified in his actions because the League of Corinth had decreed that no Greek should take up arms against another Greek. His action against the mercenaries after the battle was won was a statement to the rest of the Greek world, and every unemployed mercenary, as to what would happen if they took the Great King's coin.

After the Granicus, for the next year, Alexander fought little else than Greek mercenaries in the employ of the Great King acting as garrisons in a variety of cities down the west coast of Asia Minor. The major engagement was at Halicarnassus, where the remnants from the Granicus defended the city admirably, led by Memnon and Ephialtes, but were ultimately unsuccessful.

Darius' next stand against Alexander was at Issus in 333 (the first time the two had met on the field of battle), which we examined in some detail above, and there is no need to do so again here. Of the perhaps 30,000 mercenaries Darius commanded at Issus, only one contingent decided to follow the Great King into the interior of Persia and formed part of the army that resisted Alexander again at Gaugamela in 331, by that time only 2,000 in number.[36] The remainder made their escape via the coast. At Gaugamela, the Greek mercenaries were again placed in the centre of the Persian line, but by that time they were far too few in number to have any impact on the battle. The decline in numbers was no indication of Darius' lack of faith in his mercenaries; he would have been desperate to recruit more, but evidently found it almost impossible. As Alexander conquered the western empire, Darius had little or no access to the recruiting grounds of Greece, and, even if a recruiter with sufficient funds made it to Arcadia (or somewhere similar), there was little hope that a large hostile mercenary army could reach Darius without being engaged by Alexander, even if Antipater allowed them to escape the mainland. On top of this, of course, was the fact that Darius was simply not an attractive paymaster, given Alexander's conquests. As a mercenary, it was probably much more attractive a proposition to take up employment with the Macedonians in a nice secure garrison somewhere in the growing empire.

The Greek Resistance to Alexander

Mercenary employment during the reign of Alexander was not limited to the two competing kings; there were still employment opportunities on the mainland for soldiers of fortune to seek a living. These mercenaries can be divided into three categories: those employed by Antipater (Alexander's regent); those employed by people opposing the Macedonians; and those that remained unemployed. The largest single body of anti-Macedonian mercenaries was those that escaped after the Persian defeat at Issus. These mercenaries left Persian soil via Tripolis, and destroyed every ship they could find – other than those they used to transport themselves – to prevent Alexander following them (which he showed no inclination of doing).[37] Arrian records 8,000 mercenaries escaping via this route, and that may not be too bad an estimate out of the (probably exaggerated) 30,000 that were at Issus. These mercenaries were organized along similar lines to the 10,000 of Xenophon, in that they had four separate commanders of seemingly equal status: Amyntas, Thymondas, Bianor and Aristomedes. This could indicate, as it did with the 10,000, that they were originally recruited as separate armies and then brought together, but we have no evidence on exactly how they were recruited.

Once these mercenaries were free from the immediate threat of reprisals from Alexander, they broke up into four separate armies and went their separate ways. Amyntas and Aristomedes travelled to Cyprus, where they won over a number of cities. Of Amyntas and his 4,000 mercenaries, Diodorus tells us:[38]

> He sailed over to Cyprus, took on additional soldiers and ships, and continued on down to Pelusium. Becoming master of that city, he proclaimed that he had been sent by King Darius as military commander because the satrap of Egypt had been killed fighting at Issus in Cilicia.

We do not know about Aristomedes, but if he was prepared to accompany Amyntas to Cyprus then he may well have been prepared to accompany him to Egypt. Amyntas' plan to take control of Egypt was unsuccessful, as the Persian nobility stationed in Egypt managed to muster enough local support to defeat him, even after an initial setback. If Amyntas wished to avoid Alexander, one wonders why he would have travelled to Egypt with the intention of making himself at least satrap; he must have known Alexander was marching in a southerly direction. This seems a curious choice, unless he was still acting as if in the employ of Darius and hoping for reinforcements once he had occupied the province.

Whilst Alexander was besieging Tyre and Amyntas was failing in Egypt, there were general rumblings of discontent on the mainland and a developing sentiment towards revolt from Macedonian rule. Those proponents of this policy would have been encouraged by the presence of a large Persian fleet in the Aegean (the fleet was ultimately captured by Alexander towards the end of the siege of Tyre, an act which was the turning point of the siege) and the ever-present possibility of Persian gold.[39] The majority of the states of Greece had been enrolled (not all willingly) into the League of Corinth after the battle of Chaeronea in 338, an alliance that was affirmed upon Alexander's accession in 336. The exception was Sparta, who neither Philip nor Alexander (nor Antipater) had taken the time to subdue and force into membership. It is not always easy to understand why Sparta was allowed to remain free, but she was militarily weak after the Peloponnesian War and the continuous warfare of the fourth century, and especially after Mantinea and Leuctra. Sparta had not actively, or passively, opposed either Philip or Alexander either, and this neutrality did not bring them to the attention of the Macedonians. Sparta's absence from the League of Corinth treaty, however, meant that she was not bound by its edicts and was free to seek alliance with Persia, or anyone else, if she felt it beneficial.[40] The status of the Peloponnese as a 'free state' led to Taenarum becoming the central meeting and recruitment point for anti-Macedonian mercenaries, especially from the period after Agis III's unsuccessfull revolt against Macedonia until shortly after the death of Alexander. Taenarum was a perfectly located city on the major sea routes to Africa, Asia and the Western Mediterranean, and therefore an ideal meeting place for mercenaries awaiting recruitment.

As already noted, Sparta was not a threat to Macedonia as long as she was militarily weak and without funds because of the loss of the Peloponnesian League. Within about a year of Alexander's invasion of Persia, however, we see the Spartan king, Agis, negotiating with Pharnabazus at Siphnos (333) for a loan of money, as well as naval and military support for a proposed revolt against Macedonian rule. During the negotiations, the shattering news arrived of Alexander's stunning victory at Issus. Pharnabazus immediately broke off the negotiations, gathered together the few mercenaries he had with him, and sailed for Chios to ensure that island remained loyal. Pharnabazus commanded 1,500 mercenaries, and a similar amount were already acting as a garrison within the city.[41] The city was controlled by a tyrant, loyal to Darius, but evidently unpopular amongst the citizenry, and indeed with the mercenary garrison. An argument ensued, and the city was betrayed to Alexander, who took control of it willingly. He also employed all of the mercenaries present, destroyed the pirates on the island and enrolled those pirates he had captured into his own fleet. One wonders what he must have done to upset the mercenaries, but the withholding of pay was always a good way to make them question their loyalty, and ultimately switch sides, as here.

Despite the negotiations between Pharnabazus and Agis being both cut short and unsatisfactory from either perspective, Agis did secure some small level of assistance from the Persian satrap. Agis received the small sum of thirty talents, along with ten triremes for his resistance to Alexander in Greece. Agis sent these to his brother, Agesilaus, with instructions to sail to Crete and stir up a pro-Persian rebellion.[42] The news of the disaster at Issus was a crippling blow for the anti-Macedonian forces in Greece and on the islands. Alexander was starting to look more powerful and a more attractive potential paymaster every day. All Agesilaus was able to do was stir up some local difficulties, but there seems never to have been a serious risk of revolt. Agis had little choice in the immediate future but to employ as many of the mercenaries formally in Darius' service at Issus as he could and wait for the opportune moment to strike at the Macedonians.

The next real anti-Macedonian act of resistance was in 331/0. The Spartans had been preparing for war for around two years, and had already gathered to their banner a significant body of mercenaries, presumably at least partly funded by Persia. After his victory at Gaugamela, Alexander continued further into the Persian Empire, and it started to look increasingly likely that he either would not return, or that he was so far away that there was little he could do to impact proceedings on the mainland. When Agis finally revolted – although he was not in fact under the nominal control of the League of Corinth – he forced Antipater, Alexander's regent, into a battle at Corragus, where the Macedonians were defeated. Following this success, the Spartans moved to create a formal anti-Macedonian alliance, as Diodorus describes:[43]

> There was also an upheaval in Thrace at just this time which seemed to offer the Greeks an opportunity for freeing themselves. Memnon, who had been designated governor-general there, had a military force and was a man of spirit. He stirred up the tribesmen, revolted against Alexander, quickly possessed a large army, and was openly bent on war. While Antipater was occupied with this, the Lacedaemonians thought that the time had come to undertake a war and issued an appeal to the

Greeks to unite in defence of their freedom. The Athenians had been favoured beyond all the other Greeks by Alexander and did not move. Most of the Peloponnesians, however, and some of the northern Greeks reached an agreement and signed an undertaking to go to war. According to the capacity of the individual cities they enlisted the best of their youth and enrolled as soldiers not less than twenty thousand infantry and about two thousand cavalry.

Antipater saw the growing threat and, using the huge resources that Alexander had sent back to Macedonia, raised more mercenaries himself to support the core of the Macedonian home guard.[44] Once both sides had prepared their forces, they met at Megalopolis. For the first time in twenty years, the Spartans were in command of a major army marching to battle. That the army was largely mercenary in origin and to an extent paid for by Persian gold would not have concerned them greatly; overthrowing Macedonian rule in Greece and reasserting their own dominance was at the front of their minds. The battle was hard-fought, but the numerical advantage, as well as the superior discipline, of the Macedonians won the day, and the Spartan alliance was defeated. Agis himself died after distinguishing himself during the height of the fighting. Curtius describes the aftermath of the battle and the tensions that remained:[45]

> This victory broke the spirit, not alone of Sparta and her allies, but of all those who had awaited the fortune of the war. Antipater did not fail to notice that the expression of those who congratulated him did not correspond with their feelings, but since he desired to end the war, he was constrained to let himself be deceived, and although the success of the affair pleased him, yet he feared envy, for what he had done was more important than suited the limitations of a prefect.

Neither Antipater nor Alexander would have been overly concerned by the underlying hostility to Macedonian rule, as long as the city-states remained loyal. Antipater had smashed Greek resistance completely, and there was no further organized armed resistance to Macedonian rule until after the death of Alexander in 323.

The loyalty (or obedience) of the city-states was severely tested when the deserter Harpalus arrived in Greece with a large sum of money and a mercenary army of 6,000. He at first made for Athens, where he received a frosty reception, after which he retired with his army to Taenarum, which was still not under Macedonian rule, even after Megalopolis.[46] Harpalus left his army there and returned to Athens, but after Antipater complained he was forcibly removed from that city, and he returned again to Taenarum.

His second spell there saw him murdered by one of his subordinates, a Spartan called Thibron. Thibron took control of the financial reserves that Harpalus had stolen from Alexander, as well as the 6,000 mercenaries Harpalus had hired, and set off for a life of piracy and pillage.[47] The army's first stop was Cyrene, where they pillaged the land and blackmailed the populace. As was so often the case, however, an internal struggle arose over the distribution of the plunder, and one of Thibron's subordinates, Mnasicles of Crete, deserted the army along with an unspecified number of mercenaries. Thibron summoned reinforcements from Taenarum and continued his campaign against Cyrene. He was ultimately defeated and killed by troops sent from Egypt to support the Macedonian governor.

During his career, Alexander would have required ever more troops to act as garrisons in his newly won empire. This does not appear, however, to have reduced the numbers available at Taenarum. As already noted, this kind of garrison service was probably highly prized amongst some mercenaries, as it represented a regular income with little likelihood of being killed or of having to engage in any real combat. The opportunities for plunder were virtually nil, however.

The death of Alexander in 323 led to two serious rebellions against Macedonian rule, one in the east and one in the west, both of which had mercenaries at their core. In the north-eastern satrapies, as soon as news arrived of Alexander's death, the mercenaries that had been left in those provinces or settled there against their will rose up against the Macedonian authority with the intention of marching back to Greece. This was the second such attempted rebellion by these mercenaries, the first taking place during Alexander's lifetime when inaccurate rumours spread of the king's death. That rebellion was put down ruthlessly. Diodorus tells us there were 20,000 infantry and 3,000 cavalry involved in this second rebellion, although this is certainly an exaggeration.[48] When Alexander died, Perdiccas assumed, for a time at least, the leadership of the empire and he dispatched Peithon with a number of Macedonians to rectify the situation. Peithon, however, had his own agenda and wished to recruit these mercenaries to his own banner and set himself up as ruler of an independent state with the military backing of these disaffected mercenaries. He found a willing partner in Letodorus, the commander of 3,000 of these mercenaries. The matter was not simply resolved, however, as the mercenaries were prepared to fight to gain their freedom and made a stand on the field of battle against the numerically inferior force commanded by Peithon. At the key moment, however, the desertion of Letodorus' troops caused the mercenaries' resolve to crumble and they fled the field. Peithon persuaded these mercenaries to surrender their arms as an act of submission, which they did. The Macedonians, however, had been promised by Perdiccas, unknown to Peithon, that they could take possession of all of the enemy's belongings as plunder. With this at the forefront of their minds, and unhappy with the leniency shown by Peithon, the Macedonians slaughtered the unarmed prisoners and took their possessions. This was more like the act of a mercenary army than one commensurate with the Macedonians that Alexander had commanded, and demonstrates a further decline in Greek warfare into a period of much greater violence where plunder was a way of life. The revolt, however, was crushed, as were Peithon's dreams of being ruler of his own kingdom.[49]

At virtually the same time, a general revolt began in Greece under the leadership of the Athenian, Leosthenes. Diodorus blamed the rebellion on the unemployed mercenaries that were roaming Greece and Asia as a direct result of Alexander's mercenaries' decree disbanding the mercenary armies of the satraps.[50]

> During this period Greece was the scene of disturbances and revolu-
> tionary movements from which arose the war called Lamian. The
> reason was this. The king had ordered all his satraps to dissolve their
> armies of mercenaries, and as they obeyed his instructions, all Asia was
> overrun with soldiers released from service and supporting themselves
> by plunder. Presently they began assembling from all directions at
> Taenarum in Laconia, whither came also such of the Persian satraps
> and generals as had survived, bringing their funds and their soldiers, so
> that they constituted a joint force.

Pausanias lays the blame more firmly at the door of Leosthenes, claiming a great personal enmity between him and Alexander.[51]

> All the Greeks that were serving as mercenaries in the armies of
> Darius and his satraps Alexander had wished to deport to Persia, but
> Leosthenes was too quick for him, and brought them by sea to Europe.

Whoever was to blame, the result was rebellion in Greece and the so-called Lamian War. Athens had seemingly been preparing for rebellion since 324 and had gathered together a force of 8,000 mercenaries at Taenarum, paid for by the gold they had confiscated from Harpalus (which he in turn had stolen from Alexander). As soon as the news of Alexander's death reached Athens, they sent Leosthenes to Aetolia, where he was joined by his 8,000 mercenaries and 7,000 local levies. From here they marched to Plataea, where they engaged and defeated a combined Macedonian and Boeotian garrison at Thebes.[52]

Whilst the Athenians were strengthening their position in southern and central Greece, Antipater sent for aid from Leonnatus, satrap of Phrygia, and awaited the return of Craterus with the Macedonians discharged from the mobile field army. Antipater needed to act, but he was militarily relatively weak, having only 14,000 Macedonians under arms. He left Sippas in Macedonia with a small force to guard against potential rebellion from Thrace, along with a sum of money to recruit mercenaries as necessary, and marched south. His forces were too small to risk a set-piece battle, however, so when he arrived at Lamia he fortified the city and awaited the arrival of the rebels.

Leosthenes began the siege with vigour, but with little skill in siegecraft, and it quickly descended into little more than a blockade maintained by the mercenaries over the winter months into 322. There were a number of small-scale engagements as the defenders occasionally sortied from the city, and, during one of these, Leosthenes was killed. Whatever limited vigour the besiegers had before the death of their commander, it virtually disintegrated upon his death.

When Craterus and Leonattus joined forces with Antipater, the Macedonians felt strong enough to offer battle, and were victorious at the resulting Battle of Crannon. The battle itself was indecisive, but the political outcome was not. The Athenian forces melted away after the battle and Athens sued for peace, accepting Antipater's terms. The battle was decisive in the short term, but Greece remained highly unstable for much of the next fifty years, partly due to uncertainty as to who was to be the ruler of Macedonia in the long term.[53]

Chapter 7

The West: Syracuse and Carthage

The history of conflict between Syracuse and Carthage, the two great western mercenary employers, began in earnest with the Carthaginian invasion of 480. It is possible that this invasion was deliberately timed to coincide with the Persian invasion of Greece, although the details of the question are beyond the scope of this book. A Carthaginian army under Hamilcar landed on Sicily and besieged the city of Himera. The Himerans appealed for help to Syracuce, and Gelon, its tyrant, dispatched an army that was partly citizen and partly mercenary. It has been suggested that he commanded a total of around 15,000 troops, even at this early date.[1] When the two armies met outside of Himera, the Carthaginians were decisively defeated and Hamilcar was killed. In 474, the Syracusans again used their mercenary army to defeat an Etruscan force at Cyme in southern Italy. It appears the aim of the Etruscans may have been to ally themselves with Carthage in order to carve up Sicily between themselves.[2] The Peloponnesian War saw the ambitious and ultimately failed Sicilian expedition from Athens, and its attempt to capture Syracuse. The invasion was almost successful, as has already been described, but Syracuse emerged victorious. The victory came at a cost, however. Syracuse was seriously weakened militarily and financially, and the Carthaginians were not long in attempting to exploit that weakness.

At the end of the fourth century, the democratic faction in Syracuse was in the ascendancy, having won much kudos for the victory over the Athenians. They acted against some of their anti-democratic opponents by exiling them, the most notable being Hermocrates. At the time of his exile, he was commanding the Syracusan fleet in Asia Minor, and those he commanded did not take kindly to the news.[3] In 410/09 a second Carthaginian invasion of Sicily began. Upon hearing the news of the invasion, Hermocrates did not immediately return home, but:[4]

> He now went to visit Pharnabazus; and since he had once brought
> an accusation against Tissaphernes at Lacedaemon, in which Astyochus

supported him as witness, and had been adjudged to speak the truth, he received money from Pharnabazus before he asked for it, and busied himself with collecting mercenaries and triremes with a view to his restoration to Syracuse. Meanwhile the Syracusans who succeeded the banished generals arrived at Miletus and took over the ships and the troops.

Once his mercenary army had been gathered, he sailed for Sicily and landed at Messana, where his force was bolstered by 100 fugitives from Himera, which the Carthaginians, under the command of Hannibal, had sacked. Hermocrates appears to have wanted the tyranny of Syracuse as his first priority, the defeat of Carthage as second. His first action was a raid into Carthaginian-controlled territory with the aim of gathering plunder, which he used to bolster the size of his mercenary force. When it reached a strength of around 6,000, he marched on Syracuse and attempted to besiege the city and to force entry. His attempt failed and he withdrew to occupy Selinus, which had previously fallen into Carthaginian hands.

Hermocrates attempted to ingratiate himself into the hearts of the Syracusans by marching to Himera, recovering the bones of the Syracusan dead, and returning them in specially decorated wagons.[5] Hermocrates intended to follow up this act by arriving at the city with 3,000 of his mercenaries, at which point he had arranged for his local supporters to betray the city to him. After some kind of miscommunication (there is no reason to suspect treachery), the mercenaries did not arrive, and he entered the city with only a small contingent of friends. When the citizens realized what was happening, they surrounded his party and slew the would-be ruler and most of his followers.[6] The most important of the small number who escaped the attempt to snatch power was Dionysius, the future tyrant, who was himself a Syracusan citizen with wealthy and powerful friends.

In 406, the Carthaginians made another attempt to invade Sicily, this time in far greater numbers and with the conquest of the whole island as their goal. They first began a siege of Acragas, a city which had remained neutral during previous invasions. This time, however, she both requested help from Syracuse, and hired a number of Campanian mercenaries. The city's defence was conducted by the elected generals, and a mercenary general from the Peloponnese called Dexippus. The defenders fought stoically as they awaited the hoped-for assistance from Syracuse, but before that could arrive the Carthaginians were overtaken by a plague and many were killed, including their leader, Hannibal.[7] The plague left the defenders in the ascendancy, and, although food within the city was running short, the inhabitants were receiving regular shipments from Syracuse. Probably by luck rather than good judgement, the Carthaginians intercepted a grain shipment to the city, which turned the tables against the defenders. Food shortages began almost immediately amongst the populace, the soldiers and mercenaries alike. For mercenary troops, food or a stipend provided to purchase food (and its availability) were key elements of mercenary service. Once the food started to run out, the loyalty of the Campanian mercenaries similarly expired. They deserted to the Carthaginian side and, since they were the backbone of the defensive forces, the city quickly fell to the invaders.

The Carthaginians had aided the defenders of Acragas by providing provisions to allow them to withstand the siege, but had given limited actual military aid. In the spring of 405, the year following the fall of Acragas, Syracuse elected ten new generals, including Dionysius himself.[8]

> Having become elated, therefore, in his hopes, he tried every device to become tyrant of his country. For example, after assuming office he neither participated in the meetings of the generals nor associated with them in any way; and while acting in this manner he spread the report that they were carrying on negotiations with the enemy. For in this way he hoped that he could most effectively strip them of their power and clothe himself alone with the office of general. While Dionysius was acting in this fashion, the most respectable citizens suspected what was taking place and in every gathering spoke disparagingly of him, but the common crowd, being ignorant of his scheme, gave him their approbation and declared that at long last the city had found a steadfast leader.

Dionysius believed that a mercenary bodyguard would be his surest route to the tyranny, and so he set about tricking the populace by faking an assassination attempt upon himself, after which he was voted a bodyguard of 600 foreign mercenaries, a force he later increased to 1,000. Gradually, Dionysius established himself as a military dictator, and eventually tyrant. He replaced the leaders of the citizen militia with his own men, and also sent Dexippus back to the Peloponnese. After this, he set about trying to win over the mercenaries formally employed by Dexippus, and with some success. This did not prove difficult, as the pay of Dexippus' mercenaries was in arrears and he won them over by simply paying off that debt. The mechanism for doing so is interesting, however. Dionysius did this by confiscating the property of the wealthiest citizens of Gela:[9]

> And when Dionysius on arrival found the wealthiest citizens engaged in strife with the people, he accused them in an assembly and secured their condemnation, whereupon he put them to death and confiscated

their possessions. With the money thus gained he paid the guards of the city under the command of Dexippus the wages which were owing them, while to his own troops who had come with him from Syracuse he promised he would pay double the wages which the city had determined.

Dionysius' first major internal difficulty was in 403, when his newly constructed fortress within the city was besieged by citizens who were opposed to tyranny, and more specifically to his tyranny. Dionysius had very few mercenaries with him at that point, and he was not prepared for a lengthy siege. For a time, the situation looked bleak indeed; some of his mercenaries had been seduced by offers of citizenship and had deserted, but despite the blockade he managed to smuggle a letter to his Campanian mercenaries, those who had deserted Acragas, and summoned them to his aid. The citizen rebels felt victory was within their grasp, and some began to disperse. As they did, the Campanian mercenaries arrived, forced their way into the city and broke the siege. It is an interesting side note that we see many more examples of mercenaries deserting their paymasters in the west than we do on the mainland or in the east.

Once Dionysius broke the siege, he had the opportunity to suppress the rebels brutally if he so chose, but he enhanced his reputation amongst the Syracusans by not doing so. In fact, he treated the rebels with a great deal of respect and exacted no punishments that we are aware of for the rebellion. Perhaps Dionysius realized that to treat the citizens harshly was to store up trouble for the future. He did not, however, do nothing. Whilst the citizen farmers were in the fields by day, his mercenaries were searching their homes and confiscating any weapons they found, to reduce the chances of another armed uprising. The citizens seem to have accepted this as being considerably milder punishment than they might have expected.

Dionysius made further moves to increase the size of his mercenary forces. At this time, the Peloponnesian War had just ended in Greece and there were large numbers of unemployed former mercenaries adding to the tension and political unrest on the mainland. Dionysius also had an alliance with Sparta, the victor in that war and therefore the most powerful city-state in Greece, at least for the time being. The Spartans were happy for Dionysius to recruit as many mercenaries as he required from Greece and specifically from the Peloponnese. There were also fertile recruiting grounds in Italy and Spain, as well as the availability of Sicels and Greeks from Sicily itself. In short, Dionysius was in the privileged position of being able to create as large an army as he had money to pay for. On top of these mercenaries, Dionysius could, of course, call upon the citizenry of his various subject states to bolster his forces. He even recruited a citizen force from Syracuse, although he took the precaution of only arming them when they were outside of the city, and of disarming them before they returned, in order to prevent an ugly reoccurrence of the disturbances he had already experienced.

The army Dionysius gathered was huge by any standards, and certainly by the standards of the ancient world:[10]

> He had eighty thousand infantry, well over three thousand cavalry, and a little less than two hundred warships, and he was accompanied by not less than five hundred merchantmen loaded with great numbers of engines of war and all the other supplies needed.

How many of these 83,000 troops were mercenaries is not recorded, and any estimate would be nothing more than a guess. At the same time as he was gathering together this enormous army, Dionysius also hired huge numbers of craftsmen from both the Greek world and the dominions controlled by Carthage by offering larger wages than were available elsewhere. We usually do not hear of this occurring during warfare, or in the build up to it, but craftsmen were just as important as the soldiers themselves in terms of the provision of weapons and armour.[11]

> ... there were made one hundred and forty thousand shields and a like number of daggers and helmets; and in addition corselets were made ready, of every design and wrought with utmost art, more than fourteen thousand in number.

We can reasonably assume that mercenary soldiers would be expected to bring their own weapons and armour, and perhaps be expected to purchase their own replacements. The numbers of helmets, shields and daggers may indicate that many of the 83,000 were citizen soldiers, and the lack of corselets produced may imply that many of those were perhaps equipped as peltasts rather than hoplites. The mercenaries hired may have been equipped as the heavily armed hoplites, much as was the practice of the Persians. Greeks on the mainland, by contrast, typically hired peltast mercenaries rather than hoplites. These manufacturing figures may imply that, in the hiring of mercenaries, the Syracusans acted more like the Persians than the mainland Greeks.

Dionysius' military effort was on an enormous scale, particularly given such a short timescale. These preparations, personally supervised by Dionysius himself, along with the liberal application of bonuses, included two significant military innovations. These were the quinquereme and, perhaps more importantly, the catapult.[12] Diodorus' mention of catapults is the first certain mention of them in history.

Dionysius must have had vast funds in order to make this manufacturing effort happen, and to pay for the huge army. Having said this, he was not profligate with his money. We are told that he ensured that he had the weapons and armour produced before he hired any mercenaries or gathered the citizen soldiers together, which was obviously financially astute. Why hire mercenaries before he was ready to use them, after all?

Once Dionysius' army was ready, equipped and trained, the tyrant lost no further time in his attempt to both conquer Sicily and drive out the Carthaginians. He first captured Aetna, a local rival, before failing to capture the Sicel city of Herbita. From this set-back, he moved onto the Ionian cities of Catane and Naxos.[13] Diodorus tells us that these two cities fell to the Syracusans by means of the treachery of some of the citizens, who opened the gates for the promise of a significant payment in gold. Philip of Macedon became famous for capturing cities by treachery, but he was not the first to do so. Polyaenus, on the other hand, presents a different version of the capture of Naxos:[14]

After agreeing with certain individuals on the betrayal of Naxos, Dionysius approached the walls with 7,000 soldiers late in the day. The Naxians, realizing the threat of betrayal, rushed to the towers. The betrayers called from the towers, telling Dionysius to attack with his entire force. He in turn threatened the men on the walls that if they did not surrender the city voluntarily, he would kill them all. About the same time, at Dionysius' command, one of his fifty-oared ships sailed into the Naxians' harbour, carrying pipers piping and signallers counting time, as if each were directing one trireme. The Naxians, thinking that as many triremes were approaching as the signallers they perceived, became frightened and voluntarily surrendered the city to Dionysius.

Dionysius was of Dorian Greek descent, and he behaved with considerable savagery towards the Ionian cities which he captured. They were both razed to the ground, and the inhabitants, those that survived, were sold into slavery, although the rebels in each city were spared these excesses. The territory of Naxos was given to the Sicels in an attempt to win greater loyalty, and later Catane was given to some of his Campanian mercenaries.[15]

After the sack of these Ionian Greek cities, Dionysius began a siege of Leontini. This city had long been a rival of Syracuse, and this campaign was partly about reducing a rival and partly about expanding his own sphere of influence. The citizens of the city had heard about the fate of the citizens of Catane and Naxos, and they feared what resistance to Dionysius might bring. Their city was fortified, but their citizen numbers were nowhere near what the Syracusans were capable of putting into the field. Dionysius realized that he had an opportunity to capture the city by guile rather than force, seemingly always his prefered option, so he offered the populace of the city citizenship of Syracuse; many accepted and the city fell into his hands. Shortly after this, the city was given to 10,000 of his mercenaries in allotments in lieu of payment. These mercenaries were apparently happy to settle down, which is an interesting statement about their desire to abandon the life of a mercenary when safer, more stable options were presented to them.

In many ways, Dionysius was acting exactly the same as were the Carthaginians, conquering, annexing and sacking where necessary. It is a sobering thought that Dionysius probably destroyed just as many Sicilian cites as did the Carthaginians.[16] Dionysius' war of expansion went well, and occupied his attentions for probably two years from 403.

For some years, Dionysius avoided direct confrontation with the Carthaginian army, preferring to expand his own domain by capturing largely neutral cities. He also invested a great deal of time and money into fortifying Syracuse itself. The Athenian had almost succeeded in capturing the city during their great expedition, thus revealing significant weaknesses in its defences. Dionysius had no intention of allowing another foreign invader the opportunity to exploit those weaknesses a second time. Whilst this work was underway, and whilst Dionysius was consolidating his own position, an uneasy peace reigned between the two rival powers. This also gave the Carthaginians the opportunity to consolidate their own gains in the parts of Sicily they had conquered.[17]

> When Dionysius observed that some of the Greeks were deserting to the Carthaginian domain, taking with them their cities and their estates, he concluded that so long as he was at peace with the Carthaginians many of his subjects would be wanting to join their defection, whereas, if there were war, all who had been enslaved by the Carthaginians would revolt to him. And he also heard that many Carthaginians in Libya had fallen victims to a plague which had raged among them.

By the end of 398, Dionysius' preparations were complete. The army was at full strength, the navy was prepared, and there was a multitude of weapons and armour, along with provisions and finances, for the coming campaign against the Carthaginians. Dionysius' first act was to expel all Phoenicians from the cities under his control and to seize all of their assets, no doubt adding a welcome boost to his treasury. Along with this, he sent a messenger to the Carthaginians offering an ultimatum: free the Greek cities under their control – essentially leave Sicily – or he would declare war.

The Carthaginians were not in a position to go to war with Dionysius. Their homeland had been suffering from plague, with the consequent reduction in their available manpower. The Carthaginians were also not prepared for war logistically. It has been recently noted that it is hard to see how this could have been the case. Dionysius was making open preparations for war for two years, and numerous Phoenician traders must have carried that news back to the Carthaginian hierarchy, yet they had not felt the need to prepare.[18] However unprepared they were, they were not willing to sacrifice their gains in Sicily without a fight, so they dispatched recruiters to Europe to hire a mercenary army as a matter of urgency.

With allies flocking to his banner, Dionysius made first for the Elymian city of Eryx. The city occupied a naturally strong defensive position, but the Syracusans were not required to test their new army quite yet, since the city surrendered at their approach:[19]

> Since the armament was on the great scale we have described, the people of Eryx were awed by the magnitude of the force and, hating the Carthaginians as they did, came over to Dionysius.

Eryx was around 30km north of the main Carthaginian base at Motya, which was Dionysius' real target, and he wasted no further time in approaching it.[20]

> The inhabitants of Motya, however, expecting aid from the Carthaginians, were not dismayed at Dionysius' armament, but made ready to withstand a siege; for they were not unaware that the Syracusans would make Motya the first city to sack, because it was most loyal to the Carthaginians. This city was situated on an island lying six stades off Sicily, and was embellished artistically to the last degree with numerous fine houses, thanks to the prosperity of the inhabitants. It also had a narrow artificial causeway extending to the shore of Sicily, which the Motyans breached at this time, in order that the enemy should have no approach against them.

The causeway that Diodorus mentions could be crossed at low tide, but the Motyans destroyed as much of it as they could before the siege began as part of their very hurried preparations. They also sent messengers to the Carthaginians asking for military aid, and were evidently confident of its arrival; they also felt confident as to the strength of their naturally very defensible position.

Dionysius' troops arrived and made camp to the north side of the city. The Syracusan general then took a detailed survey, along with his engineers, to look for weak points in the defences of the city. In what was an eerie foreshadowing of Alexander the Great's siege of Tyre, Dionysius' response to an island fortress was to begin the construction of a mole that would connect the island to the mainland and allow him to assault the walls directly.[21]

Dionysius also beached his fleet close to the island and constructed a defensive palisade around them. In many ways this was a curious decision, since the Carthaginians still possessed a strong fleet, and we might imagine he needed his own ships to try to prevent reinforcements and supplies from reaching the island fortress, or to blockade key ports. It also seems unlikely that he needed the manpower to build the mole given the size of his army, but that may well have been what the crews ended up doing as the army stood guard, or campaigned elsewhere.

The construction of the mole was not an engineering project that would be completed quickly, and Dionysius was not keen to stand idle whilst the preparations were underway.[22]

> After this he left Leptines his admiral in command of the works, while he himself set out with the infantry of his army against the cities that were allies of the Carthaginians. Now the Sicani, fearing the great size of the army, all went over to the Syracusans, and of the rest of the cities only five remained loyal to the Carthaginians, these being Halicyae, Solus, Aegesta, Panormus, and Entella.

Of those cities that remained loyal to the Carthaginians, their territory was ravaged by the Syracusans:[23]

> Hence Dionysius plundered the territory of Solus and Panormus, and that also of Halicyae, and cut down the trees on it, but he laid siege to Aegesta and Entella with strong forces and launched continuous attacks upon them, seeking to get control of them by force. Such was the state of the affairs of Dionysius.

The Syracusan offensive met with very little Carthaginian resistance, other than from the garrisons in the towns that chose to resist. They were clearly not yet ready to directly contest the control of Sicily after they had failed to prepare adequately for the inevitable war.

The Carthaginians, despite not being prepared at the very outset of the war, recovered quickly, and Himilcon (the Carthaginian general), whilst himself busy with the mustering of the army, dispatched his admiral with ten fast triremes and as many marines as they could carry with instructions to sail to Syracuse, enter the harbour at night and burn any ships left there.[24]

> This he did, expecting to cause a diversion and force Dionysius to send part of his fleet back to the Syracusans. The admiral who had been dispatched carried out his orders with promptness and entered the harbour of the Syracusans by night while everyone was ignorant of what had taken place. Attacking unawares, he rammed the vessels lying at

anchor along the shore, sank practically all of them, and then returned to Carthage.

The destruction at Syracuse did not distract Dionysius from his offensive:[25]

> Dionysius, after ravaging all the territory held by the Carthaginians and forcing the enemy to take refuge behind walls, led all his army against Motya; for he hoped that when this city had been reduced by siege, all the others would forthwith surrender themselves to him. Accordingly, he at once put many times more men on the task of filling up the strait between the city and the coast, and, as the mole was extended, advanced his engines of war little by little toward the walls.

As with Alexander's later mole, Diodorus presents a picture that its construction was fairly rapid, but in reality an engineering project of this scale must have taken several months, time enough for Dionysius to conduct any secondary expeditions.

When Himilcon's scouts reported back to him that Dionysius had grounded his fleet intentionally, he saw an opportunity to deliver a crippling blow to Syracusan naval power. Having already scored a major victory in the harbour at Syracuse, a second victory here would leave him master of the seas around Sicily, a dominant position that would make supporting the land army far easier. Diodorus even tells us that Himilcon felt that if this plan was successful be could attack Syracuse in force and transfer the war to Dionysius' home city.[26]

The Carthaginians manned one hundred of his best triremes and immediately set off for Motya. They sailed during the night to Selinus, skirted the promontory of Lilybaeum, and arrived at Motya at daybreak, taking the enemy completely by surprise. He attacked immediately and destroyed a number of ships that were still in the harbour either by ramming or burning. The Syracusans could do nothing to prevent the loss of these ships; they were unprepared for such an attack and taken utterly by surprise.[27]

> After this he sailed into the harbour and drew up his ships as if to attack the vessels which the enemy had drawn up on land. Dionysius now massed his army at the entrance of the harbour; but when he saw that the enemy was lying in wait to attack as the ships left the harbour, he refused to risk launching his ships within the harbour, since he realized that the narrow entrance compelled a few ships to match themselves against an enemy many times more numerous. Consequently, using the multitude of his soldiers, he hauled his vessels over the land with no difficulty and launched them safely in the sea outside the harbour. Himilcon attacked the first ships, but was held back by the multitude of

missiles; for Dionysius had manned the ships with a great number of archers and slingers, and the Syracusans slew many of the enemy by using from the land the catapults which shot sharp-pointed missiles. Indeed this weapon created great dismay, because it was a new invention at this time. As a result, Himilcon was unable to achieve his design and sailed away to Libya, believing that a sea-battle would serve no end, since the enemy's ships were double his in number.

Himilcon had lost a golden opportunity to strike a decisive blow against the Syracusans, and he was forced to withdraw back to North Africa with his tail between his legs. His retreat is itself interesting, as evidently his new mercenary army had either not yet arrived from Greece, or it was not yet fully equipped and ready for battle.

After defeating Himilcon's surprise naval assault, Dionysius put greater efforts into the completion of the mole. He did this by hiring huge numbers of labourers, and most likely using the sailors from the fleet, as noted earlier. When the mole was finally complete, he moved his war machines into position and began to assault the fortress in earnest.[28]

> ... he advanced war engines of every kind against the walls and kept hammering the towers with his battering-rams, while with the catapults he kept down the fighters on the battlements; and he also advanced against the walls his wheeled towers, six stories high, which he had built to equal the height of the houses.

It is an interesting note that the catapults were being employed to suppress the infantry on the battlements rather than to directly assault the walls; stone-throwing torsion catapults were not invented until the mid to late fourth century, probably in Macedonia. The catapults constructed by Dionysius were bolt throwers, essentially large crossbows.

The inhabitants of Motya were not cowed by the Syracusan mercenary army with its array of new weapons, or the vast number of troops at their gates. They still held out hope that the Carthaginians would arrive with their own force of mercenaries to reinforce their defences. Much like the defenders of Tyre when faced with the same situation, the Motyans were incredibly inventive in their own defence, but their efforts were ultimately futile:[29]

> Surpassing the besiegers in thirst for glory, they in the first place raised up men in crow's-nests resting on yard-arms suspended from the highest possible masts, and these from their lofty positions hurled lighted fire-brands and burning tow with pitch on the enemies' siege

engines. The flame quickly caught the wood, but the Sicilian Greeks, dashing to the rescue, swiftly quenched it; and meantime the frequent blows of the battering-rams broke down a section of the wall. Since now both sides rushed with one accord to the place, the battle that ensued grew furious. For the Sicilian Greeks, believing that the city was already in their hands, spared no effort in retaliating upon the Phoenicians for former injuries they had suffered at their hands, while the people of the city, envisioning the terrible fate of a life of captivity and seeing no possibility of flight either by land or by sea, faced death stoutly.

Once the Syracusans broke into the city the defenders did not give up; the Carthaginian defenders knew they would likely suffer badly at the hands of Dionysius, and the Motyans equally feared the consequences, and besides were fighting for their homes. Diodorus gives us a vivid description of the hand-to-hand fighting, of running battles that were street by street, but once the besiegers were inside the walls the fate of the city was sealed. The Syracusans greatly outnumbered the defenders, and the mercenaries and Sicilian Greeks alike took out their frustrations on the defenders of the city, unleashing the full horrors of warfare upon the citizen population. Dionysius tried to stop the worst excesses, not out of some humanitarian sympathies, but because he viewed the city as now belonging to him, and therefore they were destroying his property. On top of which, he also wanted to sell the surviving inhabitants into slavery and raise funds to pay for his mercenaries.

In the days after the capture of the island fortress, once the dust had settled and the fires had been extinguished, Dionysius left Biton in charge of what remained of the city with a garrison of Sicel mercenaries. On top of these would likely have been a detachment of engineers and labourers who would endeavour to rebuild the defences in case the Carthaginians counter-attacked. Along with Biton was Leptines with 120 warships, with orders to oppose any further attempt by the Carthaginians at crossing from Africa to Sicily. Leptines was also charged with the continued sieges of Aegesta and Entella. Having successfully captured Motya, Dionysius then marched his mercenary army back to Syracuse.[30] Diodorus notes that the campaigning season was coming to a close, but why a standing army of mercenaries needed to retire to Syracuse at this point is an oddity. They could easily have continued the war against the remnants of the Carthaginian forces still in Sicily whilst they had the advantage.

At the time, the Syracusans would have seen the capture of the main Carthaginian base on Sicily, coupled with the defeat of their naval forces in the area, as a major victory. In reality, however, it solved little.

Dionysius did not sit back and await the Carthaginian response to his capture of their key strategic towns, but in the following year:[31]

> In the year [396] Dionysius, the tyrant of the Syracusans, set out from Syracuse with his entire army and invaded the domain of the Carthaginians. While he was laying waste the countryside, the Halicyaeans in dismay sent an embassy to him and concluded an alliance. But the Aegestaeans, falling unexpectedly by night on their besiegers and setting fire to the tents where they were camped, threw the men in the encampment into great confusion; for since the flames spread over a large area and the fire could not be brought under control, a few of the soldiers who came to the rescue lost their lives and most of the horses were burned, together with the tents. Now Dionysius ravaged the Carthaginian territory without meeting any opposition, and Leptines his admiral from his quarters in Motya kept watch against any approach of the enemy by sea.

Dionysius, after a winter's rest and recuperation, was again trying to drive the Carthaginians out of Sicily. The Carthaginians had done little in reality to oppose the Syracusans to this point, save for the naval operations. This seems to be because they were inexplicably unprepared for the Dionysian offensive. This time, however, they had spent their time wisely:[32]

> Consequently, lawfully according Himilcon sovereign power, they gathered armaments from all Libya as well as from Iberia, summoning some from their allies and in other cases hiring mercenaries. In the end they collected more than three hundred thousand infantry, four thousand cavalry in addition to chariots, which numbered four hundred, four hundred ships of war, and over six hundred other vessels to convey food and engines of war and other supplies. These are the numbers stated by Ephorus. Timaeus, on the other hand, says that the troops transported from Libya did not exceed one hundred thousand and declares that an additional thirty thousand were enlisted in Sicily.

The Carthaginians had finally gathered together a sizeable force; the mercenary recruiters had obviously returned, and their allies were providing troops rather than simply financial aid. The new Carthaginian army was comparable to that of Dionysius and perhaps somewhat stronger (even taking into account the obvious exaggerations in Diodorus regarding the size of each).

Dionysius began his campaign of 396 with a march towards Aegesta. He was not prepared for their bold counter-attack, however, and many of his tents and most of his horses were lost. The setback was minor, however, and he continued on to pillage the territory of Panormus and Soluntum, no doubt keeping his mercenary forces happy. The Syracusans met no further resistance during this time.

Himilcon and the Carthaginians did not sail until late summer. In an intriguing episode, the king gave sealed orders to his naval captains that were only to be opened when they had set sail, for fear that Greek spies would uncover his strategic plans and communicate them to Dionysius. Their destination was likely to be one of two places: Syracuse, for a bold surprise attack as they had attempted previously, or the largest of the surviving Carthaginian bases in Sicily, Panormus. The latter was the chosen destination. When the Carthaginians came within sight of Sicily, Leptines sailed out to oppose them, as were his orders.[33]

> The wind continued favourable, and as soon as the leading vessels of the transports were visible from Sicily, Dionysius dispatched Leptines with thirty triremes under orders to ram and destroy all he could intercept. Leptines sailed forth promptly and straightway sank, together with their men, the first ships he encountered, but the rest, having all canvas spread and catching the wind with their sails, easily made their escape. Nevertheless, fifty ships were sunk, together with five thousand soldiers and two hundred chariots.

Leptines accomplished more than Dionysius could realistically have hoped with only 30 triremes. The loss of 5,000 soldiers was a significant blow to the Carthaginians. Although we do not know of their origins, the impact on morale would likely have been far from negligible. Once the remainder of the fleet reached Panormus, Himilcon disembarked his army and immediately marched out to engage the enemy. As already noted, it was late in the campaigning season and he could not afford to waste any more time. He first captured Eryx by treachery, but his ultimate goal was the recapture of the iconic island stronghold of Motya. We know very little of the Carthaginian campaign against Motya, but they appear to have recaptured it without the struggle Dionysius had had. This is likely because the mole was already constructed and the walls were probably still in a poor state of repair. The garrison of Sicel mercenaries also evidently did not put up a particularly heroic resistance.

Fearing the length of his supply lines, Dionysius did not march to engage Himilcon, but withdrew back to the vicinity of Syracuse. Himilcon had no such defensive strategy in mind. He made plans for the capture of Messene; its harbour was one of the largest on Sicily and capable of housing the whole of his 600-vessel fleet. It would also control the potential supply of aid to Syracuse from both southern Italy and the Peloponnese. Before he marched on Messene, Himilcon made an alliance with the Himeraeans and those defenders of the fort at Cephaloedium, 15 miles east of Himera. The Carthaginians also captured the island of Lipara and exacted a tribute of 30 talents that would be most welcome to the treasurers of the army.[34]

> Then he set out in person with his entire army toward Messene, his ships sailing along the coast beside him. Completing the distance in a brief time, he pitched his camp at Peloris, at a distance of one hundred stades from Messene. When the inhabitants of this city learned that the enemy was at hand, they could not agree among themselves about the war. One party, when they heard reports of the great size of the enemy's army and observed that they themselves were without any allies – what is more, that their own cavalry were at Syracuse – were fully convinced that nothing could save them from capture. What contributed most to their despair was the fact that their walls had fallen down and that the situation allowed no time for their repair. Consequently, they removed from the city their children and wives and most valuable possessions to neighbouring cities.

The Messenians were determined to resist the invaders, and appear to have received no help from Syracuse in this. They marched out to face the Carthaginians, presumably greatly outnumbered. Himilcon, however, rather than simply engaging the enemy, with the inevitable loss of life that that would entail, instructed 200 of his ships to sail around the coast, land troops near Messene and capture the city whilst their troops were on campaign. Some Messenians made it back in time to help the defence of the city, but the attacking force was too strong, and the Messenian walls too weak to resist. Himilcon easily captured the city by a brilliant tactic that involved minimal loss to his army, or to the city. Diodorus preserves a vivid description of the chaos at the fall of the city to the Carthaginians:[35]

> Of the Messenians, some were slain as they put up a gallant fight, others fled to the nearest cities, but the great mass of the common people took to flight through the surrounding mountains and scattered among the fortresses of the territory; of the rest, some were captured by the enemy and some, who had been cut off in the area near the harbour, hurled themselves into the sea in hopes of swimming across the intervening strait. These numbered more than two hundred and most of them were overcome by the current, only fifty making their way in safety to Italy.

Himilcon moved his entire army into the city and made camp there. He detached groups of mercenaries to reduce the forts that were in the vicinity, but these were all strongly held and well situated and he made little head-way. Not wishing to lose troops unnecessarily, he retired to the city again to gather his forces for the final push on Syracuse. Again, it is noticeable that Dionysius made no move to arrest the advance of Himilcon, or to aid any of the cities and fortresses in his path. Some well-timed and directed aid could have caused the Carthaginians significant losses and made any future battle or siege that much easier for the Syracusans, but the opportunity was missed. Himilcon separated his forces for the final stages of the advance, with Magon commanding a fleet of some 500 ships, whilst the land army marched towards Syracuse. Leptines, still the commander of the Syracusan fleet, sailed to meet Magon. Initially, Leptines attacked with only thirty handpicked ships.[36]

> Leptines advanced with his thirty best vessels far ahead of the rest and joined battle, in no cowardly fashion, but without prudence. Attacking forthwith the leading ships of the Carthaginians, at the outset he sank no small number of the opposing triremes; but when Magon's massed ships crowded about the thirty, the forces of Leptines surpassed in valour, but the Carthaginians in numbers. Consequently, as the battle grew fiercer, the steersmen laid their ships broadside in the fighting and the struggle came to resemble conflicts on land. For they did not drive upon the opposing ships from a distance in order to ram them, but the vessels were locked together and the fighting was hand to hand. Some, as they leaped for the enemy's ships, fell into the sea, and others, who succeeded in their attempt, continued the struggle on the opponents' ships. In the end, Leptines was driven off and compelled to flee to the open sea, and his remaining ships, attacking without order, were overcome by the Carthaginians; for the defeat suffered by the admiral raised the spirits of the Carthaginians and markedly discouraged the Sicilian Greeks.

In an action more reminiscent of a land battle, the Carthaginians followed the retreating Syracusan ships and destroyed many more ships that had been held in reserve. Magon also stationed his smaller vessels along the coastline with orders to kill any enemy sailors or marines who tried to swim to shore. Diodorus tells us the losses on the Syracusan side were over 100 ships and 20,000 men; exaggeration of course, but the losses would have been significant.[37] The Carthaginians had not only succeeded in disabling a major part of the Greek fleet, but they also towed into port any damaged Greek ships that they had partially sunk or otherwise captured, and repaired them, bolstering their own fleet in the process.

The Greeks must now have expected a lengthy siege, but Dionysius' advisors urged him to march out against the Carthaginians, partly to save the city from the privations of siege warfare, and partly because they felt

Himilcon would not be expecting a direct assault, given the Syracusans' unwillingness to engage the enemy to that point. Dionysius initially was persuaded by this, but ultimately refused for fear Magon would simply sail into the harbour and capture the city while the army was away. Dionysius did not have the strength to leave a major proportion of his mercenary forces in Syracuse to defend against that possibility, and still have a large enough land army to defeat Himilcon. Dionysius was aware that the Carthaginians had captured Messene with little bloodshed precisely because their army ill-advisedly marched out to meet the enemy host; he would not make the same mistake.

Himilcon paused in his advance upon Syracuse at Catane, where he beached his ships to protect them from a storm. Whilst here, he sent an embassy to the Campanian mercenaries in Dionysius' employ at Etna in an attempt to ferment rebellion. He told them of the other Campanian mercenaries already in his army, and of the good treatment that they had received. The Campanians appear to have been open to these advances, but ultimately remained loyal because of the hostages that Dionysius had taken, and also to ensure the safety of their countrymen currently stationed with the Syracusans.

Seeing the Carthaginians inexorably approaching, evidently intent now on forcing a conclusion with Syracuse, Dionysius sent his brother-in-law, Polyxenus, as ambassador to the Italian Greeks, and then onto the Peloponnese and Corinth, requesting aid against the common enemy. Whilst Polyxenus was attempting to garner the support of allied states, others were sent to the Peloponnese with funds sufficient to recruit another large mercenary army. There they were told to 'enlist as many soldiers as they could without regard to economy.'[38]

Himilcon's navy now sailed into the harbour of Syracuse, to some an act reminiscent of the Athenian expedition during the Peloponnesian War.[39]

> Himilcon decked his ships with the spoils taken from the enemy and put in at the great harbour of the Syracusans, and he caused great dismay among the inhabitants of the city. For two hundred and fifty ships of war entered the harbour, with oars flashing in order and richly decked with the spoils of war; then came the merchantmen, in excess of three thousand, laden with more than five hundred ... and the whole fleet numbered some two thousand vessels. The result was that the harbour of the Syracusans, despite its great size, was blocked up by the vessels and it was almost entirely concealed from view by the sails.

At the same time as the Carthaginian navy were occupying the harbour, the land army advanced upon the city in what was no doubt a deliberately coordinated act. It made camp close to the city, and soon after advanced towards the walls in battle order in a challenge to the defenders. The Syracusans did not march out to meet them; if they were struggling for manpower (hence the diplomatic and recruitment missions) then they would have been foolish indeed to sacrifice the advantage of their walls for a set-piece battle. The Carthaginians retired to their camp and spent the next thirty days ravaging the countryside, gathering as much plunder and supplies as were available.[40] During this time, Himilcon allowed his mercenaries to virtually run riot over the local area, and he appears not to have made any attempt to siege the city, other than to blockade it. As the blockade entered its second month:[41]

> Himilcon seized the suburb of Achradine; and he also plundered the temples of both Demeter and Core, for which acts of impiety against the divinity he quickly suffered a fitting penalty. For his fortune quickly worsened from day to day, and whenever Dionysius made bold to skirmish with him, the Syracusans had the better of it. Also at night unaccountable tumults would arise in the camp and the soldiers would rush to arms, thinking that the enemy was attacking the palisade. To this was added a plague which was the cause of every kind of suffering. But of this we shall speak a little later, in order that our account may not anticipate the proper time.

The act of looting the temples was again likely because of the need for plunder to swell his coffers, to allow him to pay for his huge mercenary army. This is probably also the reason that he allowed them to plunder the locality of the city with impunity. The 'tumult' of which Diodorus speaks is perhaps some form of internal dissent, but we know nothing of the causes, if it even existed at all.

The sorties of the Syracusans were starting to have an impact upon the Carthaginians, not in terms of the losses they inflicted, as the host was large enough to deal with minor losses, but upon the morale of the besiegers. To defend his troops, Himilcon built a wall around their camp using materials salvaged from the tombs of the area, among them that of Gelon (the former tyrant) and his wife Demarete. He also built three forts in the area to strengthen the blockade of the city. Himilcon also made every effort to gather grain and as much water as he could, both from the surrounding areas and by sending merchantmen back to North Africa; a rare glimpse into the logistics of an ancient army. Whilst Himilcon was strengthening his stranglehold by land, Polyxenus arrived back with thirty warships from the Peloponnese commanded by a Lacedaemonian called Pharacidas. We do not hear of any further mercenary reinforcements arriving with these ships; the recruiting mission was evidently going slowly. The Carthaginian fleet must have with-drawn from the immediate vicinity of the harbour, but where they were stationed is not mentioned.

The Syracusans were themselves running short of supplies, but merchant-men were still prepared to attempt access to Syracuse, despite the presence of a major Carthaginian fleet. Dionysius himself, along with his admiral Leptines, left the safety of the harbour with a part of the fleet to escort a supply convoy back to Syracuse. The Syracusans were temporarily left under the command of an unnamed subordinate of the tyrant, but the leading citizens clearly felt they had an opportunity to act independently and to attempt to influence events.[42]

> The Syracusans, who were thus left to themselves, seeing by chance a vessel approaching laden with food, sailed out against it with five ships, seized it, and brought it to the city. The Carthaginians put out against them with forty ships, whereupon the Syracusans manned all their ships and in the ensuing battle both captured the flag-ship and destroyed twenty-four of the remainder; and then, pursuing the fleeing ships as far as the enemy's anchorage, they challenged the Carthaginians to battle. When the latter, confused at the unexpected turn of events, made no move, the Syracusans took the captured ships in tow and brought them to the city. Elated at their success and thinking how often Dionysius had met defeat, whereas they, without his presence, had won a victory over the Carthaginians, they were now puffed up with pride.

Dionysius was still implementing his policy of not arming the citizens, but had been forced to temporarily relax the rules because of the siege. The citizens now saw something of an opportunity to make a break for freedom, as they were armed and Dionysius was away from the city escorting the transport vessels. As they were contemplating a coup, however, Dionysius sailed back into the harbour with the supply ships. Recognizing the mood, Dionysius held an assembly meeting where strong views were expressed as to his abilities and the likelihood of his wining the current war. Amongst the stinging criticism, we are told:[43]

> Because of him [Dionysius] Gela and Camarina were subdued, Messene lies in total ruin, twenty thousand allies are perished in a sea-battle, and, in a word, we have been enclosed in one city and all the other Greek cities throughout Sicily have been destroyed. For in addition to his other malefactions he sold into slavery Naxos and Catane; he has completely destroyed cities that were allies, cities whose existence was opportune. With the Carthaginians he has fought two battles and

has come out vanquished in each. Yet when he was entrusted with a generalship by the citizens but one time, he speedily robbed them of their freedom, slaying those who spoke openly on behalf of the laws and exiling the more wealthy; he gave the wives of the banished in marriage to slaves and to a motley throng; he put the weapons of citizens in the hands of barbarians and foreigners. And these deeds, O Zeus and all the gods, were the work of a public clerk, of a desperate man.

The speaker goes on to say that they had previously been guarded by a multitude of mercenaries, almost reduced to slavery in their own city because of Dionysius' policy of refusing to allow them to carry (or own) arms, a policy that did not apply to the mercenary soldiers.[44] Since they were now armed, however, the speaker urged the citizenry to remove the tyrant, allowing them to be free, although not taking into account the enormous mercenary army at their gates.

At the end of the anti-Dionysian speeches, the Lacedaemonian admiral spoke to the assembly, stating that he had been sent to aid Syracuse and Dionysius, not to overthrow him. At this the mercenaries which Dionysius had no doubt stationed close by rushed to surround the tyrant to protect him lest the assembly turn violent. The citizenry made no move against the tyrant, save for the shouting of abuse. Worried the situation could descend into violence, and fully aware the city was under siege, Dionysius dismissed the assembly and resumed his position, backed as always by his mercenaries.

Whilst the Carthaginians were fortifying their camp with building material from the desecrated Greek tombs, a plague began to take hold in their camp. Diodorus tells us that the siege was occurring at the most prolific time of year for diseases to take hold, that it had been particularly warm, and that with so many men in close proximity it spread more quickly; very astute observations.[45] The plague spread quickly and the Carthaginians were overwhelmed by the casualties. The plague caused death in the fifth or sixth day after contracting the disease, and people were dying faster than their bodies could be disposed of. Even those handling the corpses while carrying them to the funeral pyres were contracting the disease.[46]

When Dionysius heard of the disaster that had struck the Carthaginians, he manned eighty ships and ordered Pharacidas and Leptines the admirals to attack the enemy's ships at daybreak, while he himself, profiting by a moonless night, made a circuit with his army and, passing by the temple of Cyane, arrived near the camp of the enemy at daybreak before they were aware of it. The cavalry and a thousand infantry from the mercenaries were dispatched in advance against that part of the Carthaginian encampment which extended toward the interior. These mercenaries were the most hostile, beyond all others, to Dionysius and had engaged time and again in factional quarrels and uproars.

The situation Dionysius was trying to control was not an easy one. His citizenry were prepared to take every opportunity to try to overthrow him, and his position was only maintained by his mercenary forces. Even these, however, were not a coherent, disciplined unit; there was factional infighting amongst them too. In a remarkable act of betrayal, Dionysius:[47]

> had issued orders to the cavalry that as soon as they came to blows with the enemy they should flee and leave the mercenaries in the lurch; when this order had been carried out and the mercenaries had been slain to a man, Dionysius set about laying siege to both the camp and the forts. While the barbarians were still dismayed at the unexpected attack and bringing up reinforcements in disorderly fashion, he on his part took by storm the fort known as Polichna; and on the opposite side the cavalry, aided in an attack by some of the triremes, stormed the area around Dascon.

After the capture of two of the Carthaginian forts, Dionysius ordered a general assault by land and sea. The Carthaginians were depleted by the plague and utterly unprepared for a fight. The Syracusan navy, supported by land forces, attacked the compound where Himilcon had stationed his triremes; some were set on fire, others rammed and sunk. On the day of the attack there was a strong wind which fanned the flames, spreading them quickly from ship to ship. After victory over the troops guarding the Carthaginian ships, and against those ships that had managed to put to sea, Dionysius was unable to contain the plundering that followed:[48]

> Forthwith elated by the Syracusan successes, both the oldest youths and such aged men as were not yet entirely incapacitated by years manned lighters, and approaching without order all together made for the ships in the harbour. Those which the fire had ruined they plundered, stripping them of anything that could be saved, and such as were undamaged they took in tow and brought to the city. Thus even those who by age were exempt from war duties were unable to restrain themselves, but in their excessive joy their ardent spirit prevailed over their age. When the news of the victory ran through the city, children and women, together with their households, left their homes, everyone hurrying to the walls, and the whole extent was crowded with spectators.

With the loss of their fleet, the Carthaginians sued for terms. They offered Dionysius 300 talents if the army were allowed to return to North Africa unmolested. Dionysius could not agree to these terms, but he did agree to allow the Carthaginians to escape, but only the Carthaginian nationals. The mercenaries and any other allies were to remain behind. The payment of 300 talents was also to be paid. Diodorus argues that Dionysius was happy to allow the Carthaginians to escape to ensure there was still an enemy, and thus a focus for the citizens of Syracuse. He worried that if they were to experience a prolonged state of peace, a revolt might be more likely. He ordered his troops to withdraw from the crippled Carthaginian fleet, and several days later, during the night (as agreed), the Carthaginian nationals made for their ships and sailed back to North Africa with as much as they could carry, having first deposited 300 talents with Dionysius' representatives. To keep up appearances, Dionysius led his army out of Syracuse in a belated attempt to stop the fleeing Carthaginians, but they succeeded in allowing them to escape as per the agreement between Himilcon and Dionysius. This left the Carthaginian camp populated by the mercenaries who had so far survived the plague. Without their paymaster, and without any offer of employment from Dionysius, they fled immediately. For the time being, the war against the Carthaginians was over.

The Carthaginians recovered slowly from their defeat, and the deprivations of the plague, but by 392 they were ready for another attempt to exert their influence over Sicily. This time their invasion force consisted of:[49]

> ... only a few warships, but brought together troops from Libya and Sardinia as well as from the barbarians of Italy. The soldiers were all carefully supplied with equipment to which they were accustomed and brought over to Sicily, being no less than eighty thousand in number and under the command of Magon.

They landed in western Sicily and immediately began to win over by force, deception or threats some of the cities in that region loyal to Dionysius, but they did not advance far into the interior, as Dionysius, unlike during the earlier invasion, gathered his forces quickly and marched out to confront this new threat. The Syracusan tyrant gathered to his banner as many citizen soldiers as he could arm, and hired a large mercenary army (from where and how this was achieved so quickly we are not told); his forces numbered around 20,000.[50]

> When he came near the enemy he sent an embassy to Agyris, the lord of the Agyrinaeans. This man possessed the strongest armament of any of the tyrants of Sicily at that time after Dionysius, since he was lord of practically all the neighbouring fortified communities and ruled the city of the Agyrinaeans which was well peopled at that time, for it had no less

than twenty thousand citizens. There was also laid up on the acropolis for this multitude which had been gathered together in the city a large store of money which Agyris had collected after he had murdered the wealthiest citizens. But Dionysius, after entering the city with a small company, persuaded Agyris to join him as a genuine ally and promised to make him a present of a large portion of neighbouring territory if the war ended successfully.

This was a vital alliance for Dionysius to have concluded as he approached the enemy; it secured for him not only extra front-line troops but also supplies to feed his existing army during the campaign.

Magnon and the Carthaginians were at a significant disadvantage now, being in hostile territory with long supply lines. The troops of Agyris were harrying them at every opportunity, laying ambushes at opportune positions, and not allowing their foraging parties to work unmolested. The Syracusan generals wanted to attack Magnon, but Dionysius held back, saying that 'time and want would ruin the barbarians without fighting.'[51] Dionysius' strategy proved very astute; the Carthaginians could not survive for long in hostile territory without supplies, and so Magnon sued for peace. Once the treaty was concluded, Magnon sailed back to North Africa without a major engagement. The treaty ceded to Dionysius the territory of the Sicels, the majority of whom he banished; in their place, he settled the best of his mercenaries. By 383, Dionysius was ready to finally drive the Carthaginians out of Sicily.[52]

> This year Dionysius, the tyrant of the Syracusans, after preparations for war upon the Carthaginians, looked about to find a reasonable excuse for the conflict. Seeing, then, that the cities subject to the Carthaginians were favourable to a revolt, he received such as wished to do so, formed an alliance with them, and treated them with fairness. The Carthaginians at first dispatched ambassadors to the ruler and asked for the return of their cities, and when he paid no attention to them, this came to be the beginning of the war.

When Dionysius ignored the Carthaginian ambassadors, it became obvious to Magnon, their king, that war was inevitable. Realizing the potential severity of the coming war, Magnon reaffirmed alliances with some of the southern Italian states, armed his citizen soldiers and hired as many mercenaries as his treasury would allow. Once his army was ready, he shipped 'many tens of thousands of soldiers across to Sicily and Italy, planning to wage war on two fronts.'[53] Dionysius responded by also dividing his forces; some he sent to Italy, but the majority remained behind in Sicily. The first few months of the campaign saw many minor skirmishes on both fronts, but no decisive encounters. Each side was wary of the other and looking for both weaknesses and opportunities. There were, however, two major engagements:[54]

> In the first, near Cabala, as it is called, Dionysius, who put up an admirable fight, was victorious, slaying more than ten thousand of the barbarians and capturing not less than five thousand. He also forced the rest of the army to take refuge on a hill which was fortified but altogether without water. There fell also Magnon their king after a splendid combat.

With their forces in Sicily defeated twice, and their king dead, the Carthaginians sued for peace. Unlike in previous campaigns, however, Dionysius saw an opportunity to rid Sicily of the Carthaginian presence permanently. His reply to the envoys was that he would accept peace only on condition that all Carthaginians left Sicily and their cities be handed over to him. The Carthaginians were loathe to accept such terms, but requested a few days in which to gather the views of the cities in question; a request that Dionysius readily agreed to, as he thought their acceptance was a formality. The Carthaginians used the time to give Magnon a great funeral and to replace him as their supreme commander with his son. They then spent the whole of the time of the truce drilling and training their troops to a higher state of competence than they had demonstrated during their two defeats at the hands of the Greeks. When the period of the truce expired, the Carthaginians set up their troops in battle array and awaited the Syracusan response. Seeing that the truce was nothing more than a ruse, Dionysius ordered his troops to take to the field as well. The ensuing battle was fought at Cronium in 379:[55]

> Leptines, who was stationed on one wing and excelled in courage, ended his life in a blaze of glory, fighting heroically and after slaying many Carthaginians. At his fall the Phoenicians were emboldened and pressed so hard upon their opponents that they put them to flight. Dionysius, whose troops were a select band, at first had the advantage over his opponents; but when the death of Leptines became known and the other wing was crushed, his men were dismayed and took to flight.

Once the Greeks were routed and fleeing, the Carthaginians pursued them with orders to take no one alive. The slaughter was terrible; perhaps up to 14,000 Greeks were killed, the majority of that number during the flight after the defeat. The bloodshed was only stopped by nightfall. The surviving Greeks had made it to their camp, and the Carthaginians retired to Panormus. The Carthaginians, happy with their victory, chose not to press the issue with the Syracusans, perhaps feeling they were ultimately not strong enough to capture Syracuse, given their lack of a large-enough fleet. Embassies were dispatched to Dionysius offering to end the war:[56]

> The tyrant gladly accepted the proposals, and peace was declared on the terms that both parties should hold what they previously possessed, the only exception being that the Carthaginians received both the city of the Selinuntians and its territory and that of Acragas as far as the river called Halycus. And Dionysius paid the Carthaginians one thousand talents.

Dionysius had little choice but to accept terms, since he lacked the strength to drive the Carthaginians out of Sicily. This treaty ended what could have proved to be a long and indecisive war, but it did not end the ambitions of Dionysius to control the whole of Sicily. In 367, Dionysius made his final attempt to seize Sicily in its entirety, but again achieved nothing of note. He died during the campaign and, whilst the cause is debated, it appears not to have been on the battlefield. The passing of Dionysius was the end of an era in mercenary service; he had been one of the largest and most consistent employers of mercenaries the ancient world had seen. Whilst he used them to maintain his power base, they were ultimately unsuccessful in achieving his aim of controlling the whole of Sicily.

In 366, Dionysius I was succeeded by his son, Dionysius II. The new tyrant had none of his father's ability or ambition, and he immediately sued for peace with the Carthaginians. With a series of expensive foreign wars conducted by his father having seriously depleted the treasury, Dionysius II tried to reduce the wage paid to his mercenaries, with very nearly disastrous results. The mercenary forces that he inherited threatened revolt at the prospect of lower wages. Dionysius II was, however, wise enough to understand that he needed them and backed down before he was abandoned. The leader of the miniature mercenary rebellion was Heracleides, who left Syracuse immediately after these difficulties. He reappeared in 357 in Corinth with Dion, another exile from Syracuse. Together they formulated a plot to overthrow Dionysius II. The two appear to have had something of a history of this, one reason why both were in the Peloponnese.[57] They agreed to sail in two separate detachments with the intention of overthrowing Dionysius II. They gathered small groups of mercenaries without informing them of their ultimate goal, not wholly unusual, as Cyrus' 10,000 were in the same boat when initially hired. Dion met up with his mercenaries on route to Sicily:[58]

> The rendezvous was the island of Zacynthus, and here the soldiers were assembled. They numbered fewer than eight hundred, but they

were all well known in consequence of many great campaigns, their bodies were exceptionally well trained, while in experience and daring they had no equals in the world, and were capable of inciting and inflaming to share their prowess all the host which Dion expected to have in Sicily.

Although Dion's mercenary army was small, it consisted of highly trained veterans and would have the advantage of a certain amount of stealth. Dion set sail for Sicily in midsummer of 357 in perhaps only five vessels, again with stealth being paramount.[59] Whilst in the ships bound for Sicily, Dion revealed to his mercenaries their true destination, and again, as with Cyrus' 10,000 when they became aware of their goal, they thought their mission mad and were only persuaded to continue with difficulty.

They eventually landed to the west of Sicily in Carthaginian-controlled territory, but their force was small enough to go unnoticed. They anticipated gathering local dissidents to their cause and carried with them several thousand panoplies of spare armour.[60] Recruits were not hard to find. Once Dion marched into territory controlled by Dionysius II, thousands flocked to the rebel banner.[61] Either by good fortune or blind luck, Dion was marching upon Syracuse whilst Dionysius II was campaigning in Italy, and the citizens of that city were not unhappy to see his approach. We can assume this from the numbers of volunteers that joined him as he marched. Dionysius' mercenaries, mostly Campanians from Leontini, felt no such desire to rid themselves of their paymaster. In an excellent display of tactical awareness, Dion let it be known that he intended to attack Leontini.[62] This had exactly the desired effect of encouraging the mercenaries to flee to protect their homes and families. Dion, of course, waited until the mercenaries were removed and marched on Syracuse. He entered the city as a liberator, but was flanked by a mercenary bodyguard.

Dionysius retuned around a week after Dion occupied the city, and the latter had not spent that week idly. He had fortified his position within the city, and he rejected Dionysius' initial attempts at diplomacy.[63]

> For this reason on both sides men outstanding in gallantry met in the action and since Dionysius' mercenaries, by the size of the promised rewards, and the Syracusans, by the hope of freedom, were wrought up to a high pitch of rivalry, at first the battle stood equally poised, as the valour of both sides in the fight was equal. Many fell, and not a few were wounded, receiving all the blows in front; for on the one hand those in the front rank courageously met death defending the rest, and those arrayed behind them covering them with their shields as they

fell and holding firm in the desperate peril took the most dangerous risks to win the victory.

The mercenaries on both sides fought ferociously, Dionysius' because of the promises he had made of huge rewards, Dion's men partly because they had no escape and partly after an inspirational individual act from Dion himself:[64]

> After this engagement Dion, wishing to display his valour in the battle and eager to win the victory by his own deeds, forced his way into the midst of the enemy and there in an heroic encounter slew many and having disrupted the whole battle line of the mercenaries was suddenly cut off and isolated in the crowd. Many missiles hurled at him fell upon his shield and helmet, but he escaped these owing to the protection of his armour, but receiving a wound on his right arm he was borne down by the weight of the blow and barely escaped capture by the enemy. The Syracusans, fearing for their general's safety, dashed into the mercenaries in heavy formation and rescued the distressed Dion from his perils, then overpowering the enemy, forced them to flee. Since likewise in the other part of the wall the Syracusans had the superiority, the tyrant's mercenaries were chased in a body inside the gates of the Island. The Syracusans, who had now won victory in a significant battle and had securely recovered their freedom, set up a trophy to signalize the tyrant's defeat.

Heracleides then arrived with the second wave of troops: 1,500 mercenaries to bolster their now combined position. This was not a blessing for Dion as the bulk of the work had already been completed and Heracleides immediately set about trying to win favour with the populace with a view to becoming sole ruler. He even persuaded the assembly to elect him admiral instead of Dion. Dion objected on the grounds they had already offered that role to him, and the assembly retracted the offer to Heracleides.[65] Dion essentially won the day, although Heracleides was also voted a bodyguard of mercenaries like Dion. Despite Dion's success, he gave the command of the naval forces to Heracleides. The new admiral gained some significant early success with a victory over a contingent of the Dionysian fleet. This compelled Dionysius to offer terms again, but the conditions he was offered were unacceptable (the surrender of the acropolis, which he still controlled, and the disbanding of his mercenary army).

The democrats in Syracuse held rather more power than under either tyrant, and Dion had not managed to replicate their position, although he seemingly tried. The differences between Dion and the democrats only widened through his time in Syracuse. The democrats realized that to undermine a potential tyrant they needed to remove his bodyguard, and so they allowed the pay of the mercenaries to fall into arrears. Once this was done, they also refused to elect Dion general for the following year, and the latter was forced to retire to Leontini after the situation became more dangerous for him in Syracuse. When Dion left the city, Syracuse was left in a position where it employed no mercenaries at all, probably the first time since before the reign of Dionysius I that that had happened. They were also still besieging Dionysius II's mercenaries on the acropolis. The position of these mercenaries was becoming increasingly desperate and they decided to establish a democracy within their ranks in an attempt to rectify their problems.[66] The mercenaries held an assembly meeting at which they voted to ask for terms from the Syracusans. Whilst the embassy was negotiating, however, a shipment of grain and troops arrived from Dionysius, along with a new commander, Nypsius.

Heracleides inflicted another naval defeat upon the new arrivals, but ultimately could not prevent the troops and supplies reaching the besieged mercenaries. The Syracusans, not being professional soldiers, retired for the evening to celebrate their victory and soon most were in a somewhat inebriated state. Biding their time, the mercenaries on the acropolis waited for the merriment to die down and broke out of the acropolis, slaughtered the guards that were still on duty, and set about the citizens of Syracuse in an orgy of rape and slaughter. Diodorus describes events:[67]

> The bravest of the mercenaries climbed on the wall with these, slaughtered the guards, and opened the gates. As the men poured into the city, the generals of the Syracusans, becoming sober after their drunkenness, tried to bring aid, but, their efforts being hampered by the wine, some were slain and some fled. When the city had been captured and almost all the soldiers from the citadel had rushed inside the circuit-walls, since the Syracusans were panic-stricken by the sudden-ness and confusion of the attack, a great slaughter took place ... Once the market-place had come into possession of the enemy, the victors straightway attacked the residences. They carried off much property and took off as slaves many women and children and household servants besides. Where the Syracusans formed to meet them in narrow alleys and other streets, continuous engagements occurred and many were killed and not a few wounded. So they passed the night slaying one another at random in the darkness, and every quarter teemed with dead.

The citizens had no option but to beg Dion to return from Leontini and rescue them. There, the mercenaries had enjoyed both full pay and the benefits of citizenship, but Dion persuaded them to return with him to Syracuse.[68]

> Dion, a man noble in spirit and civilized in his judgements because of his philosophical training, did not bear a grudge against his fellow citizens, but, after winning the mercenaries over, straightway set out and, having quickly traversed the road to Syracuse, arrived at the Hexapyla [the gate to the north of the city].

When Dion arrived, the mercenaries of Dionysius were still plundering and ravaging the marketplace area of the city, their appetites and desire for gold not yet sated. Their undisciplined looting was their undoing, however:[69]

> At this very moment Dion, rushing into the city in several places and attacking the enemy as they were busily engaged in their looting, slew all whom he met as they were lugging furnishings of various sorts off on their shoulders. And because of the unexpectedness of his appearance and the disorder and confusion, all of those who were making off with their plunder were easily overpowered. And finally, after more than four thousand had been slain, some in the houses, and others in the streets, the rest fled in a body to the citadel and closing the gates escaped the danger.

After succeeding in driving the mercenaries back into the acropolis, Dion ingratiated himself to the citizenry by ordering his troops to help put out the fires. He also ordered the fortifications repaired and constructed defences to prevent a recurrence of this mercenary sortie. The siege continued for some time, but eventually the mercenaries of Dionysius, with no further help evident or expected, surrendered the acropolis to the Syracusans.

Dion initially acquiesced to a power-sharing agreement with Heracleides, which seemed to work for a short while, but Dion eventually ordered the assassination of the latter. Dion himself was in turn assassinated in 354 by a friend, Callippus, and a group of mercenaries from Zacynthus. Dion's assassination encouraged Dionysius to return to Syracuse and attempt to regain his former position. Syracuse appealed for help from their founding city, Corinth, and she agreed by sending, in 344, a mercenary army of 700 Phocians commanded by Timoleon.[70] These mercenaries were some of the remnants of the Phocian mercenary army that occupied and sacked the sacred precinct at Delphi. The Syracusans also appealed to the tyrant of Leontini (Hicetas) for assistance. Dionysius had some initial success (his forces managed to occupy the fortress in the bay at Syracuse), but he was soon hard pressed by Hicetas.

Hicetas, either upon receiving the appeal from Syracuse or not long before, concluded a treaty with Carthage. He even invited a Carthaginian army to Sicily to aid his cause. Of the Carthaginian host we hear:[71]

They prepared and transported to Sicily a large sea and land force of their own, and appointed Hanno to the command as general. They had one hundred and fifty battleships, fifty thousand infantry, three hundred war chariots, over two thousand extra teams of horses, and besides all this, armour and missiles of every description, numerous siege engines, and an enormous supply of food and other materials of war. Advancing first on Entella, they devastated the countryside and blockaded the country people inside the city. The Campanians who occupied the city were alarmed at the odds against them and appealed for help to the other cities that were hostile to the Carthaginians. Of these, none responded except the city of Galeria. These people sent them a thousand hoplites, but the Phoenicians intercepted them, overwhelmed them with a large force, and cut them all down.

Hicetas also reacted quickly to the Syracusan call for aid and marched upon the city. He did not attempt a potentially lengthy siege, but engaged in a series of skirmishes with the mercenaries of Dionysius, which proved inconclusive.[72]

Now at the time when Dionysius was still master of Syracuse, Hicetas had taken the field against it with a large force, and at first constructing a stockaded camp at the Olympieium carried on war against the tyrant in the city, but as the siege dragged on and provisions ran out, he started back to Leontini, for that was the city which served as his base.

Dionysius was not prepared to simply allow Hicetas to walk away, however. He followed the tyrant out of Syracuse and, after further skirmishing, a major battle developed.

Hicetas wheeled upon him, joined battle, and having slain more than three thousand of the mercenaries, put the rest to flight. Pursuing sharply and bursting into the city with the fugitives, he got possession of all Syracuse except the Island. Such was the situation as regards Hicetas and Dionysius.

Plutarch gives more detail on the situation in Syracuse and with Timoleon:[73]

For Hicetas, after defeating Dionysius in battle and occupying most of the outlying portions of Syracuse, had shut the tyrant up in the acropolis and what was called The Island, where he was himself helping to besiege and wall him in, while he ordered the Carthaginians to see to it that Timoleon should not land in Sicily, but that he and his forces should be repulsed, and that they themselves, at their leisure, should divide the island with one another. So the Carthaginians sent twenty triremes to Rhegium, on board of which were envoys from Hicetas to Timoleon carrying proposals which conformed to his proceedings.

Three days after the capture of the major part of the city, Timoleon and his mercenary army landed at Rhegium after dodging a Carthaginian fleet. From there they again outmanoeuvred the enemy and landed at Tauromenium, an ally of the Syracusans, and from there they marched against Hicetas.[74]

Hicetas now put himself at the head of five thousand of his best soldiers and marched against the Adranitae, who were hostile to him, encamping near their city. Timoleon added to his force some soldiers from Tauromenium and marched out of that city, having all told no more than a thousand men. Setting out at nightfall, he reached Adranum on the second day, and made a surprise attack on Hicetas's men while they were at dinner. Penetrating their defences he killed more than three hundred men, took about six hundred prisoners, and became master of the camp. Capping this manoeuvre with another, he proceeded forthwith to Syracuse. Covering the distance at full speed, he fell on the city without warning, having made better time than those who were routed and fleeing.

Hicetas escaped this embarrassing disaster by fleeing to the relative safety of Syracuse. Timoleon followed closely behind, and as he approached the city he received an offer of surrender from Dionysius, the only condition being that he be allowed to leave peacefully along with his personal possessions.[75] Timoleon readily agreed to this, and he then took possession of the fortress that Dionysius had been occupying, along with the huge arsenal of weapons stored there. He also accepted into his ranks the 2,000 mercenaries that were formally employed by Dionysius. This campaign had been very rapid, taking only fifty days from the landing at Rhegium to the surrender and flight of Dionysius.[76] Timoleon was riding high after his against-the-odds victory, and his supporters in Corinth sent another 2,000 mercenaries to further demonstrate their commitment. Hicetas responded by requesting the Carthaginian army become more involved in the conflict. Mago, the Carthaginian general, responded by marching on Syracuse and making camp close to the city.[77]

But when Mago got tidings of his approach, disturbed and fearful as he was, he was made still more suspicious for the following reason. In the shoals about the city, which receive much fresh water from springs, and much from marshes and rivers emptying into the sea, great numbers of eels live, and there is always an abundance of this catch for anybody. These eels the mercenary soldiers on both sides, when they had leisure or a truce was on, used to hunt together. And since they were Greeks and had no reason for private hatred of one another, while in their battles they risked their lives bravely, in their times of truce they would visit and converse with one another. And so now, as they were busy together with their fishing, they conversed, expressing their admiration of the richness of the sea and the character of the adjacent lands. And one of those who were serving on the Corinthian side said: 'Can it really be that you, who are Greeks, are eager to barbarize a city of such great size and furnished with such great advantages, thus settling Carthaginians, who are the basest and bloodiest of men, nearer to us, when you ought to pray for many Sicilies to lie as a barrier between Greece and them? Or do you suppose that they have collected an army and are come hither from the pillars of Heracles and the Atlantic sea in order to risk their lives in behalf of the dynasty of Hicetas? He, if he reasoned like a true leader, would not be casting out his kindred people, nor would he be leading against his country her natural enemies, but would be enjoying a befitting amount of honour and power, with the consent of Timoleon and the Corinthians.' Such speeches as these the mercenaries disseminated in their camp, and made Mago suspicious of treachery, though he had long wanted a pretext for going away.

This passage of Plutarch is an interesting insight into the Greek mercenaries on Sicily. They had no personal animosity towards the mercenaries employed by the enemy of their chosen employers, and would socialize with them when 'off duty'. Mago, however, did not understand the mercenary psyche and, suspecting treachery, he left the vicinity of Syracuse without offering a battle.

Hicetas and the Carthaginians had been driven back, but it was far from clear that this would be permanent and, given that no Syracusan citizen came forward to offer his services as general, Timoleon continued in command of the mercenary troops. He was now also offered the command of some citizen levies to supplement his mercenary forces, but he declined, perhaps preferring the professionalism of a small, mobile and highly skilled army for the raiding operations that he had planned. Funding, as so often with a mercenary army, remained a problem. Neither Syracuse nor Corinth were prepared or able to foot the bill for the entire army, and the traditional mechanism of pillaging was not immediately available to Timoleon, as doing so against fellow Greeks would potentially have been highly unpopular with his employers. Timoleon's only option was to raid the territory controlled by the Carthaginians in the hope of gathering enough plunder to pay his mercenaries for the immediate future.[78]

> ... he sent forth the troops under Deinarchus and Demaretus into that part of the island which the Carthaginians controlled, where they brought many cities to revolt from the Barbarians, and not only lived in plenty themselves, but actually raised moneys for the war from the spoils they made.

Diodorus adds that the raiding party consisted of only 1,000, but that they were the best of the forces available, and the plunder that they gathered was taken to Timoleon, who sold everything that was gathered, raising a significant sum of money. This he used to pay his mercenaries.

Timoleon was undoubtedly a tactician of great skill, and he must have understood what the inevitable reaction from the Carthaginians would be to his raid.[79]

> In the west, the Carthaginians prepared great stores of war materials and transported their forces to Sicily. They had all told, including the forces previously on the island, more than seventy thousand infantry; cavalry, war-chariots, and extra teams of horses amounting to not less than ten thousand; two hundred battleships; and more than a thousand freighters carrying the horses, weapons, food and everything else.

It hardly needs saying that the numbers are exaggerated, but the army was not put together with the intention of a reciprocal raid into Greek territory; this was an army of invasion. Timoleon now gathered together what mercenaries he could, around 4,000 in total. He also accepted the previous offer of citizen levies and mustered as many citizen hoplites and cavalry as were available from Syracuse and the other allied states, perhaps 4,000 infantry and 1,000 cavalry in total. He was still massively outnumbered, however, and so he took the unlikely step of offering an alliance with Hicetas, which the latter (very surprisingly) accepted, and provided 3,000 mercenaries to the Greek army.[80]

Timoleon was bolstered by his recent success against a numerically superior enemy, and he chose not to allow the Carthaginians to advance upon Syracuse and risk a siege of the city. As soon as his forces were gathered, he marched out to confront the invaders. He did not get too far, however, before a mutiny broke out over non-payment of wages.[81]

> He had reached the territory of Agrigentum when unexpected confusion and discord broke out in his army. One of his mercenaries named Thrasius, who had been with the Phocians when they plundered the

shrine at Delphi, and who was remarkable for his mad recklessness, now perpetrated an act that matched his former outrages.

Thrasius appears to have attempted to instigate this revolt only partly because of the issue of their wages having fallen into arrears, but also partly because of the realization of the size of the Carthaginian army ranged against them.[82]

> He said that Timoleon was out of his mind and was leading his men to certain destruction. The Carthaginians were six times their number and were immeasurably superior in every sort of equipment, but Timoleon was nevertheless promising that they would win, gambling with the lives of the mercenaries whom for a long time because of lack of funds he had not even been able to pay. Thrasius recommended that they should return to Syracuse and demand their pay, and not follow Timoleon any further on a hopeless campaign.

Thrasius spoke to the mercenaries and tried to persuade them to abandon Timoleon, a speech that was apparently persuasive and received enthusiastic-ally by the Greeks who heard it. Timoleon managed to quell the rebellion only with great difficulty, with the liberal distribution of gifts and promises of more in the future. He was not entirely successful, however, as Thrasius did desert along with 1,000 of his fellow mercenaries, a perfect illustration of the dangers of relying too heavily on this type of soldier. Timoleon sent messengers to Syracuse with instructions that these deserting mercenaries should receive the full pay that they were owed, a generous act but a necessary one to calm those that remained. Timoleon's army was thus reduced in numbers, but he was not distracted from the coming battle, and in early June of 339 the two armies met at the River Crimisus.

The Greeks arrived on the battlefield early in the morning, probably around dawn, as it was still dark, and there was a heavy fog that shrouded the enemy. Timoleon could not see their preparations or dispositions, and could only hear the clamour of men and arms preparing for battle. The Greeks took up a position on a hillside overlooking where the enemy army were camped. As the morning wore on and midday approached, the fog burned off and the enemy became visible for the first time. Timoleon now realized that the enemy had camped on the far side of the river and were endeavouring to cross it as quickly as they were able. Any chance he may have had of gaining a tactical advantage by using the river as a defensive line and attempting to stop their crossing had been lost by the presence of the all-concealing fog of the morning.[83]

> ... in the van [of the Carthaginian army] their four-horse chariots formidably arrayed for battle, and behind these ten thousand men-

at-arms with white shields. These the Corinthians conjectured to be Carthaginians, from the splendour of their armour and the slowness and good order of their march. After these the other nations streamed on and were making the crossing in tumultuous confusion.

Whilst Timoleon had lost the chance of opposing the crossing, he realized that he could still use the river to his tactical advantage, as only some of the enemy had crossed, and the others were either struggling to do so or were waiting their turn.[84]

> [Timoleon] ordered Demaretus to take the horsemen and fall upon the Carthaginians and throw their ranks into confusion before their array was yet formed. Then he himself, descending into the plain, assigned the wings to the other Sicilian Greeks, uniting a few of his mercenaries with each wing, while he took the Syracusans and the best fighters among his mercenaries under his own command in the centre. Then he waited a little while, watching what his horsemen would do, and when he saw that they were unable to come to close quarters with the Carthaginians on account of the chariots which coursed up and down in front of their lines, but were forced to wheel about continually that their ranks might not be broken, and to make their charges in quick succession after facing about again, he took up his shield and shouted to his infantrymen to follow and be of good courage; and his voice seemed stronger than usual and more than human, whether it was from emotion that he made it so loud, in view of the struggle and the enthusiasm which it inspired, or whether, as most felt at the time, some deity joined in his utterance. Then, his men re-echoing his shout, and begging him to lead them on without delay, he signalled to his horsemen to ride along outside and past the line of chariots and attack the enemy on the flank, while he himself made his vanguard lock their shields in close array, ordered the trumpet to sound the charge, and fell upon the Carthaginians.

The Carthaginians held up to the initial charge well, owing largely to the quality of their equipment, but as the battle turned into a hand-to-hand skirmish the superior quality of the Greeks started to show through. As the fighting wore on into evening, a thunderstorm started, accompanied by wind and torrential rain. The Greeks fought on but Plutarch tells us the Carthaginians became fearful and confusion reigned.[85]

> Then the darkness hovering over the hills and mountain summits came down to the field of battle, mingled with rain, wind, and hail. It enveloped the Greeks from behind and smote their backs, but it smote

the Barbarians in the face and dazzled their eyes, a tempest of rain and continuous flames dashing from the clouds. In all this there was much that gave distress, and most of all to the inexperienced; and particularly, as it would seem, the peals of thunder worked harm, and the clatter of the armour smitten by the dashing rain and hail, which made it impossible to hear the commands of the leaders.

The heavy armour of the Carthaginians was also acting against them, as the ground became muddy and their armour and clothing filled with water. The lighter-armed Greeks appear to have struggled slightly less with the deteriorating conditions, and they began to push the Carthaginians back towards the river. Before the onset of the battle, the river was swollen with rain that had fallen over the previous few days, and the storm caused it to quickly flood its banks. The many streams feeding into the river also began to flood and added to the confusion in the Carthaginian ranks, as many in their army were still trying to cross as those in the vanguard fighting the Greeks were being pushed back towards the river.[86]

Many were overtaken in the plain and cut to pieces, and many the river dashed upon and carried away to destruction as they encountered those who were still trying to cross, but most of them the light-armed Greeks ran upon and despatched as they were making for the hills. At any rate, it is said that among ten thousand dead bodies, three thousand were those of Carthaginians – a great affliction for the city. For no others were superior to these in birth or wealth or reputation, nor is it recorded that so many native Carthaginians ever perished in a single battle before, but they used Libyans for the most part and Iberians and Numidians [mercenaries] for their battles, and thus sustained their defeats at the cost of other nations.

Timoleon did not follow up this great victory by harrying the retreating Carthaginians and inflicting even heavier losses.[87] His mercenaries were too intent on plundering the dead and the enemy camp to follow. This continued for three days before Timoleon was able to regain control and erect a trophy; the vanquished army was long gone by that time.[88]

The rank of those who had fallen was made known to the Greeks from the spoils. For those who stripped the bodies made very little account of bronze and iron; so abundant was silver, so abundant gold. For they crossed the river and seized the camp with its baggage-trains. As for the prisoners, most of them were stolen away and hidden by the soldiers, but as many as five thousand were delivered into the public stock; there were also captured two hundred of the four-horse chariots. But the most glorious and magnificent sight was presented by the tent of Timoleon, which was heaped about with all sorts of spoils, among which a thousand breast-plates of superior workmanship and beauty and ten thousand shields were exposed to view. And as there were but few to strip many, and the booty they came upon was great, it was the third day after the battle before they could erect their trophy.

This victory demonstrated once and for all, if it still needed demonstrating, that Greek mercenaries were superior in quality to both citizen soldiers and mercenaries from other regions. The Carthaginians learned this lesson well and resolved to begin to hire Greek mercenaries alongside their more traditional mercenaries from Spain and North Africa. They also decided not to risk any more citizen soldiers in overseas wars, but to allow their mercenary troops to conduct all of their battles.[89] By the spring of the following year, 338, the Carthaginian army did indeed contain a detachment of Greek mercenaries. The speed with which they were hired and incorporated into the Carthaginian land forces speaks to the ubiquity of Greek mercenary soldiers in the fourth century.

Timoleon left the mercenary army under the command of his subordinates to continue the plunder of Carthaginian-controlled territory whilst he returned to Syracuse. Once he arrived, he immediately dismissed the 1,000 mercenaries who had deserted him, along with the instigator Thrasius. These mercenaries stayed together as a group and sailed to Italy, where they pillaged the territory of the Bruttians. After some initial success, they were slaughtered by a detachment of Bruttian soldiers, however.[90]

After he had settled matters with Thrasius and his mercenaries, Timoleon set about removing tyrants from the cities of Sicily. We hear very little of his actual activities; Diodorus only provides us with a list of those removed from power. The main tyrant of interest is Hicetas. He had decided to once more side with the Carthaginians, although we are not told why the change of heart. Timoleon approached Leontini and apparently offered some form of bribe (the details are unknown) to Hicetas' mercenaries, who readily betrayed him and handed him over, along with his family and senior commander, to the Syracusans.[91]

After this, he concluded his war with Hicetas and put him to death, and then attacked the Campanians in Aetna and wiped them out. Likewise he overbore Nicodemus, tyrant of Centuripae, and ousted him from that city; and putting an end to the tyranny of Apolloniades in Agyrium he gave Syracusan citizenship to its freed inhabitants. In a word, all of the tyrants throughout the island were uprooted and the cities were set free and taken into his alliance.

After the death of Timoleon in 337, we know little of the following twenty years of history in Sicily, and some have (probably rightly) suggested that this was a relatively quiet period of recovery after the deprivations of a series of major wars, both between the Greek states of Sicily and against repeated Carthaginian invasions.[92]

Notes

Introduction

1. Griffith, 1935, p. 1.
2. Parke, 1933, p. 1*ff.*
3. Aymard, 1967, p. 487.
4. Plutarch, *Themistocles* 10.3; Trundle, 2004, p. 22.
5. Trundle, 2004, p. 22.
6. Cited in Trundle, 2004, p. 22.
7. Krasilnikoff, 1992, p. 27; McKechnie, 1989, p. 92; Griffith, 1935, pp. 310–11; Trundle, 2004, p. 22; Aristotle, *Politics* 1256a–b.
8. Trundle, 2004, p. 23.
9. Trundle, 2004, p. 10.
10. Xenophon, *Hellenica* 4.5.11-18; *cf.* Trundle, 2004, p. 15.
11. Van Wees, 2004, pp. 71–6 on *epikouroi*.
12. *Cf.* Herodotus 2.152–4.
13. Herodotus 1.61.3–4; Aristotle, *Ath. Pol.* 15.1–3.
14. Herodotus 5.55, 65, 71, 91; 6.35, 102, 103, 107, 123; 7.6. Diodorus 11.48.3; 53.2, 67.5. Trundle, 2004, pp. 28–9; Hunt, 2007, p. 141 notes that this use for internal stability ran from the Archaic period to the fourth century.
15. Plutarch, *Agesilaus* 22.2. For general works on peltasts see Best, 1969; Hunt, 2007, pp. 119–22; Webber, 2011 on Thracians generally.
16. Thucydides 1.115.4; 2.33.1; 70.3; 79.3; 3.18.1; 34.2; 73.1; 85.3; 109.2; 6.46.2; 129.3; 130.3; 131.3; 7.43.1; 57.3; 57.9; 57.11; 58.3; 8.25.2; 28.4; 38.3. Trundle, 2004, p. 30.
17. Plato, *Laws* 630a–b; the first sentence being a quotation of Theognis 77–8.
18. Aristotle, *Nicomachean Ethics* 3.8.9.
19. Diodorus 19.40–3.9; Plutarch *Eumenes* 17–17; *cf.* Trundle, 2004, p. 35.
20. Diodorus 14.19.1–34.3 (Cyrus); 14.7.5—8, 14.41.4–96.4 (Dionysius).

Chapter 1

1. This chapter relies heavily on the excellent works of Pritchett, 1974 and Trundle, 2004.
2. Trundle, 2004, pp. 82–3.

3. Diodorus 16.36.1; 16.56.5.
4. Marinovic, 1988, pp. 270–4 cited in Trundle, 2004, pp. 83–4.
5. Examples of Alexander's garrisons in Greece include: Corinth (Polybius 38.3.3), Sicyon (Demosthenes 17.16) and in Ambracia (Diodorus 17.3.3). Examples of garrisons in Persia are almost too numerous to mention.
6. Krasilnikoff, 1993, p. 78.
7. For the Syracusans see Plutarch, *Dion* 31. For Cyrus see Xenophon, *Anabasis* 1.4.13. The context of the quote being that the mercenaries had just found out that the target was the Great King himself; they had not been told their real target before this point.
8. Diodorus 16.64.6; Curtius 5.1.45.
9. Diodorus 14.78.2–3.
10. van Wees, 2004, pp. 26–8; Trundle, 2004, pp. 99–103; Hanson 1998, pp. 185–94; Sage, 1996, pp. 121–7; Krasilnikoff, 1992, pp. 22–36; Pritchett, 1991, pp. 68–203; Griffith, 1935, p. 273; Parke, 1933, p. 233.
11. Sage, 1996, p. 121.
12. Sage, 1996, p. 127 on treaties between Hierapytnia and the cities of Priansus and Rhodes.
13. Diodorus 17.14.4; Green, 1991, p. 149.
14. Xenophon, *Anabasis* 5.3.6–9.
15. Trundle, 2004, p. 99 for this section.
16. Isaeus 4.
17. Aeneas Tacticus 16.4–8 (both quotes).
18. Trundle, 2004, p. 100.
19. Sage, 1996, p. 125.
20. Xenophon, *Anabasis* 7.8.9-24; *cf.* Trundle, 2004, p. 100.
21. Xenophon *Anabasis* 5.6.23. The Cyzicicene mentioned being a gold coin from a city in the Propontis region.
22. Trundle, 2004, p. 90.
23. For Callicratidas, see Xenophon, *Hellenica* 1.6.12–13; for the quotation, see Xenophon, *Anabasis* 6.4.8.
24. Diodorus 15.14.4.
25. Diodorus 15.15.2.
26. Trundle, 2004, p. 91.
27. Parke, 1933, pp. 231–3; Griffith, 1935, p. 273, p. 298, generally agrees with Parke's wage deflation argument.
28. This is the general argument of Loomis, 1998, pp. 47–8; Krasilnikoff, 1993, p. 95; McKechnie, 1989, p. 89; Miller, 1984, p. 155.
29. *Contra* Parke, 1933, pp. 231–2, who argues that there was a shortage of available mercenaries as wages fell in the fourth century.
30. Trundle, 2004, p. 92.
31. As argued by Griffith, 1935, pp. 294–7; *contra* Loomis, 1998, p. 60, who notes this as speculation.
32. Thucydides 3.17.4 (quote); 6.8.1; 6.31.3; 7.27.2; 8.29; 8.45.2; 8.101.

33. Rhodes, 1981, p. 306.
34. Aristophanes, *Acharnians* 159; *Wasps* 682–5, 1188–9; *cf.* Trundle, 2004, p. 91; Griffiths, 1935, p. 295. Athenian rates of pay during the Peloponnesian War are very controversial. For a recent discussion, see Hornblower, 2010, on 3.17.4; 6.31.3; 8.45.2.
35. Demosthenes 4.28–9.
36. Plutarch, *Alcibiades* 35.4; *cf.* Rhodes, 2011, p. 88.
37. Xenophon, *Hellenica* 1.5.4–7.
38. Trundle, 2004, p. 93.
39. Diodorus 14.44.2; *cf.* 14.8.6; 14.62.1; 15.47.7; 15.91.4.
40. Xenophon, *Anabasis* 1.3.21; *cf.* Trundle, 2004, p. 93.
41. Xenophon, *Anabasis* 1.2.19.
42. Trundle, 2004, pp. 94–5, for an excellent analysis of both sources.
43. Xenophon, *Hellenica* 5.2.21.
44. Rhodes, 1981, p. 306.
45. Demosthenes 4.28. The actual date is still debated.
46. Mckechnie, 1989, p. 98, believes this passage has no value, whilst Parke, 1933, p. 232, believes it has little value, although still uses it to support his view of very low mercenary wages during the fourth century.
47. Diodorus 16.25.1 (355/4); 16.30.1 (354/3); 16.31.1 (353/2).
48. Trundle, 2004, p. 96.
49. Parke, 1933, p. 233.
50. English, 2011.
51. English, 2009a, p. 63.

Chapter 2
1. A very controversial subject well beyond the scope of this book.
2. For agriculture and food supply in the Greek world, Murray, 1980, pp. 42–5; 191*f*; *cf.* Garnsey, 1988.
3. Herodotus 2.52.3.
4. Herodotus 2.52.4. Note that Ionians and Carians were Greeks from Asia Minor, not the mainland.
5. Parke, 1933, p. 4.
6. Herodotus 2.54.1.
7. Parke, 1933, p. 5.
8. Herodotus 2.163.1.
9. Herodotus 2.154.3.
10. Herodotus 3.4.2.
11. Herodotus 3.4.3.
12. Herodotus 3.9.
13. Herodotus 3.11.
14. Yalichev, 1997, p. 60.
15. Aristotle, *Politics* 1313b.
16. Parke, 1933, p. 7; this section relies heavily upon Parke.

17. Aristotle, *Politics* 1305a 24; *cf.* Parke, 1933, p. 8.
18. Aristotle, *Politics* 1315b 28; *cf.* Parke, 1933, p. 8.
19. Aristotle, *Politics* 1315b 11; *cf.* Parke, 1933, p. 8.
20. Pisistratus was ousted from power in Athens c.555 and was in exile for between three and six years. When he returned he ruled for between one and six years before being exiled again. After ten years in exile he returned again and this time he held power until his death in 527 BC.
21. Herodotus 1 61.2–62.1.
22. Polyaenus 5.47. For criticism see Parke, 1933, p. 10.
23. Parke, 1933, p. 10.
24. Herodotus 7.155.1.
25. Herodotus 7.155.2.
26. Herodotus 7.155–156.
27. Herodotus 7.157.
28. Herodotus 7.158.3.
29. Diodorus 11.21.1–22.1.
30. Diodorus 11.22.1.
31. Diodorus 11.48.3.
32. Parke, 1933, p. 12.
33. Diodorus 11.72.1–3.
34. Parke, 1933, pp. 12–13.
35. Yalichev, 1997, p. 86.
36. Yalichev, 1997, p. 86.
37. Herodotus 1.76–77.
38. Burn, 1984, p. 40. It could be argued, however, that these Ionians were fighting as subject allies rather than strictly as mercenaries.
39. Farrokh, 2007, p. 41.
40. Farrokh, 2007, p. 41.
41. Yalichev, 1997, p. 87.
42. Osborne, 1996, p. 319.
43. Best, 1969.
44. Yalichev, 1997, p. 87.

Chapter 3

1 The two most recent discussions of Marathon are: Krentz, 2010 and Billows, 2010.
2. Krentz, 2010, p. 101.
3. Herodotus 7.186.
4. For example: Burn, 1984, pp. 326–32; Lazenby, 1993, pp. 90–6.
5. Bradford, 1993; Lazenby, 1993; Cartledge, 2006.
6. Herodotus 8.26.
7. Lazenby, 1993; Strauss, 2005.
8. Lazenby, 1993.
9. Herodotus 9.28 puts the Greek strength at 110,000 and at 9.32 the Persian strength at 300,000.

10. Lazenby, 1993, p. 244.
11. Lendon, 2007, pp. 499–500.
12. Although the chronology of Plataea and Mycale is disputed.
13. Rhodes, 2010, p. 22 on Eurymedon.
14. Thucydides 1.115.4; *cf.* Diodorus 12.27.3, who is less positive about these 700 being mercenaries, although it does seem likely.
15. Rhodes, 2010, p. 73.
16. Parke, 1933, p. 15, does not cite finances directly.
17. Gabrielsen, 2007, pp. 265–6 and Delbrück, 1975, pp. 144–8 on the Athenian use of mercenaries.
18. Thucydides 1.60.
19. Thucydides 2.70.
20. Parke, 1933, p. 16.
21. Thucydides 4.80.5.
22. Thucydides 4.81–83.
23. Thucydides 4.84.
24. Thucudides 4.84; for the speech 4.85–87.
25. Thucydides 4.103–104.
26. Thucydides the historian, that is. See 4.104.4.
27. Thucydides 4.105.
28. Thucydides 4.108.
29. Thucydides 4.108. The island in question being Sphacteria, where a number of Spartans had been captured by Athens in 425 BC.
30. Thucydides 4.113.
31. Thucydides 4.117.
32. Thucydides 4.81; 108.
33. Thucydides 6.43; *cf.* 7.57–8.
34. Thucydides 7.19.4.
35. Parke, 1933, p. 16. Quote from Thucydides 6.24.3.
36. Thucydides 7.27.1–2.
37. Thucydides 8.28.
38. Diodoris 14.33.5; Xenophon, *Hellenica* 2.4.28; *cf.* Parke, 1933, p. 19.
39. Xenophon, *Hellenica* 2.4.43; *cf.* Parke, 1933, p. 19.

Chapter 4

1. Xenophon, *Anabasis* 1.1.2.
2. Xenophon, *Anabasis* 1.2.11.
3. Parke, 1933, p. 25.
4. Xenophon, *Anabasis* 1.4.3.
5. Diodorus 14.19.5. Diodorus also puts the figure at 800 hoplites.
6. Yalichev, 1997, p. 128.
7. Xenophon, *Anabasis* 1.2.25 for *lochoi* of 50 troops; Xenophon, *Anabasis* 4.7.8 for *lochoi* of 100 troops.

8. For Cyrus' route to Cunaxa see Yalichev, 1997, p. 129*f*.
9. Xenophon, *Anabasis* 1.2.6.
10. Xenophon, *Anabasis* 1.2.1–2; *cf.* Yalichev, 1997, p. 129.
11. Xenophon, *Anabasis* 1.2.11.
12. Xenophon, *Anabasis* 1.2.14–18.
13. Xenophon, *Anabasis* 1.2.19.
14. Xenophon, *Anabasis* 1.2.20.
15. Because of evident cooperation between the two.
16. Xenophon, *Anabasis* 1.2.26.
17. Xenophon, *Anabasis* 1.3.1.
18. Xenophon, *Anabasis* 1.3.3–6. For the authenticity of ancient speeches see Shrimpton, 1985.
19. Xenophon, *Anabasis* 1.3.8.
20. Xenophon, *Anabasis* 1.3.9–12.
21. Xenophon, *Anabasis* 1.3.15.
22. Xenophon, *Anabasis* 1.3.20.
23. Xenophon, *Anabasis* 1.4.7.
24. Xenophon, *Anabasis* 3.1.10.
25. Xenophon, *Anabasis* 1.5.1–5.
26. Xenophon, *Anabasis* 1.5.5.
27. Xenophon, *Anabasis* 1.5.11.
28. Xenophon, *Anabasis* 1.5.12–13.
29. Xenophon, *Anabasis* 1.5.14.
30. Xenophon, *Anabasis* 1.7.5.
31. Xenophon, *Anabasis* 1.7.14; *cf.* Barnett, 1963, pp. 1–26.
32. Xenophon, *Anabasis* 1.7.15.
33. Xenophon, *Anabasis* 1.7.19–20.
34. Xenophon, *Anabasis* 1.8.14.
35. Xenophon, *Anabasis* 1.8.4–7.
36. Xenophon, *Anabasis* 1.8.13.
37. Xenophon, *Anabasis* 1.8.18–20.
38. Xenophon, *Anabasis* 1.8.24.
39. Xenophon, *Anabasis* 1.8.25–7. Quote is from Xenophon, *Anabasis* 1.9.1.
40. Xenophon, *Anabasis* 2.2.1–2; *cf.* Parke, 1933, p. 32.
41. Xenophon, *Anabasis* 2.2.7.
42. Xenophon, *Anabasis* 2.5.27.
43. Xenophon, *Anabasis* 2.5.30. Quote is from Xenophon, *Anabasis* 2.5.31–34.
44. Xenophon, *Anabasis* 2.5.40–42.
45. Yalichev, 1997, p. 137.
46. Xenophon, *Anabasis* 3.3.1–5.
47. Xenophon, *Anabasis* 3.3.6–10.
48. Xenophon, *Anabasis* 3.4.5.
49. Xenophon, *Anabasis* 3.4.46–47.
50. Xenophon, *Anabasis* 3.4.48–49.

51. Yalichev, 1997, p. 141.
52. For their plans see Parke, 1933, pp. 34–5. Xenophon, *Anabasis* 5.1.4. A *navarch* was a Spartan commander abroad, but one not commanding native Spartan troops. Only one of the kings was allowed that privilege.
53. Xenophon, *Anabasis* 5.1.10–11.
54. Xenophon, *Anabasis* 5.1.17.
55. Xenophon, *Anabasis* 5.1.15.
56. Xenophon, *Anabasis* 5.1.16.
57. Xenophon, *Anabasis* 5.1.13–14.
58. Xenophon, *Anabasis* 5.2.1–18.
59. Xenophon, *Anabasis* 5.2.19–20.
60. Xenophon, *Anabasis* 5.6.15–17.
61. Xenophon, *Anabasis* 6.1.16.
62. Xenophon, *Anabasis* 6.1.17–18. Quote is from Xenophon *Anabasis* 6.1.18.
63. Xenophon, *Anabasis* 6.1.20.
64. Xenophon, *Anabasis* 6.1.26–32.
65. Xenophon, *Anabasis* 6.1.26–33; *cf.* Parke, 1933, p. 37.
66. Xenophon, *Anabasis* 6.2.3.
67. Xenophon, *Anabasis* 6.2.4–7.
68. Xenophon, *Anabasis* 6.2.8.
69. Xenophon, *Anabasis* 6.2.9–11.
70. Parke, 1933, p. 37.
71. Xenophon, *Anabasis* 6.3–4; *cf.* Parke, 1933, p. 37.
72. Xenophon, *Anabasis* 6.4.2–3.
73. Xenophon, *Anabasis* 6.4.9–10.
74. Xenophon, *Anabasis* 6.6.5–7.
75. Xenophon, *Anabasis* 7.1.2–3.
76. Xenophon, *Anabasis* 7.1.7.
77. Xenophon, *Anabasis* 7.1.13.
78. Xenophon, *Anabasis* 7.1.15.
79. Xenophon, *Anabasis* 7.1.17.
80. Xenophon, *Anabasis* 7.1.33.
81. Diodorus 14.37.1.
82. Parke, 1933, p. 41.

Chapter 5

1. Van Wees, 2000, p. 206, notes that many authors see mercenaries as ubiquitous in the fourth century, and I see no reason to disagree.
2. The Corinthian War was the war between Sparta and her allies against a coalition of Athens, Argos, Corinth and Thebes, fought between 395 and 387, ending in the peace of Antalcidas. The war was ultimately indecisive.
3. Xenophon *Hellenica* 3.1.4; Diodorus 14.36.1–2.
4. Xenophon, *Hellenica* 3.1.6; *cf.* Parke, 1933, p. 43.

5. Xenophon, *Hellenica* 3.1.8; *cf.* 3.1.10, 3.2.6.
6. Xenophon, *Hellenica* 3.2.1.
7. Xenophon, *Hellenica* 3.4.2.
8. Xenophon, *Hellenica* 3.4.20.
9. Xenophon, *Hellenica* 4.3.15.
10. Xenophon, *Hellenica* 4.3.16.
11. Xenophon, *Hellenica* 4.3.17. On the battle of Coronea, see Buckler, 2008, pp. 59–70.
12. Xenophon, *Hellenica* 4.3.20.
13. Parke, 1933, pp. 40–50.
14. Best, 1969.
15. Best, 1969, p. 90; Anderson, 1970, p. 128; Yalichev, 1997, p. 152.
16. Xenophon, *Hellenica* 4.8.33.
17. Best, 1969, p. 90; Anderson, 1970, p. 128; Yalichev, 1997, p. 152.
18. Xenophon, *Hellenica* 4.8.35.
19. Xenophon, *Hellenica* 4.8.39.
20. This was Sparta's second attempt at a peace, having failed in 392/1.
21. Best, 1969, p. 58; Anderson, 1970, p. 94.
22. Parke, 1933, p. 105; Sekunda, 1992, p. 27.
23. Xenophon, *Hellenica* 5.2.20–22.
24. A town in northern Laconia. Xenophon, *Hellenica* 5.2.24.
25. Xenophon, *Hellenica* 5.3.3–4.
26. Xenophon, *Hellenica* 5.3.5–6.
27. Xenophon, *Hellenica* 5.3.8–9.
28. Yalichev, 1997, p. 158.
29. Diodorus 15.32.2–3 wrongly attributes this to 377.
30. Diodorus 15.33.4–6.
31. Xenophon, *Hellenica* 5.4.41.
32. Xenophon, *Hellenica* 5.4.42.
33. Xenophon, *Hellenica* 5.4.64.
34. Diodorus 15.45.3–4; 46.1. Xenophon, *Hellenica* 6.2.4.
35. Xenophon, *Hellenica* 6.2.6.
36. Diodorus 15.47.4–5.
37. Xenophon, *Hellenica* 6.2.15–16.
38. Xenophon, *Hellenica* 6.2.19.
39. Xenophon, *Hellenica* 6.2.21–22.
40. Yalichev, 1997, pp. 160–1.
41. Diodorus 15.44.2-4; Nepos *Iphicrates* 9.1.3-4; Best, 1969, p. 102 (quote).
42. The most recent discussion of Iphicrates' reforms is Sekunda, 2007, pp. 326–9. *Cf.* Best, 1969.
43. English, 2009a, pp. 8–29.
44. Xenophon 6.3.18–19.
45. Diodorus 15.52.3.
46. Diodorus 15.52.2.

47. Diodorus 15.54.5. Xenophon, *Hellenica* 6.4.20–26, notes that Jason did not arrive until after the battle.
48. Diodorus 15.55.1–2. For Leuctra, see Buckler, 2008, pp. 111–26.
49. Diodorus 15.55.3–5.
50. Diodorus 15.56.1–2.
51. Yalichev, 1997, p. 163.
52. Xenophon, *Hellenica* 6.5.11.
53. Xenophon, *Hellenica* 6.5.13–4.
54. Xenophon, *Hellenica* 7.1.20; Justin 20.5.6; Diodorus 15.70.1; *cf.* Parke, 1933, p. 88.
55. Xenophon, *Hellenica* 7.1.27; Parke, 1933, p. 89.
56. Diodorus 15.70.2.
57. Yalichev, 1997, p. 165.
58. Xenophon, *Hellenica* 7.5.4.
59. Xenophon, *Hellenica* 7.5.5.
60. Xenophon, *Hellenica* 7.5.8.
61. Xenophon, *Hellenica* 7.5.9–10.
62. Xenophon, *Hellenica* 7.5.12.
63. Xenophon, *Hellenica* 7.5.15–16.
64. Xenophon, *Hellenica* 7.5.18.
65. Xenophon, *Hellenica* 7.5.21–22.
66. Diodorus 15.84.2.
67. Xenophon, *Hellenica* 7.5.22–23.
68. Xenophon, *Hellenica* 7.5.25.
69. Yalichev, 1997, p. 166.
70. Diodorus, 16.7.3–4.
71. Diodorus, 16.21.2.
72. Diodorus, 16.23*ff*; *cf.*Yalichev, 1997, p. 167.
73. Diodorus, 16.24.2.
74. Diodorus, 16.24.4–5.
75. Diodorus, 16.25.3.
76. Diodorus, 16.27.5.
77. Diodorus, 16.28.2–3.
78. Diodorus, 16.28.4; 29.1.
79. Diodorus, 16.30.2. Note that Philomelus was interestingly absolved of accusations of plundering the temple by an enquiry in 347, but his successors were not.
80. Diodorus 16.31.1.
81. Pausanias 10.2.4; Diodorus 26.31.4; *cf.* Parke 1933, p. 135.
82. Pausanias 2.38.2.
83. Diodorus 16.35.5–6.
84. Demosthenes 19.319.
85. Diodorus 16.37.3; *cf.* Parke, 1933, p. 138.
86. Demosthenes 19.230; *cf.* Parke, 1933, p. 139.

Chapter 6

1. Rhodes, 2010, pp. 236–7.
2. Diodorus 16.61.3–4.
3. Diodorus 16.62.2–4.
4. Diodorus 16.85.1–2.
5. Diodorus 16.85.5–7.
6. Diodorus 16.86.1.
7. Diodorus 16.86.3–4. *Cf.* Buckler, 2008, pp. 254–8.
8. Yalichev, 1997, p. 172.
9. The section relies heavily on English, 2009a, pp. 74–92.
10. For example, at Corinth (Polybius 38.3.3), Sicyon (Demosthenes 17.16), and in Ambracia (Diodorus 17.3.3).
11. Diodorus 17.17.3–4.
12. Arrian 2.9.
13. Arrian 2.20.5 for Sidon; Arrian 2.13.5 and Curtius 4.5.18 for Chios.
14. van Wees, 2004, pp. 41–2 notes that the mercenary explosion of the fourth century was demand led, not supply driven.
15. The table is an adaptation of that in Griffith, 1935, pp. 20–1, and was first presented in English, 2009a, p. 77.
16. See the opening chapter for a fuller discussion of the more typical use of these terms.
17. Arrian 3.12–13.
18. Diodorus 17.17.3–4.
19. Arrian 2.20.
20. Arrian 1.18.2.
21. For Satibarzanes, see Curtius 6.6.21; Arrian 3.25.6. For Spitamenes, see Arrian 4.3.7.
22. Arrian 3.5.3; Doloaspis and Petisis: each was to have control over half of the country, but Petisis refused the appointment (the reason is not known) and so Doloaspis was given the whole.
23. Curtius 4.8.4.
24. Bosworth, 1980, p. 276.
25. Arrian, 2.8.6; Curtius, 3.9.2; Polybius, 12.18.2.
26. Arrian, 2.8.6; *cf.* Polybius, 12.17.7.
27. Curtius, 3.9.5; Arrian, 2.8.8; Plutarch, *Alex.* 18.6.
28. Diodorus, 17.31.2; Justin, 9.9.1; Curtius, 3.2.4–9.
29. Arrian 2.9.3.
30. Fraser, 1996, pp. 240–3, gives all of the possible foundations, although he believes there were in fact very few.
31. Diodorus 17.49.5; Curtius 10.2.8.
32. Diodorus 16.75.2.
33. Pausanias 1.29.10.
34. Arrian 1.13.
35. English, 2011, pp. 33–60.

36. For the figure of 30,000, see Arrian 2.8.6; for the 2,000 at Gaugamela, see Arrian 3.7.1.
37. Diodorus 17.48.2; Arrian 2.13.2.
38. Diodorus 17.48.2–3.
39. Parke, 1933, p. 200.
40. Justin 9.5.3.
41. Curtius 4.5.15; 18.
42. Arrian 2.8.6; Diodorus 17.48.1; *cf.* Parke 1933, pp. 200–1.
43. Diodorus 17.62.4–7.
44. Arrian 3.16.10 for Persian gold sent from Susa after its capture.
45. Curtius 7.1.16–17.
46. Diodorus 17.108.6; *cf.* Parke, 1933, p. 202.
47. Pausanias 2.33.4; *cf.* Parke, 1933, p. 202.
48. Diodorus 18.7.1.
49. Parke, 1933, pp. 202–3.
50. Diodorus 17.111.1–2.
51. Pausanias 1.25.5.
52. Parke, 1933, p. 204.
53. *Contra* Parke, 1933, p. 205, who sees Greece as being stable in the period after the Lamian War.

Chapter 7
1. Sage, 1996, p. 148
2. Yalichev, 1997, p. 208.
3. Xenophon, *Hellenica* 1.1.27*ff.*
4. Xenophon, *Hellenica* 1.1.27–31.
5. Diodorus 13.75.2.
6. Diodorus 13.75.6–8.
7. Yalichev, 1997, p. 209.
8. Diodorus 13.92.1–3.
9. Diodorus 13.93.1.
10. Diodorus 14.47.7.
11. Diodorus 14.43.2.
12. Rihll, 2007, p. 27*ff.* *Cf.* English, 2009a, ch. 7.
13. Champion, 2010, p. 176.
14. Polyaenus 5.2.5.
15. Champion, 2010, p. 177.
16. Champion, 2010, p. 177.
17. Diodorus 14.41.1.
18. Champion, 2010, p. 184.
19. Diodorus 14.48.1.
20. Diodorus 14.48.1–2.
21. For Alexander's siege of Tyre, see Diodorus 17.40–46; Arrian 2.18–24; Curtius 4.2–4. *Cf.* English, 2009b, pp. 56–84.

22. Diodorus 14.48.4.
23. Diodorus 14.48.5.
24. Diodorus 14.49.2.
25. Diodorus 14.49.3.
26. Diodorus 14.50.1.
27. Diodorus 14.50.3–4.
28. Diodorus 14.51.1.
29. Diodorus 14.51.2–4.
30. Diodorus 14.53.5.
31. Diodorus 14.54.2–4.
32. Diodorus 14.54.5–6.
33. Diodorus 14.55.2–3.
34. Diodorus 14.56.2–4.
35. Diodorus 14.57.4–5.
36. Diodorus 14.60.2–4.
37. Diodorus 14.60.6.
38. Diodorus 14.62.1.
39. Diodorus 14.62.2.
40. Diodorus 14.62.4–5.
41. Diodorus 14.63.1–2.
42. Diodorus 14.64.1–3.
43. Diodorus 14.66.4–5.
44. Diodorus 14.67.3.
45. Diodorus 14.70–71.
46. Diodorus 14.72.1–2.
47. Diodorus 14.72.3.
48. Diodorus 14.74.1–2.
49. Diodorus 14.95.1.
50. Diodorus 14.95.3–6.
51. Diodorus 14.96.2.
52. Diodorus 15.15.1–2.
53. Diodorus 15.15.2.
54. Diodorus 15.15.3.
55. Diodorus 15.17.1–2. *Cf.* Champion, 2010, pp. 215–17.
56. Diodorus 15.17.5.
57. Plutarch, *Dion* 12 for an earlier plot to overthrow Dionysius II.
58. Plutarch, *Dion* 22.5. Diodorus gives a figure of 1,000. This may include a small number of volunteers collected in Sicily.
59. Plutarch, *Dion* 25.1.
60. Plutarch, *Dion* 25.1, notes 2,000 shields (along with 'boundless missiles and spears'); Diodorus 16.9.5 gives a figure of 5,000 shields.
61. Plutarch, *Dion* 27.3, notes 5,000 recruits. Diodorus 16.9.5 suggests 20,000, and then at 16.10.5 suggests 50,000.
62. Parke, 1933, p. 117.

63. Polyaenus 5.2.7. Quote is Diodorus 16.22.3.
64. Diodorus 16.22.4–5.
65. Plutarch, *Dion* 32.1–33.2.
66. Parke, 1933, p. 119.
67. Diodorus 16.19.2-4.
68. Diodorus 16.20.2.
69. Diodorus 16.20.4.
70. Three hundred more were added *en route* to Sicily.
71. Diodorus 16.67.1–3; *cf.* Parke, 1933, pp. 170–1.
72. Diodorus 16.68.1–2.
73. Plutarch, *Timoleon* 9.2.
74. Diodorus 16.68.9–11.
75. Plutarch, *Timoleon* 13.2.
76. Parke, 1933, p. 172.
77. Plutarch, *Timoleon* 20.1–4.
78. Plutarch, *Timoleon* 24.4.
79. Diodorus 16.77.4.
80. Diodorus 16.77.5. *Cf.* Parke, 1933, p. 173 fn.4.
81. Diodorus 16.78.3.
82. Diodorus 16.78.4–5.
83. Plutarch, *Timoleon* 27.2–3.
84. Plutarch, *Timoleon* 27.4–6.
85. Plutarch, *Timoleon* 28.2.
86. Plutarch, *Timoleon* 28.5–6.
87. Parke, 1933, p. 174.
88. Plutarch, *Timoleon* 29.1–2.
89. Diodorus 16.81.4; Plutarch, *Timoleon* 30.3.
90. Parke, 1933, p. 175.
91. Diodorus 16.82.4.
92. Parke, 1933, p. 176.

Bibliography

Anderson, JK, *Military Theory and Practice in the Age of Xenophon* (Berkeley at Los Angeles, 1970)

Anderson, JK, *Xenophon* (London, 1974)

Andrews, A, *The Greek Tyrants* (New York, 1963)

Anglim, S, *et al, Fighting Techniques of the Ancient World 3000 BC–AD 500: Equipment, Combat Skills and Tactics* (New York, 2002)

Ashley, JR, *The Macedonian Empire: The Era of Warfare Under Philip II and Alexander the Great* (London, 1998)

Atkinson, JC, *A Commentary on Q. Curtius Rufus' Historiae Alexandri Magni Books 3 and 4* (Amsterdam, 1980)

Atkinson, JC, *A Commentary on Q. Curtius Rufus' Historiae Alexandri Magni Books 5–7.2* (Amsterdam, 1994)

Austin, MM, 'Hellenistic Kings, War and Economy', in *CQ*, 36 (1986), pp. 450–66

Aymard, A, 'Mercenariat et l'historie grecque', in *Etudes d'historie ancienne* (1967), pp. 487–98

Badian, E, 'Harpalus', in *JHS*, 81 (1961), pp. 16–43

Badian, E, *Studies in Greek and Roman History* (Oxford, 1964)

Badian, E, 'The Administration of the Empire', in *Greece and Rome*, 12 (1965b), pp. 166–82

Badian, E, 'The Battle of the Granicus: A New Look', in *Ancient Macedonia 2*, (Thessaloniki, 1977), pp. 271–93

Barnett, RD, 'Xenophon and the Wall of Media', in *JHS*, 83 (1963), pp. 1–26

Bennett, B, and Roberts, M, *The Wars of Alexander's Successors: 323–281 BC vol. I: Commanders & Campaigns* (Barnsley, 2008)

Best, JGP, *Thracian Peltasts and their Influence on Greek Warfare* (Groningen, 1969)

Bigwood, JM, 'The Ancient Accounts of the Battle of Cunaxa', in *American Journal of Philology*, 104 (1983), pp. 340–57

Billows, RA, *Marathon: How One Battle Changed Western Civilisation* (London, 2010)

Bosworth, AB, 'The Government of Syria Under Alexander the Great', in *CQ*, 24 (1974), pp. 51–75

Bosworth, AB, *Commentary on Arrian's History of Alexander, vol. I* (Oxford, 1980)

Bosworth, AB, *Commentary on Arrian's History of Alexander, vol. II* (Oxford, 1995)

Bradford, E, *Thermopylae: The Battle for the West* (New York, 1993)

Buckler, J, and Beck, H, *Central Greece and the Politics of Power in the Fourth Century BC* (Cambridge, 2008)

Buckley, T, *Aspects of Greek History 750–323 BC: A Source based Approach* (London, 2010)

Burn, AR, *Persia and the Greeks: The Defence of the West c.546–478* (Stanford, California, 1984)

Campbell, DB, *Greek and Roman Siege Machinery* (Oxford, 2003)

Campbell, B, *Greek and Roman Military Writers: Selected Readings* (Oxford, 2004)

Carman, J, and Harding, A (eds.), *Ancient Warfare: Archaeological Perspectives* (Stroud, Gloucestershire, 1999)

Cartledge, P, *Thermopylae: The Battle that Changed the World* (London, 2006)

Casson, L, *Ships and Seamen in the Ancient World* (Princeton, 1971)

Champion, J, *The Tyrants of Syracuse: War in Ancient Sicily, vol. I: 480–367* (Barnsley, 2010)

Chaniotis, A, and Ducrey, P (eds.), *Army and Power in the Ancient World* (Stuttgart, 2002)

Connolly, P, *Greece and Rome at War* (London, 1981)

Cook, JM, *The Persian Empire* (New York, 1983)

Darnell, JC, and Manassa, C, *Tutankhamun's Armies: Battle and Conquest During Ancient Egypt's Late 18th Dynasty* (New Jersey, 2007)

Davis, EW, 'The Persian Battle Plan at the Granicus', in *James Sprunt Studies in History and Political Science*, 46 (1964), pp. 34–44

Delbrück, H, *Warfare in Antiquity*, tr. WJ Renfroe (London, 1975)

de Souza, P, Heckel, W, and Llewellyn-Jones, L, *The Greeks at War: From Athens to Alexander* (Oxford, 2004)

Devine, AM, 'Embolon: A Study in Tactical Terminology', in *Phoenix*, 37 (1983), pp. 201–17

Devine, AM, 'The Strategies of Alexander the Great and Darius III in the Issus Campaign', in *Ancient World*, 12 (1985a), pp. 25–38

Devine, AM, 'Grand Tactics at the Battle of Issus', in *Ancient World*, 12 (1985b), pp. 39–59

Devine, AM, 'The Battle of Gaugamela', in *Ancient World*, 13 (1986), pp. 87–116

Devine, AM, 'The Battle of the Hydaspes: A Tactical and Source-Critical Study', in *Ancient World*, 16 (1987), pp. 91–113

Devine, AM, 'A Pawn-Sacrifice at the Battle of the Granicus', in *Ancient World*, 18 (1988), pp. 3–20

Eadie, JW, 'The Development of Roman Mailed Cavalry', in *JRS*, 57 (1967), pp. 161–73

English, S, *The Army of Alexander the Great* (Barnsley, 2009a)

English, S, *The Sieges of Alexander the Great* (Barnsley, 2009b)

English, S, *The Field Campaigns of Alexander the Great* (Barnsley, 2011)

Everson, T, *Warfare in Ancient Greece* (Stroud, Gloucestershire, 2004)

Farrokh, K, *Shadows in the Desert: Ancient Persia at War* (Oxford, 2007)

Foss, C, 'The Battle of the Granicus River: A New Look', in *Ancient Macedonia 2* (Thessaloniki, 1977), pp. 495–502

Fuller, JFC, *The Generalship of Alexander the Great* (London, 1958)

Gabriel, RA, *Philip II of Macedonia: Greater than Alexander* (Washington, DC, 2010)

Gabrielsen, V, 'Warfare and the State', in P. Sabin, H. van Wees and M. Whitby (eds.), *The Cambridge History of Greek and Roman Warfare: Volume 1: Greece, the Hellenistic World and the Rise of Rome* (Cambridge, 2007)

Garnsey, P, *Famine and Food Supply in the Graeco-Roman World: Responses to Risk and Crisis* (Cambridge, 1988)

Griffith, GT, *The Mercenaries of the Hellenistic World* (Cambridge, 1935)

Griffith, GT, 'Alexander's Generalship at Gaugamela', in *JHS*, 67 (1947), pp. 77–89

Griffith, GT, 'Peltasts and the Origins of the Macedonian Phalanx', in H. J. Dell (ed.), *Ancient Macedonian Studies in Honour of Charles F. Edson* (Thessaloniki, 1981)

Hackett, J (ed.), *Warfare in the Ancient World* (London, 1989)

Hamblin, WJ, *Warfare in the Ancient Near East to 1600BC: Holy Warriors at the Dawn of History* (London, 2006)

Hamilton, JR, 'The Cavalry Battle at the Hydaspes', in *JHS*, 76 (1956), pp. 26–31

Hammond, NGL, 'Alexander's Campaign in Illyria', in *JHS*, 94 (1974), pp. 66–87

Hammond, NGL, 'The Battle of the Granicus River', in *JHS*, 100 (1980a), pp. 73–89

Hammond, NGL, *Alexander the Great: King Commander and Statesman* (London, 1980b)

Hanson, VD, *The Western Way of War: Infantry Battle in Classical Greece* (New York, 1989)

Hanson, VD, *Warfare and Agriculture in Classical Greece* (London, 1998)

Hanson, VD, *A War Like No Other: How the Athenians and Spartans Fought the Peloponnesian War* (London, 2005)

Harl, KW, 'Alexander's Cavalry Battle at the Granicus', in *Polis and Polemos* (Claremont, 1997), pp. 303–26

Heckel, W, *The Wars of Alexander the Great: 336–323 BC* (Oxford, 2002)

Herzog, C, and Gichon, M, *Battles of the Bible* (London, 2002)

Hornblower, S, *A Commentary on Thucydides*, vol. 1–3 (Oxford, 1997–2010)

Hunt, P, *Slaves, Warfare, and Ideology in the Greek Historians* (Cambridge, 1998)

Hunt, P, 'Military Forces', in P. Sabin, H. van Wees and M. Whitby (eds.), *The Cambridge History of Greek and Roman Warfare: Volume 1: Greece, the Hellenistic World and the Rise of Rome* (Cambridge, 2007)

Hutchinson, G, *Attrition: Aspects of Command in the Peloponnesian War* (Stroud, Gloucestershire, 2006)

Keegan, J, *The Face of Battle* (London, 1976)

Keegan, J, *The Mask of Command* (New York, 1987)

Kern, PB, *Ancient Siege Warfare* (London, 1999)

Krasilnikoff, JA, 'Aegean Mercenaries in the Fourth to Second Centuries BC: A Study in Payment, Plunder and Logistics of Ancient Greek Armies', in *Classica et Mediaevalia*, 43 (1992), pp. 23–36

Krasilnikoff, JA, 'The Regular Payment of Aegean Mercenaries in the Classical Period', in *Classica et Mediaevalia*, 44 (1993), pp. 77–95

Krentz, P, *The Battle of Marathon* (London, 2010)

Krentz, P, and Wheeler, EL, (eds. and tr.), *Polyaenus: Strategems of War, Vol. 1* (Chicago, 1994a)

Krentz, P, and Wheeler, EL (eds. and tr.), *Polyaenus: Strategems of War, Vol. II* (Chicago, 1994b)

Lazenby, JF, *The Defence of Greece 490–479 BC* (Warminster, 1993)

Lendon, JE, *Soldiers & Ghosts: A History of Battle in Classical Antiquity* (London, 2005)

Lendon, JE, 'War and Society', in P. Sabin, H. van Wees and M. Whitby (eds), *The Cambridge History of Greek and Roman Warfare: Volume 1: Greece, the Hellenistic World and the Rise of Rome* (Cambridge, 2007)

Lendon, JE, *Song of Wrath: The Peloponnesian War Begins* (New York, 2010)

Lloyd, AB (ed.), *Battle in Antiquity* (London, 1996)

Lonsdale, DJ, *Alexander: Killer of Men* (London, 2004)

Lonsdale, DJ, *Alexander the Great: Lessons in Strategy* (London, 2007)

MacQuitty, W, *Abu Simbel* (London, 1965)

Markle, MM, 'Macedonian Arms and Tactics under Alexander the Great', in *Studies in The History of Art*, vol. 10 (Washington, 1982), pp. 86–111

Marsden, EW, *The Campaign of Gaugamela* (Liverpool, 1964)

May, EC, Stadler, GP, and Votan, JF, *Ancient and Medieval Warfare* (Wayne, NJ, 1984)

McKechnie, P, *Outsiders in the Greek Cities in the Fourth Century BC* (London, 1989)

McKechnie, P, 'Greek Mercenary Troops and their Equipment', in *Historia*, 43 (1994), pp. 297–305

Messenger, C, *The Art of Blitzkrieg* (London, 1976)

Miller, HF, 'The Practical and Economic Background to the Greek Mercenary Explosion', in *Greece and Rome*, 31 (1984), pp. 153–60

Mockler, A, *Mercenaries* (Paris, 1964)

Montagu, JD, *Greek & Roman Warfare: Battles, Tactics and Trickery* (London, 2006)

Murison, JA, 'Darius III and the Battle of Issus', *Historia*, 21 (1972), pp. 399–423

Murray, O, *Early Greece* (London, 1980)

Nossov, K, *Ancient and Medieval Siege Weapons: A Fully Illustrated Guide to Siege Weapons and Tactics* (Kent, 2006)

Osborne, R, *Greece in the Making 1200–479 BC* (London, 1996)

Parke, HW, *Greek Mercenary Soldiers: from the Earliest Times to the Battle of Ipsus* (Chicago, 1933)

Partridge, RB, *Fighting Pharaohs: Weapons and Warfare in Ancient Egypt* (Manchester, 2002)

Pritchett, WK, *Ancient Greek Military Practices* (Berkeley, 1971)

Pritchett, WK, *The Greek State at War*, vol.1–5 (Berkeley, 1974–1990)

Ray, FE, *Land Battles in 5th Century BC Greece* (London, 2009)

Renfroe, WJ, *History of the Art of War Within the Framework of Political History* (London, 1975)

Rhodes, PJ, *A Commentary on the Aristotelian Athenaion Politeia* (Oxford, 1981)

Rhodes, PJ, *A History of the Classical Greek World: 478–323 BC* (Oxford, 2006) and second edition 2010

Rhodes, PJ, *Alcibiades: Athenian Playboy, General and Traitor* (Barnsley, 2011)

Rhodes, PJ and Osborne, R, *Greek Historical Inscriptions, 404–323 BC* (Oxford, 2007)

Rihll, T, *The Catapult: A History* (Yardley, Pennsylvania, 2007)

Romane, P, 'Alexander's Siege of Tyre', in *Ancient World*, 16 (1987), pp. 79–90

Romane, P, 'Alexander's Siege of Gaza – 332 BC', in *Ancient World*, 18 (1988), pp. 21–30

Roy, J, 'The Mercenaries of Cyrus', *Historia*, 16 (1967), pp. 292–323

Sabin, P, van Wees, H, and Whitby, M (eds.), *The Cambridge History of Greek and Roman Warfare* (Cambridge, 2007)

Sage, M, *Warfare in Ancient Greece: A Sourcebook* (London, 1996)

Santosuosso, A, *Soldiers, Citizens & The Symbols of War: From Classical Greece to Republican Rome 500–167BC* (Oxford, 1997)

Sekunda, N, *The Army of Alexander the Great* (London, 1984)

Sekunda, N, *The Ancient Greeks* (London, 1986)

Sekunda, N, *The Persian Army 560–330* (London, 1992)

Sekunda, N, *Early Roman Armies* (London, 1995)

Sekunda, N, 'Land Forces', in P Sabin, H Van Wees and M Whitby (eds.), *The Cambridge History of Greek and Roman Warfare: Volume 1: Greece, the Hellenistic World and the Rise of Rome* (Cambridge, 2007)

Sherman, N, *Stoic Warriors: The Ancient Philosophy Behind the Military Mind* (Oxford, 2005)

Sidebottom, H, *Ancient Warfare: A Very Short Introduction* (Oxford, 2004)

Sidnell, P, *Warhorse: Cavalry in Ancient Warfare* (London, 2006)

Smith, V, *The Early History of India* (Oxford, 1914)

Snodgrass, AM, *Arms and Armour of the Greeks* (Ithaca, NY, 1967)

Spanlinger, AJ, *War in Ancient Egypt* (Oxford, 2005)

Strauss, B, *Salamis: The Greatest Naval Battle of the Ancient World 480BC* (London, 2005)

Talbert, RJA (ed.), *Barrington Atlas of the Greek and Roman World* (Oxford, 2000)

Thapliyal, UP, *Warfare in Ancient India: Organizational and Operational Dimensions* (New Delhi, 2010)

Tritle, LA (ed.), *The Greek World in the Fourth Century* (London, 1997)

Trundle, M, *Greek Mercenaries: from the Late Archaic Period to Alexander* (London, 2004)

van de Mieroop, M, *A History of the Ancient Near East ca. 3000–323 BC* (Oxford, 2004)

van Wees, H (ed.), *War and Violence in Ancient Greece* (Swansea, 2000)

van Wees, H, *Greek Warfare: Myths and Realities* (London, 2004)

Vidal, J (ed.), *Studies on War in the Ancient Near East* (Münster, 2010)

Walbank, FW, *A Historical Commentary on Polybius, Vol. I–III* (Oxford, 1957–1979)

Waterfield, R, *Xenophon's Retreat: Greece, Persia and the End of the Golden Age* (London, 2006)

Waterfield, R, *Dividing the Spoils: The War for Alexander the Great's Empire* (Oxford, 2011)

Webber, C, *The Gods of Battle: The Thracians at War 1500BC–AD150* (Barnsley, 2011)

Webster, G, *The Roman Army* (Chester, 1956)

Whatley, N, 'On the Possibility of Reconstructing Marathon and Other Ancient Battles', in *JHS*, 84 (1964), pp. 119–39

Wise, T, *Ancient Armies of the Middle East* (London, 1981)

Wise, T, *Armies of the Carthaginian Wars 265–146 BC* (London, 1982)

Worthington, I, *Philip II of Macedonia* (London, 2008)

Yalichev, S, *Mercenaries of the Ancient World* (London, 1997)

Index